Larousse
On Cooking

Translation: Zachary R. Townsend

Cover design: Suzanne Sunwoo

Published by John Wiley & Sons, Inc., Hoboken, New Jersey.

Published simultaneously in Canada.

For general information on our other products and services, or technical support, please contact our Customer Care Department within the United States at 800-762-2974, outside the United States at 317-572-3993 or fax 317-572-4002.

Wiley publishes in a variety of print and electronic formats and by print-on-demand. Some material included with standard print versions of this book may not be included in e-books or in print-on-demand. If this book refers to media such as a CD or DVD that is not included in the version you purchased, you may download this material at http://booksupport.wiley.com. For more information about Wiley products, visit www.wiley.com.

Library of Congress Cataloging-in-Publication Data

Larousse de la cuisine. English
  Larousse on cooking / [translation, Zachary R. Townsend].
     p. cm.
  Includes index.
  ISBN 978-1-118-34996-0 (cloth); 978-1-118-38816-7 (ebk.); 978-1-118-38817-4 (ebk.)
  1. Cooking. I. Larousse (Firm) II. Title. III. Title: On cooking.
  TX714.L371513 2012
  641.5--dc23

                              2012004739

Originally published in French as Petit Larousse Cuisinier by Editions Larousse.

Printed in Spain by Graficas Estella, Estella

10   9   8   7   6   5   4   3   2   1

LAROUSSE
ON COOKING

WILEY

John Wiley & Sons, Inc.

Contents

Hors d'oeuvre

Two-tomato and avocado verrine

MAKES 12 VERRINES (2-OZ. GLASSES)

PREPARATION: 20 min

> 2 ripe avocados
> 1 white onion, peeled
> juice of 1 lime
> juice of ½ lemon
> 1 tsp. Cayenne pepper
> a few cilantro leaves
> a few mint leaves plus more for decoration
> 7 oz. tomatoes
> 1 tbsp. paprika
> 4 tbsp. olive oil
> 4¼ oz. sun-dried tomatoes
> a handful of alfalfa sprouts (optional)
> salt, freshly ground black pepper

Cut the avocados in half, remove the pit and scoop out the flesh with a spoon. Cut the onion into quarters.

In the bowl of a food processor, blend the avocado, onion, lemon and lime juice and Cayenne pepper until smooth; season with salt then refrigerate.

Chop the cilantro and mint leaves. Cut the tomatoes into small dice and mix them gently with the paprika, olive oil and herbs; season with salt and pepper. Finely dice the sun-dried tomatoes.

Place a layer of the tomato mixture in the bottom of twelve 2-ounce glasses, followed by a layer of the avocado mixture then finishing with a layer of the diced dried tomatoes. Garnish with mint leaves and alfalfa sprouts; serve well chilled.

low calorie · recipe ·

Puff pastry sticks wrapped in prosciutto

MAKES 24 PUFF
PASTRY STICKS
PREPARATION: **15 min**
FREEZING: **20 min**
COOKING TIME: **20 min**

> 3½ oz. emmental cheese
> 1 pre-prepared
  puff pastry sheet,
  approximately 8 oz.
> 3 tbsp. cumin seeds
> 3 tbsp. sesame seeds
> 1 egg yolk
> 12 thin slices prosciutto

Grate the emmental.

Unroll the puff pastry sheet onto a floured work surface and cut it into 12 strips, each ½ inch wide, then cut each strip in half. Twist each strip several times; they should be approximately 4 inches long.

Arrange the strips on a sheet of parchment paper and sprinkle one-third of them with the cumin seeds, one-third with the sesame seeds and the final third with the grated emmental. Place in the freezer for 20 minutes.

Preheat the oven to 400° F.

Arrange the breadsticks on a baking sheet and brush them with the lightly beaten egg yolk. Bake for 20 minutes until golden. Place them on a rack to cool then wrap them in the prosciutto slices. Serve at room temperature.

Mini puff pastry cheese pinwheels

MAKES 24 PINWHEELS
PREPARATION: **20 min**
FREEZING: **30 min**
COOKING TIME: **12 min**

> 7 oz. emmental cheese
> 7 oz. roquefort cheese
> 2 pre-prepared
  puff pastry sheets,
  approximately 8 oz. each
> 1 egg yolk

Grate the emmental. Mash the roquefort with a fork.

Unroll the puff pastry sheets and trim the edges to make them square. Spread the roquefort over the entire surface of the first square then roll it up tightly. Sprinkle the grated emmental over the entire surface of the second square then roll it up tightly. Place both rolls in the freezer for 20 minutes.

Line a baking sheet with parchment paper. Remove the rolls from the freezer then cut them into slices approximately ¼ inch thick. Place them on a baking sheet.

Preheat the oven to 400° F.

Mix the egg yolk with 1 teaspoon of water then brush the egg wash over each roll; place back in the freezer for 10 minutes.

Bake the rolls for 12 minutes. Let cool slightly before serving.

Guacamole

MAKES APPROXIMATELY
1 LB.
PREPARATION: **15 min**
REFRIGERATION: **1 hour**

> 1 small onion
> ½ bunch cilantro
> 1 tomato
> 4 medium avocados
> juice of 1 lime
> ½ tsp. Tabasco sauce
> salt, freshly ground
>   black pepper

Peel and chop the onion. Finely chop the cilantro. Immerse the tomato in boiling water for 20 seconds, then immediately put it in cold water; peel it, remove and discard the seeds, then dice it.

Cut the avocados in half, remove the pit, then scoop out the flesh with a spoon and mix with the lemon juice. Add the onion, cilantro, and Tabasco; season with salt and pepper.

In a medium bowl, mix the diced tomato with the avocado mixture.

Place the guacamole in the refrigerator for 1 hour before serving.

Aïoli

MAKES APPROXIMATELY
1 CUP
PREPARATION: **15 min**

> 4 garlic cloves
> 1 egg yolk
> 1 cup vegetable oil
> salt, freshly ground
>   black pepper

Peel the garlic cloves and remove any sprouts that have developed. In a bowl (or preferably using a mortar and pestle), crush them with a pinch of salt. Add the egg yolk and mix for 2 minutes; let stand 5 minutes.

Slowly pour the vegetable oil into the egg yolk in a thin stream while continuing to stir; season with salt and pepper.

TIP If the aïoli becomes too liquid, gradually mix in an additional egg yolk.

Tapenade

MAKES APPROXIMATELY
10½ OZ.
PREPARATION: **15 min**

> 20 salted anchovy fillets
> 9 oz. black olives
> 1¾ oz. capers
> ⅔ cup olive oil
> juice of ½ lemon

Rinse the anchovies under cold water to remove the salt. Remove and discard the pits from the olives then cut the olives into quarters; mix them with the anchovies and capers.

Add the olive oil and lemon juice, mixing well as if making a mayonnaise.

The tapenade can be kept in a small jar in the refrigerator. Serve with raw vegetables or spread on toast.

Swedish crackers

MAKES 6 SERVINGS
PREPARATION: **20 min**
COOKING TIME: **10 min**

> 10½ oz. rye flour
> ½ tsp. salt
> 1 tsp. powdered sugar
> 1 tsp. baking powder
> A pinch of seeds, such as sesame or poppy, or rosemary leaves, finely chopped

Preheat the oven to 400° F.

In a bowl, mix the flour with the salt, powdered sugar and baking powder. Add just over ¾ cup water then knead into a smooth ball.

Separate the dough into small balls. On a floured work surface, roll out each ball of dough as thinly as possible using a rolling pin. Sprinkle the dough with the seeds or herbs then roll over them once more so that the seeds or herbs adhere well to the dough.

Place the sheets of dough onto a sheet of parchment paper and bake for 10 minutes or until crispy.

Break the crackers and serve with guacamole (SEE p. 14) or any other dip.

Crackers with avocado and mascarpone spread

MAKES 12 CRACKERS
PREPARATION: **20 min**

> 4 tbsp. pumpkin seeds
> ⅓ cup mascarpone
> ⅓ cup fromage blanc (or cream cheese)
> 3 tbsp. olive oil
> 12 crackers of your choice (buckwheat, for example)
> 3 ripe avocados
> juice of 1 lemon
> 2½ oz. sprouts (such as leek or radish)
> salt, freshly ground black pepper

In a nonstick skillet, brown the pumpkin seeds; set aside.

In a small bowl, mix together the mascarpone, fromage blanc and olive oil; season with salt and pepper then mix again. Spread generously on the crackers.

Cut the avocados in half, remove the pit, then scoop out the flesh with a spoon. Cut the flesh into thin strips then sprinkle with the lemon juice. Divide the avocado among the crackers then place a pinch of sprouts on top. Sprinkle with the pumpkin seeds, season with salt and pepper and serve immediately.

quick & easy · recipe ·

Mini green and black olive cakes

MAKES 12 MINI CAKES
PREPARATION: **20 min**
COOKING TIME: **30 min**

> 3½ oz. beaufort cheese
> 1¾ oz. feta cheese
> 4 eggs
> ⅔ cup vegetable oil
> ⅔ cup dry white wine
> 2¼ cups (9 oz.) all-purpose flour, sifted
> 2 tsp. baking powder
> 1¾ oz. pitted black olives
> 1¾ oz. pitted green olives
> salt, freshly ground black pepper

Preheat the oven to 350° F.

Grate the beaufort and crumble the feta.

In a medium bowl, beat the eggs, then add the vegetable oil and wine. Add the flour, baking powder, beaufort, feta, and black and green olives and mix gently just until a smooth batter is formed; season with salt and pepper.

Grease and flour twelve 2¾ x 1½-inch individual cake molds, or use a muffin pan. Fill each one three-quarters full of batter. Bake for 30 minutes. The cakes are done when a knife inserted in the middle comes out clean.

Remove the cakes from the oven, let cool slightly, then unmold onto a rack to cool. Serve warm.

Cherry tomato tartlets

MAKES 12 TARTLETS
PREPARATION: **25 min**
COOKING TIME: **20 min**

> 4 tbsp. powdered sugar
> 3 tsp. balsamic vinegar
> 14 oz. cherry tomatoes
> 5¼ oz. mozzarella cheese
> 2 pre-prepared
  puff pastry sheets,
  approximately 8 oz. each
> 5 sprigs of basil

Preheat the oven to 400° F.

Butter the bottoms of twelve 3-inch tartlet pans. Sprinkle them with half the powdered sugar then drizzle on the balsamic vinegar. Place the cherry tomatoes up against each other in each pan, sprinkle them with the remaining powdered sugar, then bake for 5 minutes.

Remove the pans from the oven and pour off any water made by the tomatoes; set the pans aside.

Cut the mozzarella into strips and divide them equally among the tartlets, placing them on top of the tomatoes. Unroll the puff pastry sheets. Using a cookie cutter, cut out discs 4 inches in diameter and place them on top of each tartlet. Bake for 15 minutes.

Let the tartlets cool before removing them from the pans. Garnish with the fresh basil leaves and serve.

Jerusalem artichoke mousse with quail egg

low calorie · recipe ·

MAKES 12 SPOONS
PREPARATION: **30 min**
COOKING TIME: **30 min**

> 9 oz. Jerusalem
  artichokes
> juice of 1 lemon
> 2 cups chicken broth
> 3½ tbsp. butter
> 12 quail eggs
> a pinch of fleur de sel
  (sea salt)
> 3 tbsp. truffle or
  walnut oil
> 1 black truffle
> several mini beet shoots

Peel the Jerusalem artichokes and sprinkle them with the lemon juice.

In a saucepan, heat the chicken broth, then add the artichokes and cook for 20 minutes until tender. Drain and purée them in a food processor.

Heat the artichoke purée over low heat and incorporate the butter piece-by-piece with a spatula until the mixture is smooth; remove from the heat and let cool.

Bring a pot of water to a boil. Add the quail eggs and simmer on low heat for 4 minutes to cook all the way through. Cool the eggs in a bowl of ice water and gently peel off the shells.

Fill a pastry bag with the artichoke mixture. Pipe a small mound into each spoon then place a quail egg on top. Sprinkle with the fleur de sel and add a drop of truffle oil.

Grate the black truffle into very small pieces and lightly sprinkle them onto each spoon. Place small beet shoots on top and serve immediately.

Mini vegetable skewers

MAKES 12 SKEWERS
PREPARATION: **20 min**
COOKING TIME: **15 min**

> 3 zucchini
> 1 red bell pepper
> 1 yellow bell pepper
> 2 large onions
> 12 cherry tomatoes
  (red and yellow)
> 3 tbsp. olive oil
> a few sprigs of chervil
> 7 oz. basil pesto
> salt, freshly ground black
  pepper

Wash the vegetables and dry them with paper towels. Cut the zucchini into rounds approximately ½ inch thick. Cut the peppers in half, remove the seeds and the white membrane, then slice each half into strips ½ inch thick. Peel the onions and thinly slice them.

Thread the vegetables onto mini wooden skewers. In a skillet, heat the olive oil and add the vegetables to brown. Season with salt and pepper and cook approximately 10 minutes.

Chop the chervil. Just before serving, sprinkle the skewers with the chervil and serve with the chilled pesto.

Mini sweet and savory skewers

MAKES 12 SKEWERS
PREPARATION: **10 min**

> 12 radishes
> 4¼ oz. fresh goat
  cheese, slightly firm
> 12 dried apricots
> freshly ground black
  pepper

Wash the radishes and remove any leaves. Grind fresh pepper onto a plate. Shape the goat cheese into balls using your hands then roll them in the pepper; set aside, keeping chilled.

Thread the radishes, dried apricots and the goat cheese balls onto small wooden or metal skewers and serve.

Gougères (cheese puffs)

MAKES 24 GOUGÈRES
PREPARATION: **20 min**
COOKING TIME: **15 min**

> 7 tbsp. salted butter
> 1⅓ cups (5¼ oz.) all-purpose flour
> 4 eggs
> 5¼ oz. emmental cheese

Preheat the oven to 400° F. Line a baking sheet with parchment paper.

In a saucepan, melt the butter over low heat then add 1 cup of water and bring to a boil. Remove from heat then add the flour all at once and mix vigorously with a spatula. Return the pan to the heat and stir until the dough pulls away from the sides of the pan.

Remove the pan from the heat and stir in the eggs one-by-one using a spatula. Grate the emmental and carefully mix it into the dough.

Spoon the dough into balls using a tablespoon then place them on the baking sheet and bake for 25 minutes. Serve hot.

Celery gougères with caviar cream

MAKES 24 GOUGÈRES
PREPARATION: **15 min**

> 24 gougères
> 1 head of frisée lettuce (curly endive)
> 1 lemon
> 3½ oz. celery root
> 3½ oz. celery stalks
> just over ¾ cup heavy whipping cream, very cold
> 1 oz. caviar
> salt, freshly ground black pepper

Prepare gougères (SEE above) and let them cool. Slice them in half horizontally.

Sort, wash and coarsely chop the curly lettuce leaves. Juice the lemon. Season the lettuce with salt, pepper and the lemon juice.

Wash the celery root and celery stalks and cut them into small, thin sticks.

Whip the cream and add the lettuce and celery to it. Using two forks, gently incorporate the caviar into the cream to avoid crushing the eggs.

Fill the flat-bottomed gougères halves with the caviar cream then replace the top halves and serve.

You can use salmon or lumpfish roe in place of the caviar.

Goat cheese lollipops with mixed seeds

MAKES 12 LOLLIPOPS
PREPARATION: **15 min**
REFRIGERATION: **1 hour**

> 4½ oz. fresh goat cheese
> 2 tbsp. crème fraîche
> 1 tbsp. hazelnut oil
> 2 oz. of a mixture of seeds (flax, sunflower, poppy, etc.)
> salt, freshly ground black pepper

In a bowl, mix the goat cheese well with a spoon then add the crème fraîche. Season with salt and pepper then add the hazelnut oil and mix well. Refrigerate for 1 hour.

Pour the seed mixture into a shallow bowl. Using your hands, form the cheese mixture into uniform balls the size of a small walnut. Roll them quickly in the seeds. Place a small toothpick into each and serve.

Prunes with roquefort

MAKES 20 PRUNES
PREPARATION: **25 min**
REFRIGERATION: **2 hours**

> 20 pitted prunes (preferably Agen)
> 3 oz. roquefort cheese
> 2 tbsp. chopped hazelnuts
> 1 heaping tbsp. crème fraîche (or sour cream)
> 2 tsp. port wine
> freshly ground black pepper

Spread open the prunes and flatten them using the side of a knife blade or the back of a spoon.

Using a fork, finely crumble the roquefort in a bowl. Add the chopped hazelnuts, crème fraîche and the port; season with pepper.

Using a small spoon, place a dollop of the mixture into the center of each prune. Close and reshape the prunes then pierce them with a toothpick to keep them closed. Place in the refrigerator for 2 hours before serving.

Potato and chorizo tortilla

MAKES 12 SQUARES
PREPARATION: **15 min**
COOKING TIME: **10 min**

> 3½ oz. chorizo
> 1 onion
> 1 potato
> 4 tbsp. olive oil
> 3 eggs
> salt, freshly ground
  black pepper

Thinly slice the chorizo. Peel and thinly slice both the onion and the potato.

Immerse the potato and onion in boiling, salted water and cook for 5 minutes; drain and set aside.

In a skillet, heat the olive oil and fry the potato, onion and chorizo for 2 minutes.

In a small bowl, beat the eggs and season lightly with salt and pepper then pour them into the pan on top of the potatoes, onion and chorizo. Cook over low heat for 5 minutes on each side, turning the tortilla over halfway through the cooking time.

Cut the tortilla into 12 squares. Serve warm or cold, with toothpicks.

Mini bacon and cheese cakes

MAKES 8–10 MINI CAKES
PREPARATION: **25 min**
COOKING TIME: **20–25 min**

> 5¼ oz. comté cheese
> 5¼ oz. mimolette cheese
> 5¼ oz. lean, smoked bacon
> 4 eggs
> 1¾ cups (7 oz.) all-purpose flour
> 2 tsp. baking powder
> ½ cup milk
> ⅔ cup olive oil
> salt, freshly ground black pepper

Preheat the oven to 350° F.

Grate the comté and the mimolette. Cut the bacon into small strips.

In a large bowl, beat the eggs then add the flour and baking powder; season with salt and pepper and mix well. Gradually stir in the milk and olive oil to form a smooth paste. Add the comté, mimolette and bacon and stir gently.

Grease and flour eight to ten 2¾ x 1½-inch individual cake molds, or use a muffin pan. Fill each three-quarters full of batter. Bake 20 to 25 minutes—the cakes are done when the point of a knife inserted in the center comes out clean.

Remove the cakes from the oven, let cool slightly, then unmold onto a cooling rack. Serve warm.

Speck and ricotta muffins

MAKES 12 MUFFINS
PREPARATION: **25 min**
COOKING TIME: **20 min**

> 3½ oz. speck ham
> 2 tsp. chives
> 2 eggs
> 3½ oz. buckwheat flour
> 3½ oz. wheat flour
> 2 tsp. baking powder
> ⅔ cup white wine
> ½ cup olive oil
> 3½ oz. ricotta cheese
> salt, freshly ground black pepper

Preheat the oven to 350° F. Grease and flour 12 individual muffin molds or use a muffin pan lined with paper cups.

Cut the speck ham into pieces. Wash and chop the chives.

In a bowl, beat the eggs, add the two flours and the baking powder and mix well. Add the white wine, olive oil, ricotta, chives and ham. Mix again and season to taste.

Divide the batter among the muffin molds, filling each three-quarters full. Bake for 20 minutes.

Remove the muffins from the oven, let cool for 2 minutes, then unmold. Serve warm.

Asparagus bacon twists

MAKES 12 TWISTS
PREPARATION: **10 min**
COOKING TIME: **5 min**

> 12 green asparagus stalks
> 12 slices bacon
> a handful of sesame seeds
> salt

Break off the fibrous ends of the asparagus. Bring a large pot of salted water to a boil, immerse the asparagus and cook for 5 minutes; drain on paper towels and let cool.

Wrap a piece of bacon around each asparagus stalk. Fry quickly in a nonstick skillet. Sprinkle with the sesame seeds and serve immediately.

Beans with cumin

MAKES 6 VERRINES
(2-OZ. GLASSES)
PREPARATION: **10 min**
COOKING TIME: **4-7 min**

> 1 lb. fresh shelled or frozen fava or broad beans
> juice of ¼ lemon
> 1 tbsp. olive oil
> 1 tsp. ground cumin
> salt, freshly ground black pepper

Boil the beans for 5 minutes in lightly salted water. Drain them and put them in a small bowl.

Sprinkle the beans with the lemon juice and the olive oil then season with the cumin and freshly ground black pepper. Mix, then place the bowl in the refrigerator until ready to serve.

Divide the beans among six 2-ounce glasses and serve with toothpicks.

Prosciutto, fig and melon skewers

MAKES 12 SKEWERS
PREPARATION: 15 min

> 1 large cantaloupe melon
> 6 thin slices of prosciutto
> 6 fresh figs
> 1 small bunch fresh mint
> salt, freshly ground black pepper

Cut the melon in half and remove the seeds. Using a melon baller, form balls from the flesh and set aside.

Cut the slices of prosciutto into thirds and the figs into quarters.

Thread the melon balls, pieces of prosciutto, fig and mint leaves onto wooden skewers, alternating the ingredients; season with salt and pepper and serve.

low calorie · recipe ·

Mini pork and pineapple skewers

MAKES 12 SKEWERS
PREPARATION: 25 min
MARINADE: 30 min
COOKING TIME: 15 min

> 14 oz. pork tenderloin
> 2 Victoria pineapples or 1 large pineapple
> 3 tbsp. sesame seeds
> 4 tbsp. olive oil
> 2 tbsp. soy sauce
> 2 tbsp. sugar
> 1 small bunch cilantro
> freshly ground black pepper

Cut the pork into cubes.

Slice off the base and the top of the pineapple, then remove the rind and slice the flesh into cubes, removing the core and collecting the juice.

Pour the retained pineapple juice into a large bowl, add the sesame seeds and the pork then season with a little freshly ground pepper (1 turn of the pepper mill). Refrigerate for 30 minutes.

Thread alternate pieces of meat and pineapple onto toothpicks. In a skillet, heat the olive oil over medium heat, then add the mini skewers and cook for 5 minutes, turning often. Add the soy sauce and sugar and cook for another 10 minutes.

Sprinkle the mini skewers with cilantro leaves and serve hot.

Duck and prune muffins

MAKES 12 MUFFINS
PREPARATION: **25 min**
COOKING TIME: **15 min**

> 8 pitted prunes
> 5¼ oz. smoked duck breast
> 7 tbsp. butter, softened
> 3 eggs
> 2 cups (8 oz.) all-purpose flour
> 1¾ tsp. baking powder
> salt

Preheat the oven to 350° F. Grease and flour 12 individual muffin molds or use a muffin pan lined with paper cups.

Roughly chop the prunes and the duck breast.

In a medium bowl, mix the butter with the eggs, then carefully incorporate the sifted flour and baking powder. Add the duck and prunes; season with salt to taste.

Divide the batter among the molds, filling each three-quarters full. Bake for 15 minutes.

Remove the muffins from the oven, let them cool for 2 minutes, then unmold them gently using a non-serrated knife. Serve warm.

VARIATION Replace the prunes with dried apricots.

Foie gras bites in gingerbread crumbs

MAKES 12 BITES
PREPARATION: **10 min**
COOKING TIME: **12 min**

> 5 slices of gingerbread or rye bread
> ½ tsp. freshly ground black pepper
> ½ tsp. quatre-épices (or allspice)
> 7 oz. pre-cooked foie gras (whole or in blocks)

Preheat the oven to 350° F. Line a baking sheet with parchment paper.

Cut the gingerbread into pieces then place them in the bowl of a food processor along with the pepper and quatre-épices. Process into fine crumbs. Spread the crumbs onto the baking sheet and bake for 12 minutes; cool.

Cut the foie gras into 1-inch cubes then roll the cubes in the crumbs, pressing down on them to adhere the crumbs well. Serve immediately.

Gingerbread, foie gras and fig canapés

MAKES 20 CANAPÉS
PREPARATION: **15 min**
COOKING TIME: **1 min**

> 1 loaf of gingerbread or rye bread
> approximately 5¼ oz. pre-cooked foie gras (whole or in blocks)
> 1 or 2 fresh figs
> mixed peppercorns
> fleur de sel (sea salt)

Using a serrated knife, cut the gingerbread into slices approximately ¼ inch thick then cut each slice into the shape of a rectangle approximately 1½ by 2½ inches; toast lightly.

Cut the foie gras into the same size as the slices of gingerbread and divide them among the toasted slices.

Rinse and dry the figs then thinly slice them and arrange them on the foie gras. Season with the freshly ground mixed peppercorns and a little fleur de sel.

When fresh figs are out of season, use fig chutney instead.

Smoked mackerel and radish spread

MAKES 24 SERVINGS
PREPARATION: **20 min**

> ½ bunch dill
> 1 bunch radishes
> 2 smoked mackerel fillets (approximately 7 oz.)
> 3½ oz. light spreadable cheese, such as fromage frais or light cream cheese
> 2 tbsp. olive oil
> juice of 1 lemon
> 12 slices rye bread
> freshly ground black pepper

Wash and dry the dill. Wash and hull the radishes then thinly slice them.

In a small bowl, crumble the mackerel, add the cheese, then mash these together with a fork (or pulse briefly in a food processor, maintaining a thick texture). Stir in the olive oil and the lemon juice then season with pepper.

Cut the bread slices in half and spread them with the mixture, then cover them with slices of radish and a few small dill sprigs and serve.

VARIATION Try making this with tuna instead. Mix 7 ounces of tuna packed in water with 3 tablespoons of spreadable cheese. Season to taste with lemon juice and pepper. Instead of radishes, use finely chopped celery or sliced cherry tomatoes. Serve on bread or plain crackers.

Mini sun-dried tomato and tuna cakes

MAKES 12 MINI CAKES
PREPARATION: **20 min**
COOKING TIME: **15 min**

> 8 sun-dried tomatoes packed in oil
> 9 oz. canned tuna (preferably Catalan)
> 2 cups (8 oz.) all-purpose flour
> 1¾ tsp. baking powder
> 5 tbsp. olive oil
> 3 eggs
> salt, freshly ground black pepper

Preheat the oven to 350° F. Grease and flour twelve 2¾ x 1½-inch individual cake molds, or use a muffin pan.

Roughly chop the sun-dried tomatoes and drain the tuna.

In a large bowl, mix the flour and the baking powder then add the olive oil and the eggs, one-by-one. Add the tuna and tomatoes and mix gently to maintain a few whole pieces of tuna in the mixture; lightly season with salt and pepper.

Pour the batter into the molds, filling them three-quarters full. Bake for 15 minutes.

Remove them from the oven, let cool, then unmold onto a rack. Serve warm.

Scrambled egg blinis with salmon roe

MAKES 12 BLINIS
PREPARATION: **15 min**
COOKING TIME: **10 min**

> 2 tbsp. butter
> 1 tbsp. chopped chives
> 8 very fresh eggs
> 2 tbsp. port wine
> 12 mini blinis
> 1 jar salmon roe
> salt, freshly ground black pepper

Cut the butter into small pieces. Wash and chop the chives.

In a heavy-bottomed saucepan, add the eggs, salt, pepper, and half the butter. Cook over medium heat for 8 to 10 minutes, whisking constantly until the eggs become creamy. Remove from the heat and stir in the remaining butter. Pour in the port, then whisk for a few seconds longer.

Gently warm the blinis under the broiler, remove them, then top them with a spoonful of the scrambled eggs. Garnish with the salmon roe and chives. Serve immediately.

Smoked salmon mousse and cucumber purée

MAKES 12 VERRINES
(2-OZ. GLASSES)
PREPARATION: **20 min**
REFRIGERATION: **30 min**

> ½ cup heavy whipping cream, very cold
> 1 small cucumber, unpeeled
> 1 pinch pink peppercorns
> 10 oz. smoked salmon
> 3½ oz. beet shoots
> salt

Pour the heavy cream into a mixing bowl and chill for 30 minutes.

Slice the cucumber then chop it using a food processor. Season with salt and sprinkle with pink peppercorns; set aside.

Process the smoked salmon until it is slightly puréed. Whip the cream until it holds stiff peaks then fold this into the smoked salmon.

Divide the cucumber among twelve 2-ounce glasses then top with the salmon mousse. Garnish with the beet shoots and serve chilled.

Cucumber crab bites

MAKES 10 BITES
PREPARATION: **15 min**

> 1 medium cucumber
> 3 oz. crab meat (fresh or canned)
> 1 tbsp. crème fraîche (or sour cream)
> 1 tbsp. tomato pulp
> 1 tsp. chopped chives
> salt, freshly ground black pepper

Wash the cucumbers then slice off the ends to obtain a cylinder shape. Using a vegetable peeler, remove strips of the peel all the way down the cucumber, leaving alternating stripes of green peel and white flesh. Slice the cucumber into sections 1 inch thick. Using a melon baller, scoop out half the flesh from inside each piece (going only half way down inside the section) then season with a little salt. Place them on a grill or other low-heat source and turn them several times to help release their water.

Mix the crab meat with the crème fraîche, tomato pulp and the chives then season with salt and pepper.

Top each piece of cucumber with the crab filling, forming a small dome. Arrange the bites on a serving dish and refrigerate until ready to serve.

quick & easy recipe

Mini sardines
on toast

MAKES 12 TOASTS
PREPARATION: **35 min**
MARINADE: **2 hours**

> 6 oranges
> 1 lemon
> 2 garlic cloves
> 6 fresh sardines
> 2 tbsp. parsley or chervil
> 1 tsp. salt
> 3 tsp. pink peppercorns
> 3 tbsp. olive oil
> 1 sesame baguette
> 3½ oz. arugula

Juice 2 of the oranges and the lemon into a shallow bowl. Peel and chop the garlic clove.

Rinse the sardines under cold water and pat them dry with paper towels. Cut them in half lengthwise.

Wash and chop the parsley or chervil and add it to the citrus juice. Add the salt, pink peppercorns, olive oil and the garlic. Place the sardine fillets in the juice mixture and marinate, refrigerated, for 2 hours, turning the fillets several times during this time.

Preheat the broiler.

Cut the baguette into 12 slices, then place them under the broiler until lightly browned. Peel and segment the remaining oranges.

On each slice of toasted bread, place 1 or 2 slices of orange, 1 sardine fillet and 1 leaf of arugula. Serve immediately.

Avocado cream and shrimp barquettes

MAKES 10 BARQUETTES
PREPARATION: **25 min**
COOKING TIME:
15–20 min

> 10 to 20 cooked shrimp (depending on size)
> 1 pre-prepared pie or savory tart crust
> 1 avocado
> juice of ½ lemon
> Cayenne pepper
> ¼ cup mayonnaise
> salt, freshly ground black pepper

Shell the shrimp, leaving the tails attached.

Preheat the oven to 350° F. Butter ten 2½ to 3-inch-long barquette molds.

Cut out ten pieces of the dough in the shape of the molds. Line the molds with the dough, prick the dough lightly with a fork, and bake for 15 to 20 minutes, just until golden; let cool.

Cut the avocado in half, remove the pit, scoop out the flesh with a spoon and place it on a flat plate. Sprinkle with the lemon juice then mash it with a fork into a thick purée. Season with salt and pepper and add a generous amount of Cayenne pepper. Add the mayonnaise and mix.

Fill the barquette molds with the avocado cream and smooth the top. Place 1 shrimp in each mold (or 2 if they are small). Serve well chilled.

You can add a half pink grapefruit segment (white membrane removed) and a few dill leaves or fresh cilantro on top of each barquette, if desired.

Shrimp puppies

MAKES 24 BALLS
PREPARATION: **30 min**
COOKING TIME: **25 min**

> 7 oz. boiling potatoes
> ½ bunch parsley
> ½ bunch mint
> 5¼ oz. peeled shrimp
> 7 oz. fresh cod fillet
> 1 large pinch of Cayenne pepper
> 1 egg
> vegetable oil, for frying
> ½ cup (1¾ oz.) all-purpose flour
> salt

Peel the potatoes and boil them for 20 minutes in salted water. Drain and mash them with a fork or a potato masher.

Mince the parsley and mint.

In the bowl of a food processor, process the shrimp and cod fillet. Add the pinch of Cayenne pepper, minced parsley and mint, and the egg; season with salt and process again for 30 seconds.

Pour the mixture into a large bowl then mix in the mashed potatoes. Using your hands, form the mixture into balls approximately the size of a walnut.

Fill a large, heavy saucepan one-third full of vegetable oil and heat to 350° F. Roll the dough balls in the flour and fry for 2 or 3 minutes. Serve warm with toothpicks.

Spring gazpacho with crayfish

quick & easy · recipe ·

MAKES 12 VERRINES
(2-OZ. GLASSES)
PREPARATION: 15 min

> 2 spring onions
> 1⅓ lbs. cucumber
> 10½ oz. fennel
> ⅓ cup olive oil
> 3 tbsp. sherry vinegar
> 7 oz. peeled crayfish
> salt, freshly ground black
  pepper

Break off a 2½-inch long section of the green portion of each spring onion. Slice these sections into thin strips and place them in a bowl of cold water; refrigerate.

Wash the cucumber and the fennel and pat dry. Cut them into pieces along with the remainder of the onions.

In a blender, add the cucumber, fennel and onion pieces. Add 1¼ cups water, the olive oil and the vinegar then blend to form the gazpacho; season with salt and pepper to taste.

Remove the onion greens from the bowl of water and let drain. Divide the gazpacho among twelve 2-ounce glasses and add crayfish pieces on top. Decorate with strips of onion greens and serve.

VARIATION Instead of crayfish you can use shrimp, crab meat or slices of imitation crab.

Mini scallop and chorizo skewers

MAKES 12 SKEWERS
PREPARATION: **15 min**
COOKING TIME:
approximately 3 min

> 12 cleaned scallops
> 2 tbsp. olive oil
> 3 tbsp. orange juice
> 4¼ oz. chorizo
> freshly ground
  black pepper

Pat the scallops dry with paper towels then place them in a small bowl with the olive oil and the orange juice.

Cut the chorizo into 24 thin slices.

On small wooden skewers (or long toothpicks), thread each scallop between two slices of chorizo.

In a nonstick skillet, cook the skewers for 30 seconds on each side. Lightly season with the freshly ground black pepper and serve.

Marinated scallop canapés

MAKES 12–15 CANAPÉS
MARINADE: **1 hour**
COOKING TIME: **5 min**

> 12 cleaned scallops
> 3 tbsp. olive oil
> 1 tbsp. lemon juice
> 10 chive stalks, minced
> 1 small loaf of rye bread,
  sliced
> fleur de sel (sea salt)
  and freshly ground
  black pepper

Quickly rinse the scallops then pat them dry using paper towels. Cut them into strips of approximately ⅛ inch thick. Arrange them on a platter and drizzle with the olive oil and lemon juice then season with the pepper; sprinkle on a little of the minced chives. Cover the platter with plastic wrap and marinate in the refrigerator for approximately 1 hour.

Cut out round sections of approximately 1½ to 2 inches in diameter from the bread then lightly toast the rounds. Divide the strips of scallop among the toasted bread pieces then sprinkle with a little fleur de sel and serve.

To save time, use rye crackers instead.

Appetizers

Andalusian gazpacho

FOR 4 PEOPLE
PREPARATION: **25 min**
REFRIGERATION: **2 hours**

> 4 tomatoes
> 1 red bell pepper
> 1 green bell pepper
> 5¼ oz. cucumber
> 1 onion
> 2 garlic cloves
> 1 tbsp. tomato paste
> 1 tbsp. capers, drained
> 1 sprig fresh thyme
> 2 tbsp. vinegar
> 10 tarragon leaves
> 1 lemon
> 3 tbsp. olive oil
> salt, freshly ground
  black pepper

Immerse the tomatoes in boiling water for 20 seconds, then immediately put them in cold water. Peel them, remove and discard the seeds, then dice them. Do the same with the red and green bell peppers.

Peel the cucumber and cut it up into cubes. Peel and chop the onion and garlic cloves.

Add all of the chopped vegetables to a large bowl, then add the tomato paste, capers, thyme and vinegar.

Pour 4¼ cups cold water in the bowl and process with an immersion blender (or a standing blender).

Chop the tarragon and juice the lemon. Add this to the gazpacho along with the olive oil. Add salt and pepper and blend well.

Place the gazpacho in the refrigerator for at least 2 hours. Serve in very cold bowls.

low calorie
· recipe ·

Avocado and citrus salad

FOR 6 PEOPLE
PREPARATION: 15 min
REFRIGERATION: 30 min
COOKING TIME:
approximately 1 min

> 2 lemons
> 2 avocados
> 2 oranges
> 1 pink grapefruit
> 1 white grapefruit
> 1 small bunch mint
> 5 tbsp. olive oil
> 1 pinch sugar
> 2 tbsp. pine nuts
> 6 black olives
> salt, freshly ground
  black pepper

Juice the lemons. Cut the avacados in half, remove the pits then scoop out the flesh with a spoon and dice it; sprinkle with lemon juice.

Peel the oranges and grapefruit, removing all of the white membrane.

Wash and chop the mint. Place it in a bowl, pour in the olive oil, add the pinch of sugar, then season with salt and pepper; mix well.

Place the avocado and citrus segments in a large bowl. Drizzle with the dressing and mix gently. Chill for 30 minutes.

Toast the pine nuts in a dry skillet.

Divide the salad among 6 plates and sprinkle on the pine nuts and add a black olive for garnish. Serve immediately.

Arugula salad with basil and parmesan

FOR 4 PEOPLE
PREPARATION: 10 min

> 3 oz. parmesan
> 3½ oz. arugula
> 1 tbsp. olive oil
> 2 tbsp. balsamic vinegar
> 1 tbsp. chopped basil
  plus a few whole leaves
> salt, freshly ground
  black pepper

Shave off thin strips of the parmesan with a vegetable peeler or a mandoline. Wash and drain the arugula then wrap it in a dry cloth or paper towel to dry.

Pour the olive oil and 1 teaspoon of the balsamic vinegar in a small bowl, whisk lightly with a fork, then add the chopped basil and arugula; season with salt and pepper and mix.

Divide the contents of the bowl among 4 plates then arrange the strips of parmesan on each. Sprinkle with the remaining balsamic vinegar and garnish with whole basil leaves. Serve immediately.

quick & easy · recipe

Tomato and mint mille-feuilles

quick & easy · recipe ·

FOR 4 PEOPLE
PREPARATION: 10 min

> 4 large tomatoes
> 3 oz. feta (in block form)
> 3 tbsp. balsamic vinegar
> 3 tbsp. olive oil
> 20 fresh mint leaves
> freshly ground
  black pepper

Wash the tomatoes and cut them into fairly thick slices. Slice the feta into thin strips.

Pour half a tablespoon of balsamic vinegar on each of 4 plates, sprinkle with pepper then add half a tablespoon of olive oil. Place a slice of tomato on top of the seasoning then cover with a few slices of feta and a mint leaf. Continue with another slice of tomato and keep alternating the ingredients until all are used, ending with a mint leaf.

Season the mille-feuilles with pepper, a sprinkle of vinegar plus more olive oil. Keep refrigerated until ready to serve.

VARIATION **Replace the mint with basil.**

Tomatoes with mozzarella

quick & easy · recipe ·

FOR 4 PEOPLE
PREPARATION: 15 min

> 4 or 5 tomatoes
> 7 oz. mozzarella
> ½ bunch basil
> 1 tbsp. balsamic vinegar
> 3 tbsp. olive oil
> salt, freshly ground
  black pepper

Wash and slice the tomatoes.

Cut the mozzarella into thin slices. Chop the basil.

Arrange the tomato slices on a serving plate and create alternating layers with the slices of mozzarella; season with salt and pepper and sprinkle with the chopped basil. Sprinkle on a few drops of balsamic vinegar and a drizzle of olive oil. Serve at room temperature.

Celery and apple rémoulade

FOR 4 PEOPLE
PREPARATION: **20 min**
COOKING TIME: **1 min**
REFRIGERATION: **1 hour**

> 14 oz. celery root
> 2 apples
> juice of ½ lemon

**For the rémoulade sauce
(makes just over ¾ cup)**

> 1 egg yolk
> 1 tbsp. mustard
> Just over ¾ cup oil
> salt, freshly ground
  black pepper

Prepare the rémoulade sauce. In a large bowl, mix the egg yolk and mustard. Gradually pour the oil into the egg yolk/mustard mixture in a thin stream while whisking constantly; season with salt and pepper and refrigerate until ready to use.

Bring a large pot of lightly salted water to a boil. Meanwhile, peel the celery root and cut it into large quarter pieces. Grate the celery pieces with a coarse grater and immerse them immediately in the boiling water. Let the water come back to a boil and boil for 1 minute. Remove the celery and immerse it immediately in cold water. Remove it, place it in a towel, then squeeze it firmly to wring out most of the water.

Peel and core the apples. Grate them using the same sized grater as used for the celery or use a knife to cut them into a fine dice; sprinkle immediately with the lemon juice.

Put the grated apples and celery in a large bowl, add the rémoulade sauce and mix well. Refrigerate for 1 hour.

Serve with a few slices of smoked duck breast or serve inside of cored apples.

Celery root and rémoulade sauce with capers

FOR 4 PEOPLE
PREPARATION: **20 min**
REFRIGERATION: **1 hour**

> just over ¾ cup
  rémoulade sauce
> various herbs (parsley,
  chives, tarragon, chervil)
> 2 cornichon pickles
> 1 tbsp. capers
> 16 oz. celery root
> ½ lemon

Prepare the rémoulade sauce (SEE above).

Chop the herbs to achieve 3 tablespoons. Finely dice the cornichons. Add the herbs, cornichons and capers to the rémoulade sauce; season with salt and pepper.

Peel the celery root and squeeze the lemon juice over it to prevent browning. Grate it with a coarse grater. Mix it with the rémoulade sauce and sprinkle it with the parsley. Refrigerate for 1 hour then serve well chilled.

Wheat, avocado and grapefruit salad

FOR 4 PEOPLE
PREPARATION: **10 min**
COOKING TIME: **10 min**

> 5¼ oz. precooked wheat
  grain, such as bulgur
> 1 avocado
> juice of 1 lemon
> 1 pink grapefruit
> 1 tbsp. fromage blanc
  (or plain yogurt)
> 2 tbsp. olive oil
> A few leaves of fresh
  cilantro
> salt, freshly ground
  black pepper

Boil the bulgur in salted water for 10 minutes; drain.

Cut the avocado in half, remove the pit and scoop out the flesh with a spoon and slice it. Place it in a salad bowl then sprinkle it with half the lemon juice. Peel and segment the grapefruit. Add the cooked wheat and the grapefruit segments to the bowl.

In a small bowl, mix the remaining lemon juice with salt and pepper. Add the fromage blanc and whisk in the olive oil until it's well emulsified.

Pour the dressing into the salad bowl and mix; sprinkle with the chopped cilantro.

Sprouted wheat salad

FOR 6 PEOPLE
RESTING TIME: **24 hours**

+ 24 hours
PREPARATION: **30 min**
MARINADE: **30 min**

> 7 oz. whole wheat grains
> 2 thin-skinned zucchini
> ¼ cup olive oil
> 3 tbsp. lemon juice
> 4 tbsp. raisins
> 1 yellow bell pepper
  (pre-marinated)
> salt, freshly ground
  black pepper

Two days before: Place the wheat grains in a shallow dish and cover with water; let soak for 24 hours.

The day before: Wash the wheat grains then place them back in the bowl, without water, for 24 hours; they must remain a little moist.

The next day: Wash the sprouted grains. Wash and thinly slice the zucchini then drizzle them with the olive oil and the lemon juice; let marinate for 30 minutes.

Meanwhile, soak the raisins in warm water until plump. Thinly slice the pepper. In a salad bowl, place the sprouted wheat, zucchini (along with the marinade), pepper and the drained raisins; season with salt and pepper. Stir well and serve at room temperature.

Mâche lettuce and beet salad

FOR 4 PEOPLE
PREPARATION: **10 min**
COOKING TIME: **several seconds**

> 3½ oz. mâche lettuce (or field greens)
> 1 raw or cooked beet
> 1 granny smith apple
> 1 tbsp. pine nuts
> 1 tbsp. sesame seeds
> a dozen hazelnuts

For the dressing

> 1 tbsp. cider vinegar
> 2 tbsp. peanut oil
> 1 tbsp. hazelnut oil
> salt, freshly ground black pepper

Wash the mâche lettuce and squeeze out the water. If using a raw beet, peel and grate the beet.

If you are using a cooked beet, cut it into cubes. Wash the apple, core it then thinly slice it.

Prepare the vinaigrette. Pour the cider vinegar into a salad bowl; season with salt and pepper. Slowly drizzle in the oils, whisking constantly to create a smooth emulsion.

Lightly brown the pine nuts and sesame seeds in a dry, hot skillet.

Add the lettuce, apple slices and beets to the bowl. Sprinkle with the hazelnuts, pine nuts and the sesame seeds; mix and serve immediately.

VARIATION If you prefer a lower calorie salad, replace the peanut oil with 2 tablespoons of fromage blanc (or plain yogurt) or light crème fraîche.

low calorie recipe

Mint tabbouleh

FOR 4 PEOPLE
PREPARATION: **30 min**
REFRIGERATION: **3 hours**

> approximately 1⅓ cups (9 oz.) couscous or bulgur
> 1 lb. tomatoes
> 9 oz. onions
> fresh mint
> flat-leaf parsley
> ⅓ cup olive oil
> juice of 3 lemons
> 8 small white onions
> salt, freshly ground black pepper

Put the couscous in a bowl and drizzle in just over ¾ cup boiling water; set aside.

Wash and dice the tomatoes. Peel and chop the onions. Chop 4 tablespoons of both the mint and the parsley; add the herbs to the couscous then season with salt and pepper and mix.

Pour in the oil then add all of the lemon juice. Mix and refrigerate for 3 hours, stirring the tabbouleh four or five times during this time.

Just before serving, peel the small white onions and cut them into quarters. Add them to the tabbouleh with the mint leaves.

Caesar salad

FOR 4-6 PEOPLE
PREPARATION: **20 min**
COOKING TIME: **10 min**

> 3 eggs
> 2 hearts of romaine
  or frisée lettuce (curly
  endive)
> 5 thick slices of bread
> 2 garlic cloves
> 4 tbsp. olive oil
> 6 anchovy fillets in oil
> 1 lemon
> 1¾ oz. parmesan cheese
  shavings
> salt, freshly ground
  black pepper

Hard boil the eggs for 10 minutes. Separate and wash the lettuce leaves.

Cut the crust from the bread slices then cut the bread into small squares. Peel and chop the garlic cloves.

Heat 2 tablespoons of the olive oil in a skillet; add the garlic and stir. Add the bread squares and brown, 5 minutes. Place the croutons on paper towels to drain.

Cool the hard-boiled eggs, remove the shells then cut the eggs into quarters. Slice the anchovies into long strips.

In a salad bowl, prepare the vinaigrette with the lemon juice, the remaining olive oil, and salt and pepper to taste. Add the lettuce leaves and toss. Add the hard-boiled eggs, croutons, and the anchovies. Scatter parmesan shavings on top and serve.

Snow pea and crab salad

FOR 4-6 PEOPLE
PREPARATION: **10 min**
COOKING TIME: **10 min**

> 1 lb. snow peas
> 8 oz. can crab meat
> 1 organic lemon
> ½ cup heavy cream
> 2 tbsp. olive oil
> 1 tbsp. chopped parsley
  or tarragon
> salt, freshly ground
  black pepper

String the snow peas. Boil for 10 minutes in salted water or steam them.

Drain the liquid from the crab meat; remove any cartilage.

Zest and juice the lemon; drizzle some of the juice over the crab.

In a bowl, whisk together the heavy cream, olive oil, and lemon zest; season with salt and pepper.

In a serving bowl, combine the snow peas, crab meat and the remaining lemon juice. Add the heavy cream mixture, stir gently, then sprinkle with parsley or tarragon and serve.

"Soybean sprout" seafood salad

FOR 4 PEOPLE
PREPARATION: **20 min**
COOKING TIME: **1 min**

> 1 lb. mung bean sprouts ("soy bean sprouts")
> 8 long strips of imitation crab meat
> 7 oz. small peeled shrimp
> 4 or 5 sprigs of cilantro

For the sauce
> 2 small onions
> soy sauce
> 1 tsp. mild mustard
> 1 pinch of sugar
> 1 tbsp. sherry
> 1 tbsp. cider vinegar
> 3 tbsp. rapeseed or peanut oil
> Cayenne pepper

Wash the bean sprouts then immerse them for 1 minute in boiling, salted water. Place them in a colander and rinse them under cold water; drain and dry them in paper towels.

Slice the crab meat; place in a bowl with the shrimp and bean sprouts.

Prepare the sauce. Peel and finely chop the onions. Place them in a large bowl, add 1 tablespoon of soy sauce, the mustard, sugar, sherry, vinegar, oil and 2 pinches of Cayenne pepper.

Whisk vigorously to emulsify the sauce then pour over the crab meat mixture; toss well. Garnish with the cilantro.

What are frequently called "soy bean sprouts" are not real soy but instead mung bean sprouts.

low calorie · recipe ·

Niçoise salad

FOR 4-6 PEOPLE
PREPARATION: **40 min**
COOKING TIME: **10 min**

> 5 eggs
> 1 small head of lettuce
> 6-8 tomatoes
> 1 bunch of spring onions
> 12 to 18 salted anchovy fillets
> 1 bell pepper
> 3 celery stalks
> 1 lemon
> 3 or 4 purple artichoke hearts
> 2 tbsp. white wine vinegar
> 5 tbsp. olive oil
> 1 can tuna, 5 oz., packed in oil or water
> 3½ oz. small black olives (preferably Niçoise)
> salt, freshly ground black pepper

Hard boil the eggs for 10 minutes.

Wash the lettuce then pat it dry. Cut the tomatoes into quarters. Peel the onions and chop them, including the white and some of the light green portion.

Rinse the anchovies under cold water to remove the salt.

Rinse the bell pepper, remove the seeds and cut it into thin strips. Wash the celery stalks and finely dice them. Squeeze lemon juice over the artichoke hearts then cut them up. Cool the eggs under cold water then peel and quarter them.

Prepare the vinaigrette with the vinegar, olive oil, salt and pepper.

In a large shallow dish, place several lettuce leaves, tomatoes, artichoke slices, pepper strips, tuna pieces, onions, 2 or 3 pinches of celery and the chopped onion greens. Continue layering until all of the ingredients are used.

Pour the vinaigrette over the salad and toss lightly. Arrange the egg quarters and anchovies on top. Garnish with the olives.

Curly endive and bacon salad

FOR 4 PEOPLE
PREPARATION: **20 min**
COOKING TIME:
approximately 10 min

> 4 eggs
> 1 small head curly endive
  (frisée lettuce)
> 7 oz. thick-cut bacon,
  cut into small cubes

For the vinaigrette

> 1 tsp. mustard
> 1 tbsp. red wine vinegar
> ¼ cup olive oil or
  rapeseed oil
> salt, freshly ground
  black pepper

Boil the eggs for 6 minutes at a rolling boil so that they become soft-boiled; immediately immerse them in cold water then peel them.

Pull apart the endive leaves, wash them then squeeze them of excess water. Chop them up and place them in a salad bowl.

Prepare the vinaigrette. In a small bowl, mix the mustard with the vinegar; season with salt and pepper. Gradually drizzle in the olive oil in a thin stream, whisking constantly to emulsify.

Brown the bacon in a nonstick skillet over medium heat for 5 minutes. When crispy and still warm, add it to the salad bowl. Pour the dressing over the salad and toss. Arrange the eggs on top and serve.

Watercress salad

FOR 4 PEOPLE
PREPARATION: **20 min**
COOKING TIME: **10 min**

> 2 eggs
> 1 bunch watercress
> 1 lemon
> 1 apple
> 2 oz. gouda cheese

For the vinaigrette

> 1 tsp. mustard
> 3 tbsp. walnut oil
> 1 tbsp. sherry vinegar
> salt, freshly ground
  black pepper

Hard boil the eggs for 10 minutes.

Sort through the watercress, removing any large stems, then wash it several times in cold water and gently pat dry.

Immerse the eggs for several minutes in cold water then peel and slice them. Juice the lemon. Peel and core the apple, drizzle it with half the lemon juice then dice. Dice the gouda.

Prepare the vinaigrette. Mix the mustard, walnut oil and vinegar. Add the remaining lemon juice then season with salt and pepper.

Place the watercress in a bowl along with the diced apple and cheese. Drizzle with vinaigrette and toss. Add the egg slices and serve.

Zucchini flan

FOR 4 PEOPLE
PREPARATION: **20 min**
COOKING TIME: **1 hour 25 minutes**

> 1⅔ lb. small, firm zucchini
> 2 shallots
> 3 tbsp. olive oil
> 5 eggs
> 1 cup crème fraîche (or heavy cream)
> salt, freshly ground black pepper

Cut the zucchini into ½-inch cubes. Peel and chop the shallots. In a frying pan, heat the oil and sauté the zucchini for 5 minutes over medium heat. Add the shallots and cook 2 or 3 minutes. Remove the pan from the heat, season with salt and pepper and let cool.

Preheat the oven to 325° F and butter a 9-inch round cake pan. In a large bowl, beat the eggs with the crème fraîche; season with salt and pepper. Add the zucchini and mix. Pour the mixture into the cake pan and place it in a larger baking dish with a little water added to it to make a bain-marie. Bake for 1 hour and 15 minutes. Cover the top with aluminum foil during baking if the surface begins to brown too much.

Check the doneness of the flan; a knife inserted into the center should come out dry. Remove the pan from the oven, let cool, then unmold the flan by running the blade of a knife between the sides of the pan and the flan to loosen it. Slice and serve.

Asparagus flan

FOR 8 PEOPLE
PREPARATION: **15 min**
COOKING TIME: **10 min**
REFRIGERATION: **8 hours**

> 5 eggs
> 1 packet (approximately 1 oz.) gelée au madère (or 3 tbsp. powdered gelatin)
> 12 oz. asparagus from a jar
> ⅔ cup (5¼ oz.) mayonnaise
> salt, freshly ground black pepper

Hard boil the eggs for 10 minutes; let cool then peel and chop them.

If using the gelée au madère, prepare it according to the package directions but using only half the water called for. By reducing the water, the gelée will have more taste and be less liquid; let cool. If using the powdered gelatin, soak 3 tablespoons of the gelatin in ½ cup water mixed with ½ cup Madeira wine or port for 5 minutes. Melt the gelatin gently in hot water (or use the microwave on very low power for a few seconds) then let cool.

Gently mix the asparagus, hard-boiled eggs and mayonnaise; season with salt and pepper. Add the cooled, but not yet set, gelée au madère or gelatin and stir with a wooden spoon. Pour this mixture into a buttered or parchment-lined 9-inch round cake pan. Refrigerate for at least 8 hours.

Turn out before serving.

Coddled eggs in cream

quick & easy recipe

FOR 4 PEOPLE
PREPARATION: **5 min**
COOKING TIME: **6–8 min**

> 2 tbsp. butter
> 4 tbsp. crème fraîche
  (or heavy cream)
> 4 eggs
> a few pink peppercorns
> a few chive stalks
> salt, freshly ground
  black pepper

Preheat the oven to 425° F. Butter four individual ramekins and place 2 teaspoons of crème fraîche in each.

Break an egg into each ramekin. Add salt and pepper and a few crushed pink peppercorns then add the remaining crème fraîche.

Place the ramekins in a high-sided baking pan and pour in boiling water to come halfway up the sides of the ramekins; bake 6 to 8 minutes. Before serving, sprinkle with chopped chives.

VARIATION You can add 2 tablespoons of shredded cheese, tomato sauce or chopped ham to the cream base.

Coddled eggs in cream with leeks

FOR 4 PEOPLE
PREPARATION: **5 min**
COOKING TIME: **20 min**

> 2 leeks (white part only)
> 1½ tbsp. butter
> 2 tbsp. olive oil
> 4 tbsp. heavy cream
> 4 eggs
> salt, freshly ground
  black pepper

Wash and thinly slice the leeks. Heat the butter and olive oil in a frying pan; add the leeks and cook for 3 to 5 minutes while stirring; season with salt and pepper. Cook gently over low heat for 5 minutes then stir in 2 tablespoons of the heavy cream.

Preheat the oven to 425° F. Butter four individual ramekins.

Break an egg into each ramekin then add the remaining heavy cream and more salt and pepper. Bake for 10 minutes until the eggs have set; serve hot.

Eggs meurette (eggs poached in red wine)

FOR 4 PEOPLE
PREPARATION: **30 min**
COOKING TIME: **30 min**

> 2 tbsp. butter
> 3½ oz. thick-cut bacon, cut into small cubes
> 4-6 slices stale country bread (5½ oz.)
> 1 garlic clove
> 1 cup red wine
> ¼ cup vinegar
> 8 eggs

For the meurette sauce

> 3½ oz. thick-cut bacon, cut into small cubes
> 1 onion
> 1 small carrot
> 3½ oz. white button mushrooms
> 6 tbsp. butter
> 2 cups red wine
> Just over ¾ cup veal broth
> 1 bouquet garni (see p. 576)
> salt, freshly ground black pepper

Prepare the meurette sauce. Immerse the bacon in boiling water for 3 to 4 minutes, then drain. Peel and finley dice both the onion and the carrot. Clean the mushrooms and thinly slice them.

In a saucepan, melt 2 tablespoons of the butter and sauté the onion, the carrot and the mushrooms, covered, for 10 minutes. Add the bacon, stir, then pour in the red wine and reduce by three-quarters; add the veal broth and the bouquet garni. Season with salt and pepper then simmer over low heat until the sauce has reduced by two-thirds. Strain while pressing with the back of a spoon to release as much liquid as possible.

Reheat the sauce. Just before serving, remove it from from the heat and add the remaining 4 tablespoons of butter, whisking vigorously; adjust the seasoning.

Melt the 2 tablespoons of butter in a skillet and fry the bacon for 5 to 10 minutes; remove and drain on paper towels; add the bacon to the sauce.

Toast the bread slices, rub with the garlic clove, then cut them into small cubes to make croutons.

Heat the wine and vinegar in 4¼ cups of water, season with pepper, then simmer for 5 minutes. Poach the eggs in the simmering liquid then place them on paper towels to drain.

Pour some of the meurette sauce onto each plate then carefully add the poached eggs; garnish with croutons.

Vegetable terrine with pesto

FOR 6-8 PEOPLE
PREPARATION: **1 hour**
COOKING TIME: **25 min**
REFRIGERATION: **12 hours**

> 12 oz. frozen spinach, with stems
> 2 sprigs of basil
> 1 bunch chive stalks
> 2 tbsp. pesto
> 7 oz. fresh shelled or frozen peas
> 5¼ oz. fresh shelled or frozen fava or broad beans
> 4 sprigs of tarragon
> 2 packets (approximately 2 oz.) gelée au madère (or 6 tbsp. powdered gelatin)
> 1 cup vegetable broth
> salt, freshly ground black pepper

Thaw the spinach in a colander. Wash and chop the basil and chives.

Heat the pesto in a large skillet and add the spinach; cook for 5 minutes while stirring. Add the peas and the beans (if using frozen peas or beans, no need to thaw them); season with salt and pepper. Cook for 20 minutes over high heat. Add the chopped basil and chives and mix. Remove the pan from heat and adjust the seasoning.

Bring the broth to a simmer and add the gelée au madère (or the powdered gelatin), whisking constantly. Turn off the heat as soon as it reaches a boil.

Line a 8 x 4 x 2½-inch loaf pan with a large piece of plastic wrap (use enough to fold the ends over the top of the pan). In a large bowl, carefully mix the vegetables with the gelée au madère mixture. Pour the mixture into the loaf pan. Fold the excess plastic wrap over the top and refrigerate for 12 hours.

Carefully unmold the terrine onto a serving board. Remove the plastic wrap then cut the terrine into thick slices, using an electric knife, if available. Serve the terrine very chilled, drizzled with a bit of olive oil.

You can add pieces of oven-roasted or oil-packed sun-dried tomatoes, drained, and some pitted black olives to the terrine, if desired.

low calorie
· recipe ·

Roquefort puff pastry pillows

FOR 4 PEOPLE
PREPARATION: **20 min**
COOKING TIME: **20 min**

> 1½ oz. walnut halves
> 14 oz. pre-prepared puff pastry sheet
> 5 oz. roquefort cheese
> ¼ cup crème fraîche (or heavy cream)
> 1 egg
> 3½ oz. lettuce
> 1 tbsp. white wine vinegar
> 3 tbsp. olive oil
> salt, freshly ground black pepper

Coarsely chop the walnuts.

On a lightly floured work service, roll out the puff pastry sheet to approximately ⅛ inch thick. Using a fluted pastry wheel, cut out 8 squares of approximately 4 to 5 inches in size.

Cut up the roquefort into small pieces then mash it in a bowl with the crème fraîche, mixing well to form a thick, smooth paste; add the walnuts and mix.

Preheat the oven to 350° F. Line a baking sheet with parchment paper.

In a small bowl, beat the egg.

Spoon one fourth of the roquefort mixture onto 4 of the pastry squares, leaving a narrow border all the way around the edges. Lightly moisten the edge then place a second pastry square on top; seal the edges by pressing them together with your fingertips. Place the pastry squares on the baking sheet and brush with the beaten egg. Bake 20 minutes.

Meanwhile, wash the lettuce and prepare the vinaigrette by whisking together the vinegar and olive oil seasoned with salt and pepper. Lightly drizzle the lettuce with the vinaigrette and toss gently. Divide the salad among four plates and place a hot pastry pillow next to the salad. Serve immediately.

Cheese soufflé

FOR 4-6 PEOPLE
PREPARATION: **15 min**
COOKING TIME:
approximately 40 min

> 2 tbsp. butter
> ¼ cup (1 oz.) all-purpose flour
> 1⅔ cup cold milk
> 4 eggs
> 5¼ oz. comté or beaufort cheese, grated
> salt, freshly ground black pepper, and nutmeg

Make the béchamel. In a saucepan, melt the butter over medium heat. Add the flour and stir vigorously to obtain a smooth mixture; let cook for 2 minutes without browning. Remove the saucepan from the heat and pour in the cold milk all at once, whisking constantly to prevent lumps. Place back over the heat and cook for approximately 10 minutes; season with salt and pepper and a little grated nutmeg.

Preheat the oven to 425° F.

Break the eggs, separating the whites from the yolks. Beat the egg whites to stiff peaks with a pinch of salt. Stir the grated cheese into the béchamel sauce then add the egg yolks one-by-one, mixing well between each addition. Gently fold in the egg whites with a silicone spatula or wooden spoon, continuing to turn the bowl in the same direction to help prevent deflating them.

Butter an 8-inch round soufflé dish and gently pour in the mixture. Bake 30 minutes, without opening the oven door. Serve immediately.

The soufflé can be served as a main dish if served with a green salad.

VARIATION You can make this cheese soufflé with any other hard cheese, or even with a blue cheese such as roquefort or bleu d'Auvergne.

Beef carpaccio

FOR 4 PEOPLE
FREEZING: **4 hours**
PREPARATION: **20 min**

> 7 oz. beef filet
> 4 tbsp. olive oil
> 2 lemons
> 1¾ oz. aged parmesan cheese
> ¼ bunch parsley
> salt, freshly ground black pepper

Wrap the filet in plastic wrap and freeze for 4 hours. This will make it easier to slice. Brush the plates with olive oil.

Using a very sharp knife or a food processor with a slicing blade, cut the filet into slices as thin as a sheet of paper. Arrange them randomly on the plates to form the general shape of a rosette.

Squeeze 4 tablespoons of juice from the lemons. Drizzle the carpaccio with the remaining olive oil and then the lemon juice; season with salt and pepper.

Shave the parmesan into thin strips then chop the parsley; distribute these over the carpaccio. Serve along with a bottle of olive oil and additional salt and pepper so that each person can season to taste.

In addition to parmesan, various other side items can be served with carpaccio, such as crumbled blue cheese and walnut pieces, sliced raw mushrooms or anchovy fillets and capers.

Rabbit and hazelnut pâté

FOR 6 PEOPLE
PREPARATION: **40 min**
MARINADE: **30 min**
COOKING TIME: **2 hours**
REFRIGERATION:

24 hours

> 1 rabbit weighing approximately 3 lbs.
> 5¼ oz. barding fat
> 1 lb. chicken liver
> ½ cup port wine
> 2 onions
> 1 bunch chervil
> 1 lb. sausage, casing removed
> 1 egg
> 1 tsp. thyme
> ½ bay leaf
> 16 shelled whole hazelnuts
> salt, freshly ground black pepper

Debone the rabbit and cut the barding fat into thin strips (this can be prepared by a butcher).

Preheat the oven to 375° F.

Cut the chicken livers into cubes then place them in a large bowl with the port; marinate for 30 minutes.

Meanwhile, chop the onions and the chervil and cut the rabbit meat into small pieces. Place the rabbit meat in a bowl along with the sausage meat; add the egg and mix. Season with salt and pepper, add the chopped onion and chervil along with the thyme, bay leaf, hazelnuts and half of the port marinade; mix again and taste to adjust the seasoning.

Line a 8 x 4 x 2½-inch loaf pan with approximately three-quarters of the barding fat then fill it halfway with the rabbit mixture. Top with chicken livers then the remaining rabbit mixture. Top with the remaining barding fat.

Place the loaf pan inside a larger baking dish with high sides. Add hot water to the baking dish coming halfway up the sides of the loafpan and bake for 2 hours.

Let the pâté cool then cover and refrigerate for at least 24 hours.

Foie gras terrine

MAKES 2¼ LBS.
PREPARATION: **15 min**
MARINADE: **12 hours**
COOKING TIME: **40 min**

> 2¼ lbs. duck or goose foie gras
> 2½ tsp. salt
> 1¼ tsp. (⅛ oz.) white pepper
> 1¼ tsp. (⅛ oz.) quatre-épices (or allspice)
> ½ cup white port wine

make ahead · recipe ·

Devein the foie gras. Place it on a plate then season both sides with the salt, white pepper, and the quatre-épices; drizzle with the port. Marinate in the refrigerator for 12 hours, turning occasionally.

Preheat the oven to 200° F. Place the foie gras in a 6 x 4-inch ceramic loaf pan with a lid and pack it in well to eliminate any air pockets around it. Place the pan in a baking dish with high sides and pour boiling water into the baking dish, coming halfway up the sides of the loaf pan; bake for 40 minutes.

Remove the loaf pan from the oven and let cool. Place a small board along with a weight of around 9 ounces on top of the pan then refrigerate.

Remove the board and weight when the fat has congealed. Melt the fat in a saucepan or a hot oven then pour it on top of the foie gras. Unmold the foie gras before serving; serve sliced.

The terrine can be stored in the refrigerator for approximately 15 days.

1 It generally takes around ½ ounce of salt and ⅛ ounce of pepper per 2¼ pounds of foie gras for proper seasoning. You can replace the quatre-épices with nutmeg or other spices of your choice, and replace the port with other liquors such as cognac, armagnac, or a sweet wine.

2 To prevent oxidation, cover the surface of the foie gras with plastic wrap or cover it completely in melted fat.

3 To slice the foie gras, remove it from the refrigerator at least 20 minutes before serving. Slice it using a cake wire or a thin-bladed knife.

Pissaladière (anchovy and onion pizza provençal)

FOR 4–6 PEOPLE
PREPARATION: **15 min**
RESTING TIME: **1 hour**
COOKING TIME: **45 min**

> 1 lb. pre-prepared pizza dough
> ½ cup olive oil
> 2¼ lbs. onions
> 3 garlic cloves
> 1 sprig of thyme
> ½ bay leaf
> 1 tbsp. capers
> 25 salted anchovy fillets
> 20 black olives (perferably Niçoise)
> salt, freshly ground black pepper

Place the dough on lightly floured work service and flatten it out slightly. Add 4 tablespoons of olive oil to the dough then knead it by hand to incorporate all of the oil. Form the dough into a ball and let rise for 1 hour at room temperature.

Peel and thinly slice the onions. Peel and crush the garlic cloves. In a large skillet, add the remaining olive oil then add the onions and gently cook them, covered, for approximately 25 minutes, along with just a touch of salt, some pepper, the crushed garlic, thyme, bay leaf, and capers.

Preheat the oven to 475° F.

Roll out the dough into a ½-inch thick circle then place it on a baking sheet covered with parchment paper. Distribute the cooked onion mixture evenly over the dough, without going all the way to the edge.

Rinse the anchovies under running water to remove the salt, pat dry, then place them on the pizza in the pattern of a grid. Distribute the olives on top, pressing them down lightly to adhere.

Fold over the edge of the dough all around the pizza to create a thick border (this will help contain the toppings). Bake for 20 minutes; serve warm or cold.

Crispy sardine rolls

FOR 4 PEOPLE
PREPARATION: **10 min**
COOKING TIME: **15 min**

> 2 cans of sardines
  packed in oil
  (approximately 8 fillets)
> 2 small tomatoes
> 2 tsp. capers
> 4 sheets of feuilles de
  brick (or phyllo dough)

Preheat the oven to 400° F.

Drain the sardines, reserving the oil, and remove the backbones. Mash the sardines in a large bowl with a fork. Cut the tomatoes in half, clean out the seeds, then dice them. Add them to the bowl with the sardines, along with the capers; mix well.

Brush the sheets of dough with a little of the reserved sardine oil. Fold the sheet in half then place a small amount of the sardine filling in the center.

Roll each one up tightly then place on a baking sheet lined with parchment paper. Bake for approximately 15 minutes until the rolls are golden brown and crispy. Serve immediately.

VARIATION **You can add diced black olives to the filling.**

quick & easy · recipe ·

Fish terrine with basil

FOR 8 PEOPLE
PREPARATION: **20 min**
COOKING TIME:

approximately 1 hour

> 2¼ lbs. ripe tomatoes
> 4 garlic cloves
> 3 tbsp. olive oil
> 1⅓ lbs. fresh cod fillets,
  pollock or other white
  fish
> 1 bunch basil
> 6 eggs
> salt, freshly ground
  black pepper

Immerse the tomatoes in boiling water for 10 seconds, then immediately put them in cold water. Peel them, remove and discard the seeds, then coarsely chop them.

Peel and chop the garlic cloves.

Heat 2 tablespoons of the olive oil in a sauté pan and brown the garlic for 1 or 2 minutes over high heat. Add the tomatoes and cook, uncovered, for 15 minutes over medium heat, stirring occasionally.

Cut the fish into cubes approximately 1 to 1½ inches square.

Preheat the oven to 350° F. Fill a small roasting pan three-quarters full of water to prepare a bain-marie.

Chop the basil. In a large bowl, whisk the eggs then add the chopped tomatoes, cubed fish and basil; season with salt and pepper.

Pour the mixture into a 8 x 4 x 2½-inch loaf pan or terrine that has been greased and place in the bain-marie. Bake for 40 minutes. Check for doneness by sticking the point of a knife into the center of the terrine; the blade should come out moist.

Let cool before unmolding. Serve cold.

This dish is even better served with a homemade mayonnaise made with olive oil.

low calorie · recipe ·

Sea bass and scallop carpaccio with ginger

FOR 4-6 PEOPLE
PREPARATION: **15 min**
COOKING TIME: **5 min**
MARINADE: **12 hours**
REFRIGERATION: **1 hour**

> 1 lime
> 1¾ oz. fresh ginger
> ½ cup olive oil
> ½ bunch dill
> 1 lb. sea bass fillet
> 4 cleaned scallops with the coral still attached
> sel de mer or fleur de sel (sea salt)
> freshly ground black pepper

The day before: Zest the lime and chop the zest very fine. Boil it for 5 minutes. Pour it through a fine-mesh strainer then rinse it in cool water and let drain. Peel and grate the ginger. In a small bowl, combine the olive oil, ginger and the zest; marinate for 12 hours.

The next day: Wash and chop the dill.

With a sharp knife, thinly slice both the sea bass and the scallops. Arrange the slices randomly on the plates in the general shape of a rosette. Brush them with the infused olive oil and season with sel de mer and pepper. Sprinkle with chopped dill. Cover the plates with plastic wrap and chill for 1 hour.

Drizzle with freshly squeezed lime juice. Serve immediately.

Smoked salmon and spinach wheels

FOR 8 PEOPLE
PREPARATION: **20 min**
COOKING TIME: **10 min**
REFRIGERATION: **2 hours**

> 1 lb. frozen chopped spinach
> 4 eggs
> 5¼ oz. garlic and herb cheese spread
> 6 slices of smoked salmon (or trout)
> salt, freshly ground black pepper

Thaw the spinach and drain it completely.

Preheat the oven to 400° F.

Beat the eggs with a fork then mix with the spinach; season generously with salt and pepper.

Butter, or line with parchment paper, a quarter-sheet baking pan with sides. Pour in the eggs and spinach and bake for approximately 10 minutes or until the eggs become firm to the touch. Remove from the oven and let cool.

Gently turn out the sheet of baked eggs, lying it flat on a work surface covered with plastic wrap (to help roll them).

Melt the cheese in the microwave (approximately 1 minute) on medium power then spread it over the baked egg sheet. Arrange the smoked salmon on top. Roll the egg sheet up as if rolling a large crêpe, using the plastic wrap as a guide.

Refrigerate at least 2 hours. Remove 15 minutes before serving; cut into thick slices.

1 Roll the egg sheet tightly using the plastic wrap for support.

2 Once the egg sheet is rolled, wrap it completely in the plastic wrap before placing it in the refrigerator.

3 To slice the roll without crushing it, use a very sharp knife or an electric knife.

low calorie recipe

Salmon tartar with cilantro

FOR 4 PEOPLE
PREPARATION: 20 min
FREEZING: 20 min

> 14 oz. fresh salmon
> 2 small oysters (optional)
> 1 small bunch cilantro
> 2 tbsp. olive oil
> juice of ½ lime
> salt, freshly ground
>   black pepper

Ensure that all of the salmon skin is removed and that there are no bones present by passing your fingers in both directions all along the flesh. If any bones are present, remove them with tweezers. Put the salmon in the freezer for approximately 20 minutes to firm it up.

Open the oysters, if using, then remove the meat from the shell, ensuring that the foot is detached.

Wash the cilantro then pat it dry. Remove any large stems then snip off the leaves over a bowl.

Place a large bowl inside of a larger bowl containing ice. Remove the salmon from the freezer. Place the oysters and salmon on a cutting board and chop them finely using a sharp knife; place them in the cold bowl.

Pour the olive oil over the fish, season with salt and pepper and mix well. Add the lime juice and chopped cilantro and mix again.

Divide the salmon tartar among four individual ramekins; refrigerate if not serving immediately.

FOR PRESENTATION Just before serving, place the salmon tartar on lettuce leaves garnished with a few cherry tomatoes. Serve with several warm toast points.

Smoked salmon soufflé

FOR 4-6 PEOPLE
PREPARATION: **20 min**
COOKING TIME:

approximately 25 min

> 14 oz. smoked salmon
> 4 eggs
> 1 cup crème fraîche
  (or heavy cream)
> 4 egg whites
> 2 tbsp. butter
> salt, freshly ground
  black pepper

Chop the smoked salmon into very small pieces and place in a large bowl.

Preheat the oven to 400° F. Butter an 8-inch soufflé dish.

Beat the eggs with the crème fraîche and slowly pour over the salmon, stirring well with a spatula for 7 to 8 minutes.

Beat the egg whites with a pinch of salt until they reach very stiff peaks. Fold them gently into the salmon mixture in batches, always turning the bowl in the same direction while folding.

Gently pour the batter into the soufflé dish and bake for 25 minutes without opening the oven door during the cooking time.

Carpaccio of sea bream with tomatoes and coconut milk

FOR 4 PEOPLE
PREPARATION: **35 min**
REFRIGERATION: **2 hours**

> 1⅓ lbs. sea bream fillets
> 1 spring onion
> 3 limes
> 3 cherry tomatoes
> ½ bunch cilantro
> few sprigs of parsley
> just over ¾ cup coconut
  milk or coconut cream
> mixed peppercorns
> salt, freshly ground
  black pepper

Rinse the fillets thoroughly and pat dry. Ensure that there are no bones present by passing your fingers in both directions all along the flesh. If any bones are present, remove them with tweezers. Put the fillets in the freezer for approximately 10 minutes to firm them up.

Meanwhile, thinly slice the onion and juice the limes.

Using a very sharp thin, flexible knife, slice the fillets into strips as thin as possible and arrange them on a cold platter in the general shape of a rosette. Sprinkle with the lime juice and distribute the sliced onions on top. Refrigerate for 2 hours.

Slice the tomatoes. Wash then chop the cilantro and parsley.

Remove the fish from the refrigerator, pat dry and arrange onto very cold plates. Drizzle on the coconut milk or cream and garnish with a few tomato slices; season with salt and pepper and a few peppercorns. Sprinkle with chopped herbs and serve immediately.

Avocado and crab salad

FOR 4 PEOPLE
PREPARATION: **30 min**

> ⅔ cup (5¼ oz.)
  mayonnaise
> Cayenne pepper
> 9 oz. canned or frozen
  crab
> 2 avocados
> juice of ½ lemon
> pink peppercorns
> ½ bunch dill
> salt, freshly ground
  black pepper

Mix the mayonnaise with just a hint of the Cayenne pepper.

Crumble the crab meat, removing any cartilage.

Slice open the avocados, remove the pits, then scoop out the flesh using a spoon; dice then drizzle with the lemon juice; season with salt and pepper.

Mix the mayonnaise with the crab meat then gently mix in the diced avocado. Divide among serving cups and sprinkle with crushed pink peppercorns.

Wash the dill and squeeze out the excess water. Snip it with scissors over the cups to garnish the salad. Serve well chilled.

Bay scallop salad

FOR 4-6 PEOPLE
PREPARATION: **20 min**
COOKING TIME: **2 min**

- > 2 shallots
- > 12 chive stalks
- > juice of 1 lemon
- > ¼ cup hazelnut oil
- > 10½ oz. lettuce or curly lettuce
- > 4½ to 5½ lbs. bay scallops
- > Just over ¾ cup white wine
- > salt, freshly ground black pepper

Peel and finely chop the shallots. Chop the chives.

In a large bowl, combine the shallots, lemon juice, chopped chives and hazelnut oil; season with salt and pepper.

Wash the lettuce, pat dry and wrap in paper towels; set aside.

Wash the scallops several times in cold, fresh water, stirring well to remove any remaining sand. Open them over a large bowl. To make it easier, you can place them in a baking dish for 2 or 3 minutes in a hot oven; they will open up on their own. Remove the muscle, cutting away the coral, if present.

Filter the juice released from the shells by passing it through a fine-mesh strainer lined with a paper towel and suspended over a saucepan. Add the wine to the saucepan and bring to a boil. Add the scallops and simmer for 2 minutes. Remove them immediately and let drain. Place them in the bowl containing the prepared sauce and coat well.

Arrange lettuce leaves on plates. Add the scallops along with some sauce on top of the lettuce leaves and serve immediately.

VARIATION Replace the bay scallops with the larger variety of Atlantic scallops (also called Coquilles Saint-Jacques).

Prawn and zucchini salad

FOR 4–6 PEOPLE
PREPARATION: **25 min**
COOKING TIME: **3 min**

> 12–18 small prawns
  (or scampi)
> 2 thin-skinned zucchini
> 5 tbsp. olive oil
> 1¾ oz. radicchio
> 24 black olives
> 2 lemons
> 3 oz. radish shoots
> salt, freshly ground
  black pepper

Rinse the prawns with water then remove the heads. Cut away the shells by using scissors to slice through the membrane beneath the shell; place the prawns in a large bowl and set aside.

Wash the zucchini and thinly slice it, leaving the peel intact. Heat 1 tablespoon of the olive oil in a frying pan and fry the zucchini for 3 minutes over high heat; season with salt and pepper. Remove the zucchini to drain then pat them dry with paper towels.

Wash the radicchio and squeeze out the excess water. Pit the olives.

Whisk together the remaining 4 tablespoons of olive oil and 3 tablespoons of lemon juice to make a vinaigrette; season with salt and pepper. Pour half the vinaigrette over the prawns and toss. Pour the remaining vinaigrette over the radicchio and distribute the leaves among the serving plates. Add the zucchini, prawns, and the olives. Garnish with radish sprouts and serve.

Prawn beignets

FOR 4–6 PEOPLE
PREPARATION: **20 min**
RESTING THE DOUGH:

1 hour

COOKING TIME: **5 min**

> 16-24 small prawns (or scampi)
> 2 large onions
> vegetable oil, for frying
> 2 or 3 lemons

For the batter
> 2¼ cups (9 oz.) all-purpose flour
> 3 egg yolks
> ½ tsp. salt
> 1 cup beer or milk
> 1 tsp. vegetable oil
> 1 egg white

Prepare the beignet batter. Sift the flour into a bowl then make a well in the center and add the egg yolks, salt, beer (or milk) and the oil. Mix to form a smooth batter. Let stand for at least 1 hour.

Immerse the prawns for 2 or 3 minutes in boiling, salted water. Drain, let cool, then remove the head and shells, leaving the tip of the tail intact.

While the prawns are cooling, slice the onions into rings then separate the individual rings. Heat the vegetable oil in a heavy saucepan.

Whisk the egg whites to stiff peaks then fold into the beignet batter.

Dredge the onion rings and prawns in the batter. When the oil reaches 350° F, fry the onions and prawns, in small batches, for several seconds until puffed and well browned.

Drain on paper towels and serve immediately with lemon wedges.

1 Folding egg whites into the batter makes it lighter and allows it to puff better. Fold the egg whites in gently to avoid deflating.

2 Quickly dip the prawns in the batter with the aid of a spoon or by holding the end of the tail.

3 Wait until the batter has puffed and is golden brown before removing the beignets with a slotted spoon. Place them immediately on paper towels to drain.

Classic and timeless dishes

Pot-au-feu

FOR 6 PEOPLE
PREPARATION: **30 min**
COOKING TIME: **4 hours**

> 1 lb. beef ribs
> 1 lb. beef shank
> 1 lb. beef shoulder
> 1 onion
> 4 cloves
> 4 garlic cloves
> 1 bouquet garni (SEE p. 576)
> 6-8 peppercorns
> 1 tbsp. kosher salt
> 5 carrots
> 5 turnips
> 3 parsnips
> 4 leeks
> 2 celery stalks
> 4 beef marrow bones

Place the ribs, beef shank and beef shoulder in a Dutch oven and add 2½ quarts of cold water. Slowly bring to a boil (taking at least 10 minutes) and cook for 1 hour, skimming the fat from the water often.

Peel the onion and press the cloves into it. Peel and crush the garlic cloves. Add the onions and garlic to the Dutch oven with the bouquet garni, peppercorns and salt. Bring the mixture back to a boil, skim the fat from the surface then reduce the heat and simmer for 2 hours, continuing to skim off the fat from time to time.

Meanwhile, peel and wash all the vegetables and cut them into chunks. Add them to the Dutch oven and cook for 30 minutes.

Wrap the marrow bones in cheesecloth or muslin and add them to the Dutch oven and cook another 30 minutes. Keep paper towels on hand to dab any fat from the surface of the liquid.

Remove the meat, vegetables and marrow bones to drain and place them on a large warm, shallow serving dish.

Strain the broth into a soup tureen. Sprinkle the meat and vegetables with 2 or 3 tablespoons of the broth.

Serve with salt, pickles, mustard, and toast for the bone marrow.

You can also make the pot-au-feu in individual ramekins or mini crock pots.

Shepherd's pie

FOR 4-6 PEOPLE
PREPARATION: **30 min**
COOKING TIME: **35 min**

> 1¾ lbs. potatoes
> approximately 1⅓ lbs. boiled or braised beef
> just over ¾ cup beef broth
> 2 onions
> 3 shallots
> 8 tbsp. (1 stick) unsalted butter
> 1⅓ cups milk, heated
> 2 tbsp. crème fraîche (or sour cream)
> bread crumbs
> salt, freshly ground black pepper

Peel the potatoes and cut them into small chunks. Cook for 20 minutes in boiling, salted water.

While the potatoes are cooking, chop the beef, then peel and chop the onions and shallots. In a large saucepan, melt 2 tablespoons of the butter and brown the onions and shallots, season with salt and pepper then add the beef broth. Stir and cook for 15 minutes on low heat; let cool then add the beef and stir.

Process the cooked potatoes through a food mill or mash them with a potato masher. Add 3 tablespoons of the butter, the hot milk and the crème fraîche to the potatoes; season with salt and pepper.

Preheat the oven to 475° F. Butter a gratin dish.

Melt the remaining 3 tablespoons butter. Spread the beef mixture in an even layer on the bottom of the gratin dish then cover with the mashed potatoes. Sprinkle the top with the bread crumbs then drizzle with the melted butter. Broil for 15 minutes until the bread crumbs are golden. Serve with a green salad.

VARIATION Replace the beef with 4 duck legs confit that have been boned and cut into pieces.

Steak tartar

PREPARATION: **15 min**

> - 2 small onions
> - 2 shallots
> - 1½ lbs. thick sirloin or rump steak
> - Cayenne pepper
> - Worcestershire sauce
> - 4 egg yolks
> - 4 tsp. capers, drained
> - a few sprigs of parsley
> - ketchup, olive oil, mustard, and Tabasco, for seasoning
> - salt, freshly ground black pepper

Peel and chop the onions and shallots.

Chop the beef into fine pieces, season with salt and pepper and a hint of Cayenne pepper along with a few drops of Worcestershire sauce.

Shape the meat mixture into 4 balls, place each one on a separate plate, then make an impression in the center of each with your thumb to place the egg yolk.

Sprinkle 2 teaspoons of chopped onion, 1 teaspoon of capers and a large pinch of chopped parsley and chopped shallot on and around the meat.

Serve with the ketchup, olive oil, mustard, Worcestershire sauce and Tabasco on the side so that each guest can season to taste.

quick & easy · recipe ·

Beef cheek stew

FOR 6 PEOPLE
PREPARATION: **20 min**
MARINADE: **12 hours**
COOKING TIME: **3 hours**

> 2 onions
> 2 carrots
> 3 garlic cloves
> 8½ cups good red wine
> 3 or 4 cloves
> 3 sprigs of thyme
> 1 bay leaf
> 15 black peppercorns
> several strips of lemon zest
> 4½ lbs. beef cheek
> 1 tbsp. olive oil
> salt, freshly ground black pepper

The day before: Peel and chop the onions. Peel the carrots and thinly slice them. Peel and crush the garlic cloves.

Pour the wine into a large bowl, add the onions, carrots, garlic, cloves, thyme, bay leaf, peppercorns and lemon zest; mix well.

Cut the meat into 1-inch cubes and place in the marinade; store in the refrigerator for 12 hours.

The next day: Remove the meat and vegetables from the marinade to drain, while preserving the marinade liquid.

In a stovetop-safe casserole dish, heat the olive oil and brown the meat. Distribute the vegetables over the meat and cook until browned.

Add the marinade liquid then season with salt and pepper. Bring to a gentle boil then cover and cook gently for 3 hours. You may need to add a little water if the liquid reduces too much.

Remove the meat from the casserole dish and place on a warm serving dish. Strain the liquid to remove the vegetables. Add the liquid back to the pan and bring to a boil. Spoon the liquid over the meat when serving.

Serve with mashed potatoes made with olive oil. This stew is even better reheated. In the last 30 minutes of cooking, you can add 5 carrots, peeled and cut into sections, to the casserole dish.

Beef bourguignon

FOR 4-6 PEOPLE
PREPARATION: **45 min**
COOKING TIME:
approximately 2 hours
40 min

> 2½ lbs. stewing beef
> 2 carrots
> 2 large onions
> 1 garlic clove
> 2 tbsp. vegetable oil
> 5 oz. thick-cut bacon, cut
>   into small cubes
> 2 tbsp. all-purpose flour
> 2 cups veal broth
> 2 cups red wine
>   (preferably Burgundy)
> 1 bouquet garni (SEE
>   p. 576)
> 7 oz. white button
>   mushrooms
> 2 tbsp. butter
> salt, freshly ground
>   black pepper

Cut the beef into pieces of approximately 2 inches in size.

Peel and thinly slice the carrots and onions. Peel and crush the garlic clove.

Heat the oil in a stovetop-safe casserole dish and fry the bacon; remove and set aside.

Put the beef pieces in the casserole dish and brown them on all sides. Add the carrots and onions and gently sauté them for 2 to 3 minutes; season with salt and pepper. Remove all of the ingredients. Drain the fat from the casserole dish and discard it. Return the meat, carrots and onions back to the casserole dish. Sprinkle with flour, stir, then let the meat brown again, 1 or 2 minutes.

Pour the veal broth and wine into the casserole dish. Add the crushed garlic and bouquet garni. Stir and cook very gently, covered, for 2 to 2½ hours.

Meanwhile, clean the mushrooms and cut them into pieces. Sauté them in the butter for 10 minutes.

Remove the pieces of beef and place them them in a shallow serving dish.

Skim the fat from the broth and cook it until it's reduced, then strain. Add the strained liquid to a saucepan then add the bacon and sauteéd mushrooms. Taste and adjust the seasoning as needed. Reheat the liquid then spoon it over the beef. Serve immediately.

You can serve this dish as in the Burgundy region of France, with croutons and garlic.

Beef stroganoff

FOR 4-6 PEOPLE
PREPARATION: **15 min**
MARINADE: **12 hours**
COOKING TIME:
approximately 15 min

> 1¾ lbs. beef tenderloin
> 4 onions
> 3 shallots
> 1 large carrot
> 1 bay leaf
> 1 sprig of thyme
> 3 cups white wine
> 7 oz. white button
  mushrooms
> 6 tbsp. butter
> 1 shot glass of brandy
  (approximately 1½ oz.)
> ⅔ cup crème fraîche
  (or sour cream)
> salt, freshly ground
  black pepper

Cut the beef tenderloin into 1-inch long strips then season with salt and pepper.

Peel and chop the onions and shallots. Peel and dice the carrot. Put the vegetables in a large bowl. Add the sliced tenderloin, crumbled bay leaf and thyme. Pour the white wine into the bowl and add the meat and vegetables. Marinate, covered, in the refrigerator for at least 12 hours, stirring occasionally.

Clean and thinly slice the mushrooms.

Remove the meat to drain and pat dry. Add the marinade to a saucepan and reduce it by half, then strain.

In a skillet, brown the mushrooms with 2 tablespoons of the butter, then drain them and keep them warm.

Pour off the fat from the skillet and wipe it clean with a paper towel. Heat the remaining 4 tablespoons of butter until melted, add the meat and let cook over high heat for 5 minutes, turning constantly to avoid burning.

Heat the brandy and pour it into the skillet with the meat. Carefully light the brandy in the pan to flambé it. Stir to combine then remove the meat with a slotted spoon and place it in a serving dish; keep warm.

Add the mushrooms and the reduced marinade to the skillet along with the crème fraîche. Stir over high heat until the sauce has thickened. Adjust the seasoning as needed. Spoon the sauce over the meat. Serve very hot.

Goulash

FOR 6 PEOPLE
PREPARATION: **20 min**
COOKING TIME:

2½ hours

> 3 onions
> 1 lb. tomatoes
> 1 garlic clove
> 2½ lbs. chuck steak (or shoulder)
> 4 tbsp. peanut oil
> 1 bouquet garni (SEE p. 576)
> 2 tsp. paprika
> 2 cups beef broth
> 1⅔ lbs. potatoes
> salt, freshly ground black pepper

Peel and slice the onions. Immerse the tomatoes in boiling water for 20 seconds, then immediately put them in cold water. Peel them, remove and discard the seeds, then chop them into small pieces. Peel and crush the garlic clove.

Cut the chuck steak into very large pieces.

Heat the oil in a stovetop-safe casserole dish, add the meat and the onions and cook them until browned. Add the tomatoes, crushed garlic, the bouquet garni, salt, pepper and paprika; mix well. Pour in enough beef broth to just cover the meat. Bring to a boil, then reduce the heat and cook gently for 2 hours, covered.

Peel the potatoes and cut them into quarters. Add them to the casserole dish with just over ¾ cup boiling water. Bring to a boil again until the vegetables are tender and cooked through.

Taste and adjust the seasoning as needed. Serve very hot.

You can also steam the potatoes and serve them separately on the side. In this case, do not add the additional boiling water to the goulash.

Baekenofe (Alsatian meat stew)

FOR 6-8 PEOPLE
MARINADE: **12 hours**
PREPARATION: **20 min**
COOKING TIME: **4 hours**

> 1 lb. mutton shoulder
> 1 lb. pork shoulder
> 1 lb. stewing beef (shank or chuck)
> 5 large onions
> 3 cloves
> 2 garlic cloves
> 2 cups white wine (preferably Alsatian)
> 1 bouquet garni (SEE p. 576)
> 1¾ cups (7 oz.) all-purpose flour
> 2¼ lbs. potatoes
> 2 tbsp. lard
> salt, freshly ground black pepper

The day before: Cut the meat into large cubes. Peel two onions then press the cloves into one and thinly slice the other. Peel and crush the garlic cloves. Put the meat, onion and garlic in a bowl with the wine, bouquet garni, and a little salt and pepper. Marinate for 12 hours.

The next day: Place the flour in a bowl, add ½ cup of water and mix to form a smooth dough; set aside.

Preheat the oven to 325° F.

Peel and slice the potatoes and the three remaining onions. Grease a casserole dish with the lard, then place a layer of potatoes on the bottom of the dish, followed by a layer of the meat, then a layer of onions; season each layer with salt and pepper, as desired. Finish with a layer of potatoes on top.

Remove the bouquet garni and the onion with the cloves from the marinade. Pour the marinade into the casserole dish. The liquid should come just to the top of the last layer. If not, add a little water as needed.

Roll the dough into a long thin log. Place the lid on the casserole dish and use the rolled dough to seal the lid to the dish (this will prevent steam from escaping during cooking).

Bake for 4 hours. Serve in the casserole dish.

Breaded pig's feet

FOR 4 PEOPLE
PREPARATION: **15 min**
COOKING TIME: **8–10 min**

> 1¼ cups all-purpose flour
> 1 egg
> 1 tbsp. vegetable oil
> approximately 1¼ cups
  (5 oz.) bread crumbs
> 2 pig's feet, pre-cooked
> 2 tbsp. butter
> salt, freshly ground
  black pepper

Using three shallow bowls: put the flour in the first, beat the egg and oil with a little salt and pepper in the second, then place the bread crumbs in the third.

Cut each pig's foot in half, lengthwise. Roll each piece first in the flour, then in the beaten egg/oil mixture and then in the bread crumbs. Make sure each piece is well coated in the bread crumbs.

Preheat the broiler.

Melt the butter then brush it onto each one of the pig's feet halves.

Line a baking dish with parchment paper. Place the pig's feet in the baking dish and place them in the oven approximately 8 inches from the broiler. Roast gently for 8 to 10 minutes, turning several times.

Serve very hot, with mustard.

Garbure (ham and cabbage stew)

FOR 8 PEOPLE
SOAKING: **12 hours**
PREPARATION: **40 min**
COOKING TIME:
approximately 2 hours

> 1 pork heel (preferably Bayonne)
> 10½ oz. dried haricots blancs (white navy or kidney beans)
> 7 oz. fresh shelled or frozen fava or broad beans
> 1 lb. potatoes
> 2 carrots
> 2 turnips
> 2 shallots
> 3 garlic cloves
> 2 leeks
> 1 celery stalk
> ¼ green cabbage
> 2 sausages (preferably Toulouse)
> 3 duck thighs confit
> 1 bouquet garni (SEE p. 576)
> 8½ cups chicken broth
> Just over ¾ cup dry white wine
> 6-8 slices of country-style bread
> 1 tbsp. chopped parsley
> salt, freshly ground black pepper

The day before: Soak the pork heel with the haricots blancs in cold water for several hours to overnight.

The next day: Place the pork heel in boiling water for 10 minutes. Shell the fresh beans and remove the white skin that surrounds each bean. If you are using frozen beans, let them thaw.

Peel the potatoes, carrots and turnips then cut them into small pieces. Peel and chop the shallots and two cloves of garlic. Finely chop the leeks and celery. Cut the cabbage leaves into strips.

Preheat the oven to 425° F. Put the sausage and duck legs confit in a roasting pan and let them brown in the oven for 15 minutes. Remove from the pan and dab them with a paper towel to remove excess fat then cut them into chunks; set aside.

Put the pork heel, white beans and bouquet garni in a large pot. Pour in the chicken broth (or water) and bring to a boil and let cook for 45 minutes.

Deglaze the roasting pan with the white wine, then pour the deglazed liquid into the pot with the pork heel.

In a frying pan, brown the shallots, carrots, turnips, leeks and celery with a little duck fat for 5 minutes; season with salt and pepper. Add the vegetables to the large pot with the pork heel and simmer 30 minutes.

Blanch the cabbage by placing it in boiling water for 5 to 8 minutes, uncovered. Add the blanched cabbage to the large pot along with the potatoes. Simmer another 30 minutes.

Add the fresh beans and cook for 5 minutes longer. Adjust the seasoning as needed then remove the bouquet garni.

Toast the bread then rub the slices with the remaining garlic clove.

Slice the pork heel into ½-inch thick pieces and place them in bowls with pieces of the sausage and the duck. Spoon some of the hot broth and the cooked vegetables over the meat, sprinkle with chopped parsley and adjust the seasoning as needed. Serve hot with the garlic toast.

Quiche lorraine

FOR 4-6 PEOPLE
PREPARATION: **25 min**
DOUGH: **30 min**
COOKING TIME:
45-50 min

> 7 oz. smoked thick-cut
  bacon, cut into small
  cubes
> 5 eggs
> 1⅔ cups crème fraîche
> salt, freshly ground black
  pepper, nutmeg

For the tart dough

> 10½ tbsp. (1 stick plus
  2½ tbsp) butter, slightly
  pliable
> 2 cups (8 oz.) sifted
  all-purpose flour
> 2 pinches salt
> ½ cup cold water

Prepare the pastry. Cut the butter into small cubes. Place the flour in a bowl and make a well in the center with your fingers then add the salt and butter to the well. Quickly rub the butter into the flour by pinching it between your fingertips. Mix in just enough of the cold water (1 tablespoon at a time) to bring the dough together then work it quickly until it becomes smooth and supple. Turn it out onto a lightly floured work surface and knead it by pulling it with your fingers and pressing it down with your palms until the dough feels uniform and is flexible; be careful not to over work it. Form the dough into a ball then flatten it into a disk. Wrap it in plastic wrap and refrigerate for 30 minutes.

Preheat the oven to 400° F. Line a 10-inch tart pan with parchment paper.

Roll the dough into an ⅛-inch-thick circle then place it in the tart pan. Gently prick the dough all over with a fork, place a piece of parchment paper (slightly larger in diameter than the tart pan) on top of the dough then cover the parchment with a layer of dried beans. Bake the crust for 10 minutes; let cool.

Lightly brown the bacon pieces in a nonstick skillet then remove them to drain the fat. Evenly distribute them over the bottom of the crust.

Beat the eggs with the crème fraîche and season with salt and pepper. Grate a little nutmeg into the mixture then pour it over the bacon.

Bake for 35 to 40 minutes until set and lightly golden on top. Serve with a green salad.

Stuffed tomatoes

FOR 4 PEOPLE
PREPARATION: **20 min**
COOKING TIME:

30–40 min

> 4 large tomatoes
> ½ onion
> ½ garlic clove
> several parsley leaves (approximately 1 oz.)
> 2 tbsp. butter
> 5 oz. fine sausage, casing removed
> approximately ½ cup (1 oz.) fresh bread crumbs
> 2 tbsp. peanut oil
> salt, freshly ground black pepper

Choose tomatoes that are ripe but firm and regular in shape. Cut off the top of each tomato on the stem side to create a cap. Clean out the seeds and the pulp with a spoon. Lightly salt the inside, then turn them upside down on a rack to drain.

Peel and chop the onion and garlic and chop the parsley.

Melt the butter in a saucepan and add the onions to lightly brown them. Add the sausage meat, bread crumbs, parsley, and garlic then season with salt and pepper; mix well to create a uniform stuffing.

Preheat the oven to 425° F.

Using a small spoon, fill the tomatoes with the stuffing, forming a dome, then replace the caps. Place them side by side in a lightly oiled baking dish. Drizzle the tomatoes with the peanut oil then bake for 30 to 40 minutes. Serve very hot.

Belgian endives with ham

FOR 4 PEOPLE
PREPARATION: **30 min**
COOKING TIME: **30 min**

> 4 Belgian endives
> 6 tbsp. butter
> ¼ cup all-purpose flour
> 2 cups milk
> 2 oz. grated cheese, such as gruyère
> 4 slices cooked, pressed cold ham
> salt, freshly ground black pepper, nutmeg

Choose Belgian endives with a nice white color that are tightly closed. Remove the first layer of leaves and cut off any excess or tough stem from the bottom.

Heat 2 tablespoons of the butter in a skillet then add the endives to braise them.

In a saucepan, melt 2 tablespoons of the butter. Add the flour and stir quickly to get a smooth mixture. Cook for 2 minutes without browning. Remove from the heat and pour in the cold milk all at once while whisking to prevent lumps. Place back on the heat and let cook for 10 to 12 minutes to thicken; season with salt and pepper to taste, and a good pinch of grated nutmeg. Add half of the grated cheese; mix well.

Preheat the oven to 475° F. Butter a baking dish.

Drain excess butter from the endives then wrap each in a slice of ham. Place them side by side in the baking dish and top them with the béchamel sauce.

Sprinkle with the remaining cheese then evenly distribute the remaining 2 tablespoons of butter on top in small pieces. Bake for 15 minutes. Serve very hot.

Cabbage stuffed with chicken and olives

FOR 6-8 PEOPLE
PREPARATION: **40 min**
COOKING TIME: **2 hours**

> 3 chicken breasts
> just over ¾ cup crème fraîche (or heavy cream)
> 2 eggs
> 3½ oz. pitted green olives
> approximately 2 tbsp. (1 oz.) shelled pistachios
> 1 small green cabbage
> 4¼ quarts vegetable or chicken broth, homemade or store-bought
> salt, freshly ground black pepper
> walnut oil, olive oil or tomato sauce as a garnish

Cut the chicken breasts into small pieces then mix them with the crème fraîche. Add the eggs, olives and pistachios then season with salt and pepper. Stir to obtain a homogenous mixture.

Cut off the tip of the cabbage stalk without detaching the leaves. Spread the leaves and wash them with water. Carefully remove the heart of the cabbage then wash and chop it and stir it into the chicken mixture.

Bring the broth to a simmer in a Dutch oven. Spoon the chicken mixture into the center of the cabbage. Fold the leaves back into place then wrap the cabbage with cheesecloth and tie tightly to close. Place the cabbage in the simmering broth. If the pot is deep, you can tie the wrapped cabbage to a wooden spoon and suspend it across the pot to prevent it from sinking to the bottom; simmer gently for 2 hours.

Drain the cabbage, remove the cloth then cut the cabbage into thick slices. Serve hot drizzled with a dash of walnut oil or olive oil, tomato sauce or accompanied with a tomato salad with herbs.

VARIATION Instead of chicken use sausage or fish.

1 To create a smooth stuffing mixture, ensure that the crème fraîche is very cold.

2 Fill the cabbage so that there are no air pockets in the stuffing.

3 Moisten the cheesecloth before wrapping the cabbage and tie it tightly to prevent water from getting inside the cabbage while it's cooking.

Lentils with salt pork

FOR 4 PEOPLE
PREPARATION: 20 min
SOAKING: 2 hours
COOKING TIME: 2 hours

> 1⅓ lbs. salted pork
  shoulder
> 1 lb. fresh bacon, thick-
  cut
> 2 carrots
> 1 onion
> 4 smoked pork sausages
  (preferably Montbéliard)
> 12 oz. green lentils
> 1 bay leaf
> 1 sprig of thyme
> salt, freshly ground
  black pepper

Soak the meat in a bowl of cold water for 2 hours, changing the water frequently.

Drain the meat and place it in a large saucepan with one of the carrots and one of the onions that has been cut in half. Cover the mixture with cold water then bring to a boil, cooking for 1½ hours over medium heat. Occasionally skim the fat from the surface. Prick the sausage in several places then add it to the saucepan and cook for another 30 minutes.

While the meat is cooking, prepare the lentils by rinsing them then placing them in a large saucepan covered by a good amount of cold water. Cut the remaining carrot in half then add it and the bay leaf and thyme to the saucepan. Bring back to a boil and cook for an additional 30 minutes over medium heat, seasoning again once the cooking is complete.

Drain the meat and cut it into pieces. Add the meat to the saucepan with the lentils and simmer another 30 minutes over low heat before serving.

Serve the meat with different varieties of fine mustards.

You can add pork loin to this dish, if desired.

Sauerkraut

FOR 6-8 PEOPLE

PREPARATION: **20 min**

COOKING TIME:

2½ hours

> 4½ lbs. uncooked sauerkraut
> 2 cloves
> 1 tsp. black peppercorns
> 2 tsp. juniper berries (optional)
> 1 bouquet garni (see p. 576)
> 2 onions
> 2 garlic cloves
> 3½ oz. goose fat
> ½ cup white wine
> 2½ lbs. potatoes
> 1 medium smoked pork shoulder
> 1½ lbs. smoked bacon
> 2½ lbs. potatoes
> 6-8 sausages (preferably Alsatian)
> salt

Wash the sauerkraut in a pot of water several times until the water is no longer cloudy. Drain it and use your hands to squeeze out all of the water. Place in a cloth and pat dry. Lift the saurkraut several times with your fingers to loosen it.

Preheat the oven to 375° F.

Place the cloves, peppercorns, juniper berries and bouquet garni in just over ¾ cup of boiling water for 5 minutes to infuse it with the spices; strain it, retaining the water.

Peel and chop the onions. Peel the garlic cloves.

In a large Dutch oven set on the stove, melt the goose fat and sauté the onions. Add the garlic, spice-infused water, and the white wine. Cover and bring to a boil. Place in the oven and cook for 1½ hours.

Remove the Dutch oven from the oven and add the pork shoulder and the bacon by pushing them down into the sauerkraut. Cook for an additional 30 minutes.

Peel the potatoes.

Remove the smoked bacon from the Dutch oven and add the potatoes; bake for an additional 30 minutes. Approximately 5 minutes before the end of the baking time, add the sausages and again the smoked bacon back to the pot to reheat it.

Place the finished sauerkraut on a serving platter. Cut the pork shoulder and bacon into even slices and arrange them on the platter with the sausages and potatoes. Serve immediately.

Cassoulet

FOR 8 PEOPLE

PREPARATION: **40 min**

SOAKING: **2 hours**

COOKING TIME:

3½ hours

> 2 lbs. haricots blancs
  (white navy or kidney
  beans)
> 7 oz. pork rind
> 1 carrot
> 5 garlic cloves
> 4 onions
> 1 clove
> 10½ oz. bacon
> 2 bouquets garnis (SEE
  p. 576)
> 1½ lbs. pork loin
> 1 lb. boneless breast of
  lamb
> 3½ oz. goose fat
> 1¼ cups beef broth
> 1 dried or cooked garlic
  sausage
> 4 portions of goose or
  duck confit
> approximately 8 oz.
  fresh pork sausage
> bread crumbs
> kosher salt, freshly
  ground black pepper

Soak the haricots blancs in water for 2 hours.

Cut up the pork rind and tie the pieces together in bundles. Peel the carrot, garlic cloves and onions. Press the clove into one of the onions. Cut the carrot and bacon into pieces.

Put the beans in a stovetop-safe casserole dish with the pork rind, carrot, onion with the clove, 3 garlic cloves and the bouquet garni. Cover with water and cook 1 hour at a gentle boil, covered; add salt halfway through cooking.

Cut the pork loin and the breast of lamb into large pieces. Melt 2 ounces of the goose fat in a frying pan and fry the meat for 10 minutes; season with salt and pepper.

Chop the remaining 3 onions and crush the remaining 2 garlic cloves and add them to the frying pan with the second bouquet garni. Add a small amount of the beef broth and cook for 40 minutes, covered, occasionally adding more broth as needed.

When the beans are almost cooked, remove the vegetables and the bouquet garni, add the pork loin and breast of lamb, garlic sausage, goose or duck confit and the fresh pork sausage. Simmer gently for 1 hour.

Preheat the oven to 325° F.

Remove all of the meat and let drain. Cut the breast of lamb, pork loin and goose or duck confit into pieces of equal size and the pork rind into rectangles. Remove the skin from the garlic sausage and slice it. Cut the fresh pork sausage into small pieces.

Line a baking dish with a layer of the pork rind. Add a layer of beans, then a layer of different meats along with some of the meat juices. Continue by creating alternating layers of the meat and beans until all the ingredients are used. Season each layer with a little freshly ground black pepper as you go along.

On the last layer of beans, place the remaining pieces of pork rind and a few slices of the garlic sausage. Sprinkle with bread crumbs and the remaining 1½ ounces of goose fat.

Cook gently in the oven for approximately 1½ hours. When a crust forms on top, break it up gently then let it reform. Serve the cassoulet in the baking dish.

Eight-hour leg of lamb

FOR 6 PEOPLE
PREPARATION: **10 min**
COOKING TIME: **8 hours**

> 3 eggplants
> 2 fennel bulbs
> 1 shortened leg of lamb
> 10 garlic cloves
> 3 tbsp. olive oil
> salt, freshly ground
  black pepper

Preheat the oven to 200° F.

Cut the eggplants into cubes. Cut off the stems of the fennel and remove any damaged parts from the bulbs, then dice.

Place the leg of lamb in an oven-proof casserole dish and surround it with the eggplant, fennel and unpeeled garlic cloves. Drizzle with olive oil then season with salt and pepper.

Cover the casserole dish and bake for 8 hours without opening the oven door. Serve directly from the casserole dish.

VARIATION Replace the leg of lamb with lamb shank. In this case, you will need one lamb shank per person.

Lamb ragout

FOR 4-6 PEOPLE
PREPARATION: **25 min**
COOKING TIME:
approximately 1 hour

> 1⅓ lbs. lamb shoulder
> 1⅓ lbs. lamb neck
> 2 tomatoes
> 2 garlic cloves
> 2 tbsp. peanut oil
> 1 tbsp. all-purpose flour
> 1 bouquet garni (SEE
>   p. 576)
> 2 bunches baby carrots
> 7 oz. spring turnips
> 1 bunch spring onions
> 10½ oz. haricots verts
>   (string beans)
> 10½ oz. fresh peas
> 2 tbsp. butter
> salt, freshly ground
>   black pepper, and
>   nutmeg

Cut the lamb shoulder into large chunks and slice the neck.

Immerse the tomatoes for 20 seconds in boiling water, then immediately put them in cold water. Peel them, remove and discard the seeds and chop them. Peel and chop the garlic clove.

Heat the oil in a stovetop-safe casserole dish and brown the lamb pieces. Place them on paper towels to absorb the fat then pour off the fat from the casserole dish.

Place the meat back in the casserole dish, sprinkle with the flour and cook 3 minutes, while stirring; season with salt and pepper and grated nutmeg. Add the tomatoes, garlic and bouquet garni and just enough water to cover the meat. Bring to a boil then cover and simmer 35 minutes.

Peel and slice the carrots, turnips and onions. String the haricots verts and shell the peas. Melt the butter in a frying pan and brown the carrots, onions and turnips.

Steam the haricots verts for 7 to 8 minutes.

Place the carrots, turnips, onions, and peas in the casserole dish and mix. Continue cooking gently, covered, for 20 to 25 minutes. Add the haricots verts 5 minutes before serving and mix gently. Serve very hot in the casserole dish.

Veal blanquette

FOR 4-6 PEOPLE
PREPARATION: **20 min**
COOKING TIME:
**approximately 1 hour
and 10 min**

> 1½ to 2 lbs. of veal
  shoulder, collar or
  brisket or a combination
  of all three
> 1 carrot
> 1 small celery stalk
> 1 leek
> 1 onion
> 1 clove
> 1 bouquet garni (SEE
  p. 576)
> 2 quarts clarified veal
  broth or water
> 2 tbsp. butter
> ¼ cup all-purpose flour
> 1 egg yolk
> ½ cup crème fraîche
  (or sour cream)
> juice of ½ lemon
> salt, freshly ground
  black pepper

Cut the meat into large chunks.

Peel all of the vegetables. Cut the carrot, celery and leek into large pieces. Press the clove into the onion. Place all of the vegetables in a large stovetop-safe casserole dish with the meat and bouquet garni. Pour the veal broth or water into the dish and season with salt. Cook for 1 hour over low heat, occasionally skimming the fat from the surface.

Remove the meat to drain; keep warm. Strain the cooking liquid.

In a saucepan, melt the butter without letting it brown. Add the flour a little at a time and cook a few minutes, while stirring, to create a roux. Mix the cooking liquid into the roux while whisking. Bring to a boil and cook for 10 minutes.

In a small bowl, mix the egg yolk and crème fraîche with a few spoonfuls of the cooking liquid. Off the heat, add the contents of the bowl into the casserole dish and stir. Adjust the seasoning and add the lemon juice.

Put the meat back in the casserole dish. Keep warm (but do not boil) until ready to serve.

This dish is usually served with creole rice (SEE p. 400).

Osso buco milanese

FOR 4–6 PEOPLE
PREPARATION: 15 min
COOKING TIME: 1 hour 15 min

> 1 lb. tomatoes
> 2 onions
> 1 garlic clove
> 1 celery stalk
> 5 tbsp. olive oil
> 2 tbsp. all-purpose flour
> 4 or 6 slices veal shank, each 7 oz. with the bone
> 1 bay leaf
> just over ¾ cup dry white wine
> 6⅓ cups vegetable or beef broth
> ½ bunch of parsley
> 1 sprig of rosemary, leaves removed

Immerse the tomatoes for 20 seconds in boiling water, then immediately put them in cold water. Peel them, remove and discard the seeds then chop them.

Preheat the oven to 400° F.

Peel and chop the onions and garlic clove. Finely chop the celery. Heat the oil in a stovetop-safe casserole dish then add the vegetables and brown them well.

Lightly flour the veal and add them to the casserole dish to brown them on each side. Add the bay leaf and white wine to the dish. Continue cooking until the liquid is reduced by one-third then add the tomatoes. Cook for a few minutes then add the broth. When the liquid reaches a boil, place the dish in the oven for 1 hour.

Chop the parsley leaves and mix them with the rosemary leaves.

Arrange the slices of veal on a plate. Strain the cooking liquid, add the chopped herbs, then let the liquid continue to reduce by half.

Serve the osso buco with risotto.

Veal marengo

FOR 6 PEOPLE
PREPARATION: **30 min**
COOKING TIME:
approximately 1 hour

> 5 large tomatoes
> 2 onions
> 1 garlic clove
> 3⅓ lbs. veal shoulder
> 6 tbsp. butter
> 2 tbsp. cooking oil
> 1 tbsp. all-purpose flour
> just over ¾ cup white wine
> 1 bouquet garni (SEE p. 576)
> 24 pearl onions
> 1½ tsp. sugar
> 5 oz. white button mushrooms
> 5 oz. croutons
> 1 tbsp. chopped parsley
> salt, freshly ground black pepper

Immerse the tomatoes for 20 seconds in boiling water, then immediately put them in cold water. Peel them, remove and discard the seeds, then chop them.

Peel and chop the 2 onions then peel and crush the garlic clove. Cut the veal shoulder into pieces of approximately 3 ounces; season with salt and pepper.

In a stovetop-safe casserole dish, heat 2 tablespoons of the butter along with the cooking oil and brown the meat. Add the onions to sauté them. Sprinkle the flour in the pan, stir and cook 3 minutes.

Add the white wine then scrape the bottom of the dish with a wooden spoon to release the browned bits of cooked meat. Add the tomatoes, bouquet garni and garlic; season with salt and pepper. Add 1¼ cups of hot water (it should not cover the meat), bring to a boil then simmer, covered, for 45 minutes.

Meanwhile, peel the pearl onions and put them in boiling water for 1 minute; drain. In a small saucepan, melt 3 tablespoons of the butter, add the onions and cover them just to the top with water. Add the sugar and 2 pinches of salt. Cook gently for 10 to 15 minutes, letting the liquid evaporate until the consistency is syrupy; stir to coat the onions well. Remove from the heat when the onions are golden and glistening.

Slice the mushrooms and sauté them in the remaining 1 tablespoon of butter. Add them to the casserole dish approximately 5 minutes before the meat is finished cooking.

Serve in a heated, shallow dish and sprinkle with parsley. Garnish with the cooked onions and the croutons.

Roast chicken

FOR 4 PEOPLE
PREPARATION: **10 min**
COOKING TIME:
approximately 1 hour

> 1 chicken, approximately 3 lbs.
> 1 tbsp. peanut oil
> 2 tbsp. butter
> salt, freshly ground black pepper

Preheat the oven to 400° F.

Salt and pepper the inside of the chicken and truss it. Place the chicken in a roasting pan, brush it all over with the peanut oil then rub each thigh with half of the butter; season with salt and pepper then place in the oven.

After 10 to 15 minutes, add approximately ½ cup of hot water to the roasting pan. Bake the chicken for 45 minutes, basting occasionally with the pan juices. Turn it over halfway through the cooking time to brown evenly.

Turn off the oven, place a piece of aluminum foil over the chicken and let it rest for 10 minutes.

Cut up the chicken and collect the juice that comes out of it and add it to the roasting pan. Put the roasting pan on the stove, add 1 or 2 tablespoons of water and scrape the cooked bits from the bottom of the pan. Pour the liquid into a gravy boat or use it to glaze the pieces of chicken before serving.

To flavor the chicken, you can place a few twigs of thyme, savory or marjoram inside of it before roasting. If you like sweet and sour, add two small apples that will have time to cook all the way through while the chicken bakes. You can also add a dozen unpeeled garlic cloves to the roasting pan.

Basque chicken

FOR 4-6 PEOPLE
PREPARATION: **15 min**
COOKING TIME:
approximately 1 hour

> 1 chicken, approximately 3½ lbs.
> 4 tbsp. of olive oil
> 4 onions
> 3 garlic cloves
> 3 tomatoes
> 4 bell peppers
> 7 oz. ham (preferably Bayonne)
> ½ small chile pepper or a smidgen Cayenne pepper
> just over ¾ cup dry white wine
> salt, freshly ground black pepper

Cut up the chicken and brown it in a stovetop-safe casserole dish with 2 tablespoons of the olive oil.

Peel and chop the onions and the garlic cloves. Immerse the tomatoes for 20 seconds in boiling water, then immediately put them in cold water. Peel them, remove and discard the seeds then chop them. Dice the ham.

Preheat the broiler. Cut the peppers into quarters, remove the seeds and the white membrane. Place the pepper quarters on a baking sheet and place them in the oven approximately 6 inches from the broiler until the skin turns black and blisters; let cool. Remove and discard the blistered skins then slice the peppers into thin strips.

Remove the chicken from the casserole dish and pour off the fat. Heat the remaining 2 tablespoons of the olive oil in the casserole dish then add the diced ham and onions to brown while stirring.

Add the garlic, peppers, tomatoes, chili pepper and wine; season with salt and pepper. Mix and cook for 10 to 12 minutes, uncovered. Add the chicken pieces and stir. Cover and cook for an additional 30 to 40 minutes. Serve in the casserole dish.

Serve with fresh pasta.

Chicken waterzoï (chicken in cream sauce)

FOR 4-6 PEOPLE
PREPARATION: **15 min**
COOKING TIME:

approximately 1 hour
10 min

> 1 chicken, between 3 to
  3½ lbs.
> 4¼ cups chicken broth
> 5 leeks
> 2 celery stalks
> 3 onions
> 6 tbsp. butter
> 1 bunch parsley
> 2 egg yolks
> 1 cup crème fraîche
  (or heavy cream)
> juice of 1 lemon
> 6-8 slices of bread
> salt, freshly ground
  black pepper

Immerse the chicken in the chicken broth and simmer gently for 30 minutes.

Meanwhile, peel and finely chop the leeks, celery and onions. Melt 3 tablespoons of the butter in a stovetop-safe casserole dish. Add the vegetables and 5 parsley sprigs and let cook over low heat for 20 minutes; season with salt and pepper.

Cut the chicken into 8 pieces, removing as much of the bones as possible, and place the pieces in the casserole dish with the vegetables. Pour the broth into the pan up to the height of the chicken and cook another 30 minutes.

Remove the chicken pieces to drain. Mix the egg yolks with the crème fraîche, add the lemon juice, then pour into the casserole dish. Stir, without boiling, for 5 minutes. Taste and adjust the seasoning as needed. Return the chicken pieces to the pan.

Serve in the casserole dish with slices of toasted, buttered bread on the side.

Coq au vin

FOR 4-6 PEOPLE
PREPARATION: **30 min**
COOKING TIME:
approximately 1½ hours

> A large free-range roasting chicken, approximately 5½ lbs.
> 24 small white onions
> 2 garlic cloves
> 7 oz. thick-cut bacon, cut into small cubes
> 1 tbsp. vegetable oil
> 6 tbsp. butter
> 1 shot glass of brandy (approximately 1½ oz.)
> 4 cups red wine
> 1 bouquet garni (SEE p. 576)
> 7 oz. white button mushrooms
> 1 tbsp. all-purpose flour
> ¼ cup pig's blood (optional)
> salt, freshly ground black pepper

Cut up the chicken. Peel the onions then peel and crush the garlic cloves.

Place the bacon in a pan of cold water, bring to a boil and cook 2 minutes; remove to let drain.

Heat 1 tablespoon of oil and 1½ tablespoons of the butter in a stovetop-safe casserole dish and brown the bacon and onions. Remove them to let drain; set aside. Place the chicken pieces in the casserole dish and lightly brown them, turning them several times. Remove to let drain then pour off the fat from the pan. Place the onions, bacon and chicken back in the casserole dish.

Heat the brandy, pour it into the casserole dish then carefully light it to flambé it. Add the red wine, bouquet garni and garlic. Slowly bring to a boil, cover and simmer 40 to 50 minutes.

Meanwhile, wash and finely chop the mushrooms. Sauté them in 2 tablespoons of butter then add them to the casserole dish and cook for an additional 20 minutes.

In a bowl, mix the flour and the remaining 2½ tablespoons of butter (softened) with a fork until the flour is completely absorbed. Dilute this mixture with a little of the hot broth, then gradually stir it back into the casserole dish. Cook another 5 minutes, add the pork blood, if using, and allow to thicken for 5 minutes, stirring constantly.

Serve the coq au vin with boiled potatoes.

VARIATION you can replace white button mushrooms with other wild mushrooms when in season.

make ahead · recipe

Duck confit with potatoes sarladaises

FOR 4 PEOPLE
PREPARATION: **20 min**
COOKING TIME: **30 min**

> 4 portions of duck confit
> 1¾ lbs. potatoes
> 4 garlic cloves
> 1 bunch flat-leaf parsley
> 4 tbsp. goose fat
> salt, freshly ground black pepper

Open the jar of duck confit and set it in a saucepan of hot water to make a bain-marie, and heat until the fat has melted.

Peel, wash and dice the potatoes. Peel and chop the garlic cloves then chop the parsley. Mix the garlic with half the parsley; set aside.

When the fat in the confit has melted, remove the duck pieces and let them drain in a colander set over a plate.

Heat the goose fat in a stovetop-safe casserole dish, add the potatoes and cook over high heat for 10 minutes; season with salt and pepper. Cover and cook 10 minutes.

Add the parsley and garlic mixture and cook uncovered for another 10 minutes.

Meanwhile, heat a skillet on the stove and add the duck pieces. Cook gently until they are browned, turning several times. Remove the duck pieces and let some of the fat drain from them then cut them in half.

Arrange the potatoes on a serving dish, place the duck pieces next to them then sprinkle the remaining chopped parsley over the top. Serve immediately.

Rabbit in mustard sauce

FOR 4-6 PEOPLE
PREPARATION: **20 min**
COOKING TIME:
approximately 1 hour

> 1 rabbit, approximately
  3½ lbs.
> 3 tbsp. butter
> 2 sprigs of savory or
  thyme
> 3 or 4 tbsp. of mustard +
  1 tbsp. for the sauce
> 3 shallots
> just over ¾ cup white
  wine
> 1¼ cups crème fraîche
  (or heavy cream)
> salt, freshly ground
  black pepper

Cut up the rabbit.

Preheat the oven to 400° F. Butter a baking dish then crumble the savory or thyme leaves across the bottom of the dish.

Using a spoon, generously coat the rabbit pieces on all sides with a layer of mustard and place them in the dish. Bake for 50 minutes, turning the pieces halfway through the cooking time.

Peel and chop the shallots then place them in a small saucepan with the wine. Simmer gently and let the wine reduce by half. Place the shallots in a strainer and press them with the back of a spoon to drain as much of their liquid as possible.

Remove the rabbit pieces from the oven and arrange them on a serving plate; keep warm.

Pour the liquid from the baking dish into the wine/shallot reduction, add 1 cup of the crème fraîche and let it reduce by one-third. Mix 1 tablespoon of mustard with the remaining ¼ cup crème fraîche then add it to the reduction. Cook 2 or 3 minutes, stirring. Taste and adjust the seasoning as needed. Coat the rabbit with the sauce and serve.

Rabbit stewed in red wine

FOR 4 PEOPLE
PREPARATION: **30 min**
COOKING TIME:
approximately 50 min

> 1 freshly killed, unskinned rabbit, approximately 3 lbs.
> ½ cup blood from the rabbit
> ½ tbsp. red wine vinegar
> 1 small carrot
> 1 medium onion
> 1 tbsp. peanut oil
> 3 tbsp. butter
> 2 tbsp. all-purpose flour
> 2 tbsp. brandy
> 4¼ cups red wine
> 1 bouquet garni (SEE p. 576)
> ½ small baguette
> 2 tbsp. chopped parsley
> salt, freshly ground black pepper

Skin the rabbit and remove its entrails. Retain the blood and add the vinegar to it. Refrigerate the blood along with the liver and heart. Cut the rabbit into 8 pieces and season with salt and pepper.

Peel and dice the carrot and onion.

Heat the oil and butter in a stovetop-safe casserole dish over high heat then add the rabbit pieces to quickly sear them. Remove the rabbit pieces then pour off the fat from the pan. Add the vegetables and cook gently to brown.

Return the rabbit to the casserole dish, sprinkle in the flour and mix well.

Heat the brandy, then pour it into the casserole dish and carefully light it to flambé it. Add the wine and the bouquet garni, then cover and simmer for 45 minutes.

Slice and toast the bread to make croutons. Remove the rabbit pieces and allow the fat to drain from them. Place them on a serving dish and cover with aluminum foil to keep warm.

Strain the sauce and pour a small ladle of it into the blood and vinegar mixture and mix well. Remove the sauce from the heat, add the blood and vinegar to it and stir well. Adjust the seasoning as needed then reheat the sauce without boiling it; use it to glaze the rabbit pieces.

Sprinkle with parsley and serve with the croutons.

Aligot (potato and cantal purée)

FOR 6 PEOPLE
PREPARATION: **25 min**
COOKING TIME: **25 min**

> 2 lbs. potatoes
  (preferably Bintje or
  Yukon Gold)
> 1 lb. fresh cheese such
  as Tomme, Laguiole or
  Cantal
> 2 garlic cloves
> 2 tbsp. butter
> salt, freshly ground
  black pepper

Peel the potatoes and cut them into chunks. Cook for 20 minutes in boiling, salted water.

Meanwhile, cut the cheese into thin strips then peel and chop the garlic cloves.

Drain the potatoes and transfer them to a potato ricer or food mill (using the fine-mesh plate) and process.

Put the hot potato purée into a saucepan and set it over a pan of simmering water to make a bain-marie. Stir in the butter and garlic; season with salt and pepper.

Gradually add the cheese in batches while stirring continuously with a silicone spatula or wooden spoon. Wait until each batch of cheese is fully incorporated before adding the next. Lift the spoon higher and higher while mixing. When the mixture is smooth, creamy and stringy, the aligot is ready.

Taste and adjust the seasoning as needed. Serve hot.

This dish originated in Rouergue and is sometimes cut with scissors because of the stringiness of the cheese.

Potatoes savoyard

FOR 4 PEOPLE
PREPARATION: **30 min**
COOKING TIME: **50 min**

> 1⅓ lbs. potatoes
> 1 onion
> 9 oz. reblochon cheese (or any soft washed-rind cheese)
> 1 tbsp. peanut oil
> 7 oz. smoked thick-cut bacon, cut into small cubes
> 1¼ cups heavy cream

Peel and wash the potatoes. Cook 20 minutes in boiling, salted water. Drain, rinse with cold water, then slice.

Peel and chop the onion. Cut up one-fourth of the reblochon into medium pieces; set aside.

In a frying pan, heat the oil and sear the bacon.

Preheat the oven to 350° F.

Place the sliced potatoes, bacon and onion in layers in a large baking dish. Slice the remaining reblochon in half horizontally through the center so that each slice has the rind remaining on one side. Cover the top of the potato, bacon and onion layers with the reblochon slices with the rind facing down; the slices should be distributed to cover the entire surface of the top layer.

In a saucepan, heat the cream and the remaining pieces of reblochon over low heat. Mix thoroughly to melt the cheese then pour this into the baking dish.

Bake 25 to 30 minutes. Serve immediately along with a green salad.

VARIATION The reblochon can be replaced with morbier cheese. You can also place the onions in the pan with the bacon for 5 minutes to brown them slightly.

Fondue savoyard

FOR 6 PEOPLE
PREPARATION: **20 min**
COOKING TIME: **10 min**

> 4 fresh slices of country-
style bread
> 1 large garlic clove
> 1 tsp. cornstarch
> ½ cup kirsch
> 14 oz. emmental cheese
> 14 oz. comté or beaufort
cheese
> 2 cups dry white wine
> 1 large pinch of nutmeg
> freshly ground
black pepper

Cut the bread into approximately 1-inch cubes. Peel the garlic clove and cut it in half. Rub the interior walls of the fondue pot or a saucepan all over with the garlic. Mix the cornstarch with the kirsch to dissolve.

Remove the rind from the cheese and cut the cheese into thin strips. Place it in the fondue pot or a saucepan and pour in the white wine. Heat gently, stirring constantly for approximately 10 minutes until the cheese is fully melted; do not boil. When the cheese is smooth and homogeneous, add the cornstarch mixture, nutmeg and some freshly ground black pepper.

Place the fondue pot back on its heat stand over medium heat and place it in the middle of the table or, if using a regular saucepan, return it to the heat from time to time to keep the cheese warm and smooth.

Place the bread on the table so that each guest can use a fondue fork to dip it into the cheese, turning several times to coat the piece of bread completely.

quick & easy • recipe •

Mussels à la marinière (steamed mussels in white wine)

FOR 4-6 PEOPLE
PREPARATION: **20 min**
COOKING TIME: **7-8 min**

> 6½ lbs. mussels
> 1 large onion
> 1 shallot
> 2 tbsp. butter
> 1 to 1¼ cups dry white wine
> 1 sprig of thyme
> ½ bay leaf
> salt, freshly ground black pepper

Clean the mussels by removing the fibrous strands from the end of the shell, using a knife to scrape them while holding them under running water; they should not be soaked or they risk opening.

Peel and chop the onion and shallot.

Melt the butter in a saucepan, add the onion and shallot and let cook very gently for 1 or 2 minutes. Add the mussels and the white wine to the pan then season with salt and pepper. Add the thyme and bay leaf. Cook for 6 minutes on high heat, stirring frequently and shaking the pan occasionally.

When the mussels have opened, remove them from the pan and put them in a warm bowl. Remove the thyme and bay leaf and any mussels that remain closed. Pour the broth back over the finished mussels, then stir and serve.

You can strain the broth and stir in 3 tablespoons of crème fraîche (or heavy cream) before pouring it back over the mussels.

Mussels à la marinière with cream (steamed mussels in white wine with cream)

FOR 4-6 PEOPLE
PREPARATION: **30 min**
COOKING TIME:
approximiately 15 min

> 6½ lbs. mussels à la marinière
> ½ bunch parsley
> 1¼ cups crème fraîche (or heavy cream)
> salt, freshly ground black pepper

Prepare the mussels à la marinière (see above).

Drain them with a slotted spoon and put them on a serving dish to keep warm.

Chop the parsley.

Reduce the broth by a third over high heat. Reduce the heat then stir in the crème fraîche.

Reduce the liquid by another third, but at a lower heat. Taste and adjust the seasoning as needed. Pour the sauce over the mussels, sprinkle with parsley and serve.

Bouillabaisse

FOR 4–6 PEOPLE
PREPARATION: **45 min**
COOKING TIME:

approximately 15 min

> 4½ lbs. mixed fish (scorpion fish, gurnard, monkfish, conger, sea bream, saint-pierre, or silver hake)
> 10 small crabs (such as velvet crab)
> 2 onions
> 3 garlic cloves
> 2 leeks
> 3 celery stalks
> ⅔ cup olive oil
> 3 tomatoes
> 1 fennel bulb
> 1 bouquet garni (SEE p. 576)
> 2 pinches saffron
> 1 baguette
> salt, freshly ground black pepper

For the rouille:
> 3 garlic cloves
> 1 pinch kosher salt
> 2 pinches white pepper
> 1 small pinch saffron
> 2 small pinches Cayenne pepper
> 2 egg yolks at room temperature
> 1 cup olive oil

Clean the fish by removing the scales, entrails and the heads (do not discard the heads). Cut the fish into large pieces. Brush the crabs to clean them.

Chop 1 onion, 1 garlic clove, the leeks and celery then brown them in a sauté pan with ½ cup of the olive oil; season with salt and pepper. Add the fish heads and the fish pieces, cover with water, then bring to a boil and simmer for 20 minutes; strain the liquid and set it aside.

Meanwhile, blanch the tomatoes in boiling water, remove them then peel them and cut them into pieces. Peel and chop the second onion, the remaining garlic cloves and the fennel.

Prepare the rouille sauce. Peel the garlic and crush it or chop it. In a mortar or a bowl, mix it with the salt and pepper, saffron, Cayenne and the egg yolks. Slowly pour in the oil while whisking vigorously.

Add the remaining oil and the rest of the chopped vegetables to the sauté pan and brown them. Add the previously strained fish broth, tomatoes and bouquet garni. Add all of the fish pieces except the saint-pierre and the silver hake and cook 8 minutes on high heat, then add the saint-pierre and the silver hake and cook for another 5 to 6 minutes. Keep the bouillabaisse warm without letting it continue to cook.

Slice the baguette and toast the pieces in the oven.

Remove the fish and crabs with a large slotted spoon and let drain; place them on a large serving platter. Pour the broth, without straining it, into a soup tureen then add the fish and crabs. Serve with the rouille and the toasted baguette.

You can use a store-bought rouille to save time.

Seafood sauerkraut

FOR 6 PEOPLE
PREPARATION: **20 min**
COOKING TIME:

35-40 min

> 1¼ cups water
> 1¼ cups milk
> 1¾ lbs. smoked haddock
> 1¾ lbs. white fish filets, such as silver hake, cod, or monkfish (14 oz. each if using the salmon)
> 14 oz. salmon (optional)
> 3½ lbs. cooked sauerkraut
> just over ¾ cup dry white wine (optional), or use water
> 1 lb. potatoes

For the sauce:
> 3 shallots
> ½ cup white wine vinegar
> 1⅔ cups Muscadet
> 3 egg yolks
> 1 cups crème fraîche (or sour cream)
> salt, freshly ground black pepper

Pour the water and milk into a saucepan, bring just to the boil. Immerse the haddock and simmer gently to poach for 10 minutes.

Add more water to another saucepan, add salt, then bring just to a boil. Add the silver hake, cod or monkfish and the salmon, if using, and simmer gently to poach for 10 minutes.

Heat the sauerkraut in a stovetop-safe casserole dish over low heat with the white wine or water, covered, to prevent it from drying out.

Peel the potatoes and steam them (approximately 20 minutes for medium-sized potatoes).

Gently place the fish on the bed of sauerkraut in the casserole dish so that they finish cooking, no more than an additional 15 minutes.

Prepare the sauce. Peel and finely chop the shallots. Pour the vinegar and Muscadet in a saucepan and add the shallots. Reduce the liquid by half then remove it from the heat. Beat the egg yolks in a small bowl, add the crème fraîche then season with salt and pepper. Pour the egg mixture into the saucepan with the vinegar and wine and place back over low heat to thicken without boiling.

Place the sauerkraut on a serving dish then place the fish and potatoes on top. Serve the sauce separately.

You can add a few mussels or prawns for decoration.

Sea bream meunière

FOR 4-6 PEOPLE
PREPARATION: 15 min
COOKING TIME: 20 min

> 2 sea bream of 1⅓ lbs.
  each or 3 sea bream of
  14 oz. each
> 2 lemons
> 1 cup all-purpose flour
> 6 tbsp. butter
> 2 tbsp. chopped parsley
> salt, freshly ground
  black pepper

Clean the sea bream and place them on a large piece of absorbent cloth or paper towel. With a sharp knife, make small slits across their backs. Season on each side with salt and pepper then squeeze the lemons over them.

Pour the flour out onto a plate. Dredge each fish in the flour, coating both sides; gently shake them to remove the excess.

In a large skillet, heat 3 tablespoons of the butter and fry the fish for 10 minutes on each side. Remove the fish and let any excess oil drain from them. Arrange them on a long serving platter then sprinkle them with chopped parsley and a drizzle of lemon juice; keep warm.

Add the remaining 3 tablespoons of butter to the skillet and cook gently until it becomes golden brown and emits a nutty aroma (beurre noisette); be careful that it does not blacken. Pour the brown butter over the fish. Serve immediately.

VARIATION You can use sole (8½ to 10½ ounces) instead. Cook them for 6 or 7 minutes on each side. This dish is traditionally served with a side of steamed potatoes.

Cod nîmoise

FOR 4-6 PEOPLE
DESALTING: **12 hours**
PREPARATION: **30 min**
COOKING TIME:
15-20 min

> 2 lbs. salt cod fillets
> 3⅓ cups olive oil
> 1 cup milk
> 5 or 6 slices of bread,
  stale or toasted
> 2 garlic cloves
> salt, white pepper

Place the cod fillets in a colander set in a basin of cold water. Leave them for 12 hours to extract the salt, changing out the water two or three times.

In a Dutch oven or a large saucepan, bring water to a boil and immerse the cod fillets. Reduce the heat and simmer gently for 8 minutes. Remove the fillets and let them drain. Remove the skin and bones then flake off the flesh using your fingers.

In a saucepan, heat just over ¾ cup of the olive oil. When the oil is hot, add the cod flesh, lower the heat immediately then stir over gentle heat with a silicone spatula or wooden spoon, just until the flesh starts to develop a pasty texture.

Heat the milk. When the fish is ready, remove the saucepan from the heat and continue to mix, without stopping, while drizzling in 1⅔ to 2 cups of olive oil followed by the hot milk (the mixture should be approached as when making a mayonnaise); season with salt and pepper. The mixture should be homogeneous and have the consistency of mashed potatoes; keep warm.

Rub the slices of bread with the peeled garlic cloves. Cut into four square pieces or into triangles or toast them coated with the rest of the olive oil.

Serve the dish hot, garnished with the bread slices.

You can easily warm the leftovers in the microwave or in a saucepan over low heat, stirring continuously to prevent sticking.

Oven-roasted sea bass

low calorie recipe

FOR 6 PEOPLE
PREPARATION: **5 min**
COOKING TIME: **30 min**

> 1 sea bass, approximately 4 lbs., pre-cleaned
> olive oil
> 2 sprigs dried fennel
> pink peppercorns (optional)
> salt, freshly ground black pepper

Preheat the oven to 450° F.

Wash the sea bass then blot it dry with paper towels. Place it in a baking dish and brush it all over with olive oil. Salt and pepper the inside and outside. Place the sprigs of fennel in the belly then sprinkle with pink peppercorns, if desired. Bake for 30 minutes.

Remove the bass from the oven and remove the skin on one side by sliding a knife underneath it to lift it off. Using two long spatulas or two slotted spoons, turn the fish over and remove the skin on the other side. Serve immediately.

Serve with boiled potatoes and beurre blanc (**SEE** p. 562).

Grilled sea bass with anchovy butter

FOR 4 PEOPLE
DESALTING: **20 min**
PREPARATION: **15 min**
COOKING TIME:
20–25 min

> 1 sea bass, approximately 2 lbs., pre-cleaned
> 2 tbsp. olive oil
> salt, freshly ground black pepper

For the anchovy butter:
> 6-8 salted anchovy fillets
> juice of ½ lemon
> 7 tbsp. butter, softened

Soak the anchovy fillets in cold water for 20 minutes to extract the salt.

Wash the sea bass then blot it dry with paper towels.

Preheat the broiler. Add salt and pepper to the olive oil then coat the inside and outside of the fish with the oil using a brush.

Place the fish on a broiling pan and place it under the broiler, or you can place the fish on the barbecue. Broil 10 to 12 minutes on each side.

Meanwhile, prepare the anchovy butter. Purée the anchovies in a blender or mash them with a fork. Add the lemon juice and mix with the butter.

Remove the fish from the oven, open it up and remove the backbone. Spread the anchovy butter on the inside of the fish (or serve it on the side). Enjoy immediately.

Trout almandine

FOR 4 PEOPLE
PREPARATION: 15 min
COOKING TIME:
approximately 15 min

> 2½ oz. sliced almonds
> 4 trout, 9 oz. each
> ½ cup all-purpose flour
> 5 tbsp. butter
> 1 or 2 lemons
> 1 tbsp. chopped parsley
> 1 tbsp. vinegar
> salt, freshly ground
  black pepper

Preheat the oven to 400° F.

Place the almonds on a baking sheet lined with parchment paper and bake them just until lightly golden.

Clean the trout then blot them dry with paper towels. Season each side with salt and pepper. Pour the flour out onto a plate. Dredge each fish in the flour, coating both sides; gently shake them to remove any excess.

In a large skillet (preferably oval), heat 3 tablespoons of the butter and brown the trout on both sides. Reduce the heat and continue cooking 5 to 7 minutes (10 minutes if the trout are very big), turning the fish once. Add the toasted almonds to the pan while the fish are cooking.

Remove the trout and place them on a serving dish. Sprinkle with 2 tablespoons of lemon juice and the chopped parsley. Keep warm.

Add the remaining 2 tablespoons of butter and the vinegar to the skillet, heat and pour over the trout along with the almonds. Serve with lemon wedges.

Skate in brown butter

FOR 4-6 PEOPLE
PREPARATION: **10 min**
COOKING TIME:
approximately 10 min

> 1½ lbs. skate fins
> 8½ cups store-bought court-bouillon for fish
> 6 tbsp. butter
> 3 tbsp. capers
> juice of 1 lemon
> 6-8 sprigs of parsley

Wash the skate fins then blot them dry with paper towels.

Make or heat the court-bouillon (or use 2 quarts of salted water with ½ cup of vinegar added) and let it cool. Immerse the fins in the broth and bring it back to a boil. Skim the fat from the surface then lower the heat and let simmer 5 to 7 minutes.

Meanwhile, gently heat the butter in a skillet until it becomes golden brown and emits a nutty aroma (beurre noisette). Be careful that it does not blacken; season with salt and pepper.

Remove the fins and let them drain. Place them on a hot serving dish. Drain the capers and chop the parsley. Drizzle lemon juice over the fins then sprinkle on the capers and parsley. Pour the browned butter over them and serve immediately.

Serve with boiled potatoes or a green vegetable, such as broccoli.

If you have a little more time, prepare a court-bouillon at home. Peel and slice 2 carrots and 2 onions. Put them in a saucepan with a bouquet garni and pour in 8½ cups of water. Bring to a boil and cook 20 minutes. Add 2 tablespoons of salt, 10 peppercorns and just over ¾ cup of vinegar. Turn off the heat and steep for 10 minutes. Strain the broth to remove the vegetables.

Lunch and small plates

Tofu and vegetable tart

FOR 4 PEOPLE
PREPARATION: **10 min**
COOKING TIME: **35 min**

> 7 oz. mixed frozen
  vegetables (haricots
  verts, beans, carrots
  or small peas)
> 3 eggs
> ¼ cup milk (or soy milk)
> 5 tbsp. crème fraîche
> 4½ oz. firm tofu
> 3 oz. grated emmental
  cheese
> 1 pre-prepared pie crust
> salt, freshly ground black
  pepper

Boil the vegetables in salted water for 5 minutes; drain.

Preheat the oven to 350° F.

Using a fork, lightly beat the eggs with the milk and crème fraîche until mixed, then crumble the tofu and add it to the egg mixture along with the grated emmental cheese; season with salt and pepper.

Line a 9-inch tart pan with the pre-prepared pie crust. Distribute the vegetables evenly over the bottom of the tart then pour in the egg mixture and bake for 30 minutes or until set.

Serve with an endive and walnut salad.

VARIATION   Use thin slices of reblochon cheese in place of the emmental.

Herb and comté cheese omelet

FOR 4 PEOPLE
PREPARATION: **10 min**
COOKING TIME: **5 min**

> 4¼ oz. comté cheese
> 1 bunch chives
> 1 small bunch parsley
> 1 small bunch chervil
> 1 small bunch tarragon
> 12 eggs
> 2 tbsp. vegetable oil
> 2 tbsp. butter
> salt, freshly ground black
   pepper

Dice the comté cheese. Wash and finely chop the chives, parsley, chervil and tarragon.

Break the eggs into a large bowl; season with salt and pepper then beat them briefly with a fork until well mixed; add the chopped herbs and beat briefly again.

Heat the oil and butter together in a large, nonstick skillet. Pour the beaten eggs into the skillet and cook for 3 minutes over high heat while stirring gently. Stop stirring and distribute the diced comté cheese over the egg and cook for another 1 to 2 minutes over high heat. Using a spatula, loosen the edges all the way around the omelet then fold over one of the edges and roll the omelet over onto itself several times; tilt the skillet to aid in rolling the omelet.

Place on a serving plate and serve immediately.

Serve with a simple green salad.

You can make individual omelets in small skillets. Keep the finished ones warm in the oven with the door propped open slightly, covered with aluminum foil, until all are complete and ready to serve.

quick & easy · recipe ·

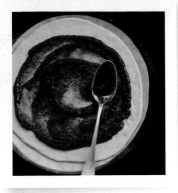

Ham and vegetable pizza

FOR 4 PEOPLE
PREPARATION: **30 min**
COOKING TIME: **10 min**

> 9 oz. pre-prepared pizza dough
> 1 large red onion
> 4 tomatoes
> 7 oz. mozzarella cheese
> 2 slightly thick slices of ham
> 4¼ oz. white button mushrooms
> 1⅔ cups tomato sauce
> 16 black and green olives
> 1 tbsp. chopped sprigs of thyme or herbes de Provence
> 3 tbsp. olive oil
> salt, freshly ground black pepper

Divide the pizza dough into 4 even pieces and roll them out into circles approximately ¼ inch thick. Place the dough circles onto a parchment-lined cookie sheet and let them rise while preparing the ingredients.

Peel and slice the onion. Slice the tomatoes and mozzarella. Cut up the ham into small pieces. Wash and thinly slice the mushrooms.

Preheat the oven to 425° F.

Spread the tomato sauce over the bottom of each circle of dough, without going all the way to the edge. Evenly distribute the ham and mushrooms over the top. Add the tomato slices then the sliced mozzarella, followed by the onions. Place 4 olives on each pizza and sprinkle all over with thyme.

Drizzle the pizzas with olive oil then season with salt and pepper; bake for 10 minutes. Enjoy while piping hot.

Instead of small pizzas, you can prepare one large, family-sized pizza.

Make your own tomato sauce. Sauté 1 onion and 2 crushed garlic cloves with a little olive oil then add 8 peeled and crushed tomatoes; simmer to soften.

Hamburger

FOR 4 PEOPLE
PREPARATION: **15 min**
COOKING TIME:
8–10 min

> 1 large red onion
> 4 tomatoes
> 1 lb. ground beef
> ¼ cup vegetable oil
> 4 sesame-seed
  hamburger buns
> 4 tbsp. mayonnaise
> 4 tbsp. ketchup
> several green lettuce
  leaves
> 3 oz. gouda cheese,
  sliced
> salt, freshly ground
  black pepper

Peel and thinly slice the onion. Slice the tomatoes.

Using your hands, form 4 beef patties the same diameter as the hamburger buns. Heat the vegetable oil in a skillet and brown each patty for 4 to 5 minutes on each side; season with salt and pepper.

Slice the buns in half horizontally and spread the bottom half of each bun with approximately ½ tablespoon each of mayonnaise and ketchup. Place several lettuce leaves on top, followed by the cooked beef patties, then the cheese, onions and tomatoes. Spread the remaining mayonnaise and ketchup on the underside of the top bun and place on top of the hamburger, pressing down lightly. Serve immediately.

Flavor the hamburger according to your own tastes, adding herbs or spices to the ground beef before forming it into patties, or flavor the mayonnaise with curry, black pepper, or ground red chili pepper.

Oxtail shepherd's pie with carrot purée

FOR 4 PEOPLE
PREPARATION: **40 min**
COOKING TIME:

3½ hours

> 1 onion
> 1½ lbs. carrots
> 2 tbsp. vegetable oil
> 4½ lbs. oxtail, cut into pieces
> 1 bouquet garni (SEE p. 576)
> 3 cups red wine
> 6⅓ cups veal broth
> 2 potatoes
> 6 tbsp. butter
> 2 tbsp. crème fraîche (or sour cream)
> 3 shallots
> 2 tbsp. bread crumbs
> salt, freshly ground black pepper

Peel the onion and one of the carrots, cutting them both into pieces. Heat the oil in a large sauté pan or stovetop-safe casserole dish and sear the meat. Add the carrot and onion pieces, the bouquet garni and the red wine; season with salt and pepper. Bring to a boil and cook for 5 minutes. Add the veal broth, cover the dish, then cook for 3 hours over very low heat, stirring occasionally. Add a little water during the cooking time if it begins to reduce too much.

Peel the remaining carrots and the potatoes and chop them; boil them for 20 minutes in salted water, drain, then process them through a potato ricer or food mill (using the fine-mesh plate). Mix in 4 tablespoons of the butter and all of the crème fraîche then season with salt and pepper; stir to obtain a smooth consistency.

When the oxtail pieces are cooked, place them on a plate to rest, reserving the cooking juices; let them cool then remove all of the meat from the bone.

Peel and mince the shallots. Sauté them in approximately 1 teaspoon of butter for 5 minutes until softened. Add the oxtail meat and ⅔ cup of the cooking juices (strained) and simmer for 10 minutes.

Preheat the oven to 350° F.

Spread the meat over the bottom of a large baking dish then cover with the puréed carrots and potatoes. Sprinkle the bread crumbs over the top then distribute the remaining butter in small pieces on top of the bread crumbs. Bake for 20 minutes. Serve very hot.

You can replace the oxtail with beef cheek, letting it simmer for several minutes. Flavor the beef cheek while it is cooking by adding a large strip of orange zest.

Pork shoulder with navy beans

FOR 4–6 PEOPLE
PREPARATION: **5 min**
SOAKING AND
DESALTING: **2–3 hours**
COOKING TIME:
2½–3 hours

> 14 oz. to 1 lb. dried haricots blancs (white navy or kidney beans)
> 2¼ lbs. lightly salted pork shoulder (upper part of shoulder)
> 1 garlic clove
> 1 onion
> 2 bouquets garnis (SEE p. 576)
> salt

Soak the beans for 2 to 3 hours. Soak the pork shoulder in cold water for 1 hour to extract the salt; change the water once during this time.

Peel the garlic clove and the onion. Cut the garlic clove into quarters.

Remove and drain the pork shoulder then make slits in the meat using the point of a knife and insert the garlic quarters into the slits. Place the pork in a Dutch oven, cover almost entirely with cold water, add 1 of the bouquets garnis, then simmer for 2 hours.

Drain the beans and add them to a saucepan with the onion and the second bouquet garni. Cover almost entirely with water and cook gently for approximately 2 hours; they should stay somewhat firm.

Remove the cooked pork shoulder and set it aside to drain. Add it to the saucepan with the beans. Adjust the seasoning as needed then cook gently, covered, until the beans are nice and soft. Remove the onion and bouquet garni before serving.

make ahead · recipe ·

Apple and cider pork roast

FOR 4 PEOPLE
PREPARATION: **30 min**
COOKING TIME: **1 hour**
15 min
RESTING TIME: **20 min**

> 1 pork roast,
> approximately 1½ lbs.
> 2 tbsp. vegetable oil
> 4 tbsp. butter
> 2 sprigs of thyme
> 2 cups hard apple cider
> (or use alcohol-free)
> 1 cup veal broth
> 2 red apples
> salt, freshly ground black
> pepper

Preheat the oven to 350° F.

Place the pork roast in a baking dish. Drizzle with the vegetable oil then distribute 2 tablespoons of the butter over the top, in little pieces; season with salt and pepper and the sprigs of thyme. Bake for 30 minutes, basting and turning the roast every 10 minutes.

In a saucepan, reduce the apple cider by two-thirds; season with salt and pepper. Add the veal broth then reduce again by half.

Wash the apples, core them, then cut them into quarters.

When the roast has baked for 30 minutes, pour the cider sauce into the baking dish and place the apple quarters around it. Bake for an additional 40 minutes, basting frequently with the sauce.

Remove the pork roast and wrap it well in aluminum foil; let rest for 20 minutes.

Place the apples on a plate and keep them warm. Pour the sauce from the baking dish into a saucepan and bring to a boil over high heat for 5 minutes; whisk in the 2 remaining tablespoons of butter.

Slice the roast and serve with the apple quarters and the cider sauce.

Use a nice cut of pork loin instead. It will be fattier than the pork roast but much more moist as a result.

Four seasons pizza

FOR 4 PEOPLE
PREPARATION: **30 min**
COOKING TIME:
approximately 40 min

> 9 oz. pre-prepared pizza
  dough
> 2 garlic cloves
> 1¾ lbs. tomatoes
> 2 tbsp. olive oil
> 3 pinches oregano
> 4 slices prosciutto
> 5¼ oz. chorizo
> 9 oz. canned artichoke
  hearts, drained
> 1 small can salted
  anchovy fillets in oil
> 5¼ oz. white button
  mushrooms
> 3½ oz. pitted black olives
> 3 oz. grated parmesan
  cheese
> salt, freshly ground black
  pepper

Divide the pizza dough into 4 even pieces and roll them out into circles approximately ¼ inch thick. Place the dough circles on a parchment-lined cookie sheet and let them rise while preparing the ingredients.

Peel and chop the garlic cloves. Immerse the tomatoes in boiling water for 20 seconds, then immediately put them in cold water. Peel them then chop them into pieces.

Heat 1 tablespoon of the olive oil in a skillet and add the tomatoes. Add the oregano and garlic; season with salt and pepper. Cook for 15 to 30 minutes until the tomatoes have lost most of their water.

Preheat the oven to 475° F.

Slice the prosciutto into small strips, slice the chorizo into thin rounds, cut the artichokes in half, and pat the anchovy fillets dry using a paper towel.

Thinly slice the mushrooms.

Spread the tomatoes over the pizza then distribute the anchovies on top. Add the remaining ingredients: artichokes, mushrooms, prosciutto and sausage, grouping them together, each on one quarter of the pizza. Scatter the olives all over the top then sprinkle on the parmesan. Drizzle with a little olive oil.

Bake for approximately 10 minutes. Serve hot.

Stuffed bell peppers

FOR 4 PEOPLE
PREPARATION: **45 min**
COOKING TIME:
45–50 min

> 4 nice red bell peppers
> 1 small bunch flat-leaf parsley
> 2 medium onions
> 7 tbsp. butter
> 5¼ oz. diced tomatoes, canned
> 3½ oz. prosciutto
> 9 oz. sausage, casing removed
> 1 egg
> salt, freshly ground black pepper

Rinse the peppers then slice off the top of each one near the stem and remove the cap. Clean out the seeds and the white membrane then place the peppers on a baking sheet just large enough to accommodate all of them.

Wash and chop the parsley.

Peel and finely chop the onions. Melt 2 tablespoons of the butter in a skillet and cook the onions over low heat for 5 to 10 minutes until they soften and become translucent. Add the diced tomatoes and cook down just until the tomatoes release enough water to create a moist mixture; transfer to a large bowl.

Preheat the oven to 350° F.

Finley chop the prosciutto. Place it in the large bowl with the tomato mixture and add the sausage meat, the egg and the parsley; season with salt and pepper and mix well (season lightly if the sausage is already well-seasoned). Fill the peppers with the stuffing mixture.

Melt the remaining 5 tablespoons of butter in a small saucepan and drizzle it over the tops of the peppers and the stuffing, then replace the pepper tops. Bake for 40 minutes, basting often with the cooking juices. Halfway through the cooking time, cover the peppers with a piece of aluminum foil to keep them moist. Serve hot in the baking dish.

The peppers can be served by themselves or with steamed rice.

Pork spareribs in bbq sauce with fried potatoes

FOR 4-6 PEOPLE
PREPARATION: **25 min**
MARINADE: **12 hours**
COOKING TIME: **45 min**

> 4 garlic cloves
> just over ¾ cup white wine
> ¼ cup ketchup
> ⅓ cup light soy sauce
> ¼ cup honey (fluid)
> 1 tbsp. herbes de Provence
> 2 whole pork spareribs, cut up into several pieces
> 1 bunch tarragon
> 4 large potatoes
> vegetable oil, for frying
> salt, freshly ground black pepper

The night before: Peel and chop the garlic cloves. In a shallow dish, stir together the white wine, the ketchup, the soy sauce, the honey, the garlic and the herbes de Provence. Add the pork pieces and marinate for 12 hours, refrigerated.

The next day: Preheat the oven to 350° F.

Remove the pork pieces from the marinade and place them in a large baking dish. Brush them well with the marinade and bake for 45 minutes, checking often while baking so that the marinade does not burn; if it does, turn the pieces of pork over and lower the temperature of the oven. At the end of the baking time, the meat should be moist with a nice caramelized crust.

Wash the tarragon then remove and mince the leaves.

Peel and grate the potatoes using a food processor or a hand-held grater with large holes.

In a large, heavy-bottomed saucepan, heat the vegetable oil to 350° F then immerse the potatoes in batches into the oil, stirring occasionally with a fork. When brown and crisp, remove them and place on a paper towel to drain; season with salt and pepper and the minced tarragon leaves; serve on the side with the pork ribs.

This dish is also delicious served with puréed potatoes.

Pork medallions with golden raisins

FOR 6 PEOPLE
PREPARATION: **5 min**
COOKING TIME:
approximately 10 min

> 1 pork filet
> 2 tbsp. vegetable oil
> 1 tbsp. dried golden raisins
> 1 tbsp. dried currants
> 3 tbsp. crème fraîche (or sour cream)
> 2 tbsp. cognac
> 1 tbsp. whole-grain mustard
> salt, freshly ground black pepper

Cut the filet into medallions approximately ½ inch thick. Heat the vegetable oil in a frying pan and cook the medallions for 3 minutes over medium heat. Turn them over then season with salt and pepper. Continue to cook over medium heat for an additional 3 minutes; remove the medallions from the pan and keep warm.

Place the raisins and currants in the frying pan along with the crème fraîche and the cognac; season with salt and pepper and cook until the sauce thickens. Remove from the heat and add the mustard; mix well and pour over the pork medallions. Serve immediately.

Serve with steamed rice or fresh pasta.

The sweet and savory flavors of this sauce marry very well with other white meat dishes.

Pork chops in maple syrup

FOR 4 PEOPLE
PREPARATION: **10 min**
COOKING TIME: **25 min**

> 2 apples, preferably reinette
> juice of ½ lemon
> 2 tbsp. butter
> 1 tbsp. vegetable oil
> 4 pork chops
> 2 tbsp. maple syrup
> 2 tbsp. crème fraîche (or sour cream)
> salt, freshly ground black pepper

Preheat the oven to 400° F.

Peel the apples then cut them in half and remove the seeds. Thinly slice them then sprinkle them with the lemon juice.

Heat the butter and the oil in a skillet; season the pork chops with salt and pepper then sear them on each side over high heat for 2 minutes. Remove them from the skillet and place them in a baking dish. Arrange the apple slices on top of them then season again with salt and pepper.

Coat the apples and pork chops with the maple syrup and the crème fraîche and bake for 20 minutes; serve very hot.

Pork chops in beer and mustard

FOR 4 PEOPLE
PREPARATION: **5 min**
COOKING TIME:
20-25 min

> 4 pork chops
> 4 tbsp. mustard
> 1 sprig of thyme
> 2 bay leaves
> 1 onion
> 1 garlic clove
> just over ¾ cup blonde beer
> salt, freshly ground black pepper

Preheat the oven to 400° F.

Brush the pork chops with the mustard then place them in a baking dish; season with salt and pepper. Sprinkle them with thyme leaves then add the bay leaves; peel and chop the onion and garlic clove and distribute them around and on top of the pork chops.

Bake for 5 minutes. When the chops begin to brown, carefully pour the beer over them and bake for another 15 to 20 minutes, basting them occasionally with the cooking juices.

Serve the pork chops with gratins potatoes or puréed celery and chestnuts.

Boudin noir normandy-style

FOR 4-6 PEOPLE
PREPARATION: **15 min**
COOKING TIME:
approximately 15 min

> 1 lb. cooking apples, such as McIntosh
> juice of 1 lemon
> 4 tbsp. butter
> 1½ lbs. blood sausage (boudin noir)
> several chive stalks
> salt, freshly ground black pepper

Peel and thinly slice the apples then toss the slices with the lemon juice.

In a skillet, melt 3 tablespoons of the butter and cook the apples over medium heat for approximately 15 minutes until soft and browned.

Cut the sausage into sections approximately 4 inches long and prick them several times with a fork.

In a second skillet, heat the remaining 1 tablespoon of butter and cook the sausage pieces for 10 to 12 minutes until browned, turning them several times; season with salt and pepper.

Wash and chop the chives.

Remove the sausages and let drain. Place them on a warm serving plate, arrange the apple slices around them then sprinkle them with the chives. Serve immediately.

Veal crumble

FOR 6 PEOPLE
PREPARATION: **30 min**
COOKING TIME: **1 hour 15 min**

> 2 onions
> 1 bunch cilantro
> 2 tbsp. olive oil
> 2 lbs. ground lamb meat
> 1 tbsp. ground cumin
> 1 tbsp. ground cardamom
> 3 zucchini
> 5 tomatoes
> salt, freshly ground black pepper

For the crumble topping

> 14 tbsp. (1 stick + 6 tbsp.) softened butter
> 7 oz. grated parmesan cheese
> 1¾ cups (7 oz.) all-purpose flour
> 3½ oz. rolled oats

Peel and mince the onions. Wash and chop the cilantro.

In a skillet, heat 1 tablespoon of the olive oil then add the onions, ground lamb meat, cumin, cardamom and cilantro and cook for approximately 10 minutes over medium heat until the onions and meat are browned; the meat must be thoroughly cooked. Mix well then set aside in a large bowl.

Preheat the oven to 300° F.

Dice the zucchini and the tomatoes. Over medium heat, add the remaining 1 tablespoon of olive oil to the skillet then add the zucchini and tomatoes. Cook for 5 minutes; season with salt and pepper.

Prepare the crumble: Cut the butter into small pieces. Using a silicone spatula, mix it with the parmesan, the flour, and the oats until the mixture has a coarse, sandy texture.

In a baking dish, spread in half the ground lamb mixture then cover it with a layer of the vegetables followed by a layer of the remaining ground lamb. Evenly distribute the crumble mixture over the top and bake for 1 hour.

The crumble topping can be prepared in advance and reheated just before using.

make ahead recipe

Sautéed lamb or veal with eggplant

FOR 4 PEOPLE
PREPARATION: **15 min**
COOKING TIME:

25–35 min

> 2½ lbs. lamb collar or veal shoulder
> 3 eggplants
> 1 garlic clove
> ¼ bunch parsley
> 2 tbsp. butter
> just over ¾ cup peanut oil
> 1¼ cups clear veal broth
> ⅔ cup white wine
> ½ cup stewed tomatoes
> salt, freshly ground black pepper

Bone the lamb collar (or the veal shoulder) and cut into pieces of equal size. Using a small knife, remove as much of the fat as possible; season with salt and pepper.

Slice the eggplants lengthwise into quarters, then thinly slice them. Peel the garlic clove and cut off the stems from the parsley; mince both the garlic and the parsley leaves.

In a sauté pan or stovetop-safe casserole dish, heat the butter and 3 tablespoons of the peanut oil. Add the meat pieces to the dish and brown them, turning several times. Remove the meat and pour off the fat from the dish.

Return the meat back to the pan or casserole dish, add the veal broth then season with salt and pepper. Cook for 15 minutes, covered (25 minutes if using the veal shoulder).

Meanwhile, fry the eggplant slices in the remaining ⅔ cup of peanut oil then season with salt; drain them on paper towels.

Remove the meat from the pan or casserole dish, pour in the white wine and add the stewed tomatoes; stir well to incorporate with the broth.

Place the meat back in the pan or casserole dish, add the eggplants, the garlic, and half the parsley. Mix and cook for an additional 5 to 10 minutes. Taste and adjust the seasoning as needed.

Serve on a large, warmed serving platter and garnish with the remaining chopped parsley.

Lamb chops and watercress

FOR 4 PEOPLE
PREPARATION: **10 min**
COOKING TIME: **8 min**

> 3 tbsp. butter, room temperature
> 1 tbsp. chopped parsley
> 1 bunch watercress
> 8 high-quality lamb chops
> salt, freshly ground black pepper

Cut up the butter into small pieces, add it to a medium-sized bowl then work it with a silicone spatula until it becomes creamy. Incorporate a pinch of salt, some pepper and the chopped parsley into the softened butter; set aside, refrigerated.

Wash and drain the watercress; separate it into small bunches.

Season the lamb chops with salt and pepper. Grill them for 3 to 4 minutes on each side then place them on a warmed serving plate. Add one quarter of the very cold herbed butter on top of each chop.

Surround the chops with the watercress bunches and serve immediately.

quick & easy recipe

You can use mâche lettuce (field lettuce) instead of the watercress.

Lamb chops with thyme

FOR 4 PEOPLE
MARINADE: **1 hour**
PREPARATION: **5 min**
COOKING TIME: **6–8 min**

> just over ¾ cup olive oil
> 1 tbsp. dried thyme
> 12 small lamb chops
> salt, freshly ground black pepper

Add the olive oil to a bowl along with the thyme. Stir and let sit at room temperature for approximately 1 hour.

Brush each lamb chop on both sides with the oil.

Just before serving, grill the chops for 3 to 4 minutes on each side; season with salt and pepper.

You can also infuse the oil with basil or rosemary instead of the thyme.

Veal shank provençal

FOR 4–6 PEOPLE
PREPARATION: **15 min**
COOKING TIME:
approximately 1 hour
40 min

> 4–6 slices veal shank (approximately 6 oz. each)
> 2 onions
> 6–8 tomatoes
> 2 garlic cloves
> 3 tbsp. olive oil
> just over ¾ cup white wine
> 1 bouquet garni (SEE p. 576)
> ⅔ cup veal broth
> salt, freshly ground black pepper

Season the veal shank with salt and pepper. Peel and chop the onions. Immerse the tomatoes in boiling water for 20 seconds, then immediately put them in cold water. Peel them, remove and discard the seeds, then finely dice them. Peel and crush the garlic cloves.

Heat the olive oil in a frying pan and brown the veal shank on both sides. Add the onions and sauté them until they start to develop color. Add the tomatoes, the white wine and the bouquet garni. Mix well and cook for 5 minutes.

Add the veal broth and the garlic to the pan. Cover and cook for 1 hour 20 minutes over gentle heat. Uncover then cook for an additional 10 minutes to reduce the sauce. Serve very hot.

make ahead recipe

Veal and onion tart

FOR 4–6 PEOPLE
PREPARATION: **25 min**
COOKING TIME:
approximately 30–40 min

> 14 oz. pre-prepared pie crust
> 1⅔ lbs. onions
> 6 tbsp. butter
> 1 egg
> just over ¾ cup crème fraîche
> 1 pinch nutmeg
> approximately 7 oz. left-over veal (or chicken) meat
> salt, freshly ground black pepper

Preheat the oven to 350° F.

Line an 11-inch tart pan with the pre-prepared pie crust. Cover the dough with parchment paper, add a layer of dried beans or pie weights on top of the parchment, then bake for 10 minutes; remove from the oven and carefully lift off the parchment paper.

Meanwhile, peel and finely mince the onions. Add 3½ tablespoons of the butter to a skillet and sauté the onions gently for 15 to 20 minutes.

Increase the oven temperature to 400° F.

In a small bowl, beat the eggs with the crème fraîche, season with salt and pepper, add the pinch of nutmeg, then add this mixture to a saucepan and cook gently over low heat until thickened; do not boil. Add the cooked eggs to the skillet.

Cut the veal (or chicken) meat into small strips. Distribute the meat over the bottom of the prebaked pie crust, still in the tart pan. Pour the onion mixture over the top of the meat then distribute the remaining 2½ tablespoons of butter, in pieces, over the top and bake for 15 to 20 minutes. Serve very hot.

Veal milanese

FOR 4 PEOPLE
PREPARATION: **25 min**
COOKING TIME:

approximately 40 min

> 7 oz. spaghetti or macaroni
> 2 white button mushrooms
> 1 thin slice of ham, approximately 3 oz.
> 4 veal cutlets, approximately 5¼ oz. each
> 6 tbsp. butter
> 2 tbsp. peanut oil
> 3 tbsp. madeira wine
> just over ¾ cup brown veal broth
> 1 oz. parmesan cheese
> salt, freshly ground black pepper

For the stewed tomatoes

> 5–6 tomatoes
> 1 onion
> 1 garlic clove
> 2 tbsp. olive oil
> 1–2 sprigs of thyme

For the bread crumbs

> 1 cup (3½ oz.) all-purpose flour
> 1 egg
> 1 cup (3½ oz.) finely ground bread crumbs
> 1 oz. parmesan cheese

Prepare the stewed tomatoes. Immerse the tomatoes in boiling water for 20 seconds, then immediately put them in cold water. Peel them, remove and discard the seeds, then dice them. Peel and chop the onions and the garlic clove. In a skillet, heat the olive oil and brown the onion. Add the tomatoes, the garlic and the thyme then cook for approximately 20 minutes over gentle heat, stirring occasionally; season with salt and pepper.

Meanwhile, boil the pasta in salted water to al dente. Clean the mushrooms and cut them into small strips. Slice the ham into thin strips.

Prepare the bread crumbs. Pour the flour out onto a flat plate. Beat the egg in a second shallow plate, then mix the bread crumbs with 1 ounce of parmesan cheese on a third plate; season the cutlets with salt and pepper. Dredge the cutlets in the flour then quickly dip them in the beaten eggs then in the bread crumbs, coating both sides thoroughly each time.

In a skillet, melt 1½ tablespoons of the butter with the peanut oil and fry the cutlets for 8 to 10 minutes, turning them once.

In a small saucepan, melt 1½ tablespoons of the butter and sauté the mushrooms for 2 minutes; add the ham and cook for another 2 minutes. Add the madeira wine and cook 1 minute more to reduce the liquid. Add the veal broth and cook for another 2 to 3 minutes to reduce the liquid again. Stir in 1½ tablespoons of the butter, taste and adjust the seasoning then set aside, keeping warm.

Drain the pasta, mix with the remaining 1½ tablespoons of butter then turn out onto a warmed serving plate.

Serve the cutlets with the pasta on warmed plates. Serve the parmesan, stewed tomatoes and the sauce on the side.

You can make this dish in the same way using veal chops instead.

Sautéed veal with lemons and cumin

FOR 6 PEOPLE
MARINADE: **12 hours**
PREPARATION: **30 min**
COOKING TIME:
approximately 35 min

> 2½ lbs. rack of veal, fat removed
> 2 tbsp. vegetable oil
> 2 tbsp. butter
> 1 packet dehydrated onion soup
> salt, freshly ground black pepper, pink peppercorns

For the marinade
> 1 garlic clove
> 5 sprigs of parsley
> 8 basil leaves
> 2 tsp. ground cumin
> 1 lime
> 1 lemon
> 1 orange

The day before: Prepare the marinade. Cut the veal into cubes then season all over with salt and pepper. Peel and chop the garlic clove. Using scissors, snip off 3 sprigs of the parsley and cut up the basil leaves. Wash the lime and remove the zest. Place the veal on a shallow serving plate and add the parsley, basil, garlic, ground cumin, and lime zest. Juice the lemon, lime and orange and pour the juice over the veal. Cover and refrigerate overnight to marinate.

The next day: Remove the lamb from the marinade and let drain. In a frying pan, heat the vegetable oil with the butter and brown the lamb.

Strain the marinade liquid then pour it into the frying pan. Cover and cook for 10 minutes over medium heat.

Empty the packet of dehydrated onion soup into a cup of boiling water and stir; pour this into the frying pan. Continue cooking, covered, for another 20 minutes over low heat. Serve very hot, garnished with additional lemon and lime quarters, chopped parsley and a sprinkle of several pink peppercorns.

Serve with plain rice or fresh pasta.

make ahead · recipe ·

Veal chops normandy-style

FOR 4 PEOPLE
PREPARATION: **25 min**
COOKING TIME: **20 min**

> 4 veal chops
> 6 tbsp. butter
> ¼ cup calvados (apple brandy)
> 1 cup crème fraîche (or sour cream)
> 4 cooking apples, such as McIntosh
> salt, white pepper

Season the veal chops with salt and pepper. Make a few small slits across the edges to prevent the chops from curling up while cooking.

Melt 3 tablespoons of the butter in a large skillet and brown the chops for 2 minutes on each side. Lower the heat, cover, and cook gently for 10 minutes.

Heat the calvados then pour it into the skillet and light it to flambé it; remove the chops and keep them warm.

Add the crème fraîche to the skillet and cook for 3 to 4 minutes while stirring, until the sauce thickens; taste and adjust the seasoning as needed.

Place the veal chops back in the skillet in the sauce and keep them warm but do not let them continue to cook.

Peel, core, and thinly slice the apples. In another skillet, sauté the apples over high heat with the remaining 3 tablespoons of butter.

Place the veal chops with the sauce on a warm serving platter. Surround the chops with the slices of cooked apple and serve.

Sautéed veal and artichokes

FOR 4 PEOPLE
PREPARATION: **15 min**
COOKING TIME:

approximately 25 min

> 1 small onion
> 4 artichoke hearts, canned
> 4 tbsp. butter
> 1⅓ lbs. cushion (upper leg) of veal
> 1 tbsp. paprika
> 4 tbsp. crème fraîche (or sour cream)
> 1 small jar truffle peels (optional)
> salt, freshly ground black pepper

Peel and chop the onion. Drain the artichoke hearts.

Melt 2 tablespoons of the butter in a saucepan and sauté the artichoke hearts for 10 minutes over low heat.

Meanwhile, cut the veal into small pieces; season with salt and pepper and sprinkle with the paprika.

In a skillet, melt the remaining 2 tablespoons of butter and fry the veal pieces over high heat. Lower the heat, add the onion and cook for approximately 10 minutes, stirring occasionally. Add 1 tablespoon of water during cooking to help prevent the meat from sticking to the bottom of the skillet.

Place the veal in a serving dish and distribute the artichoke hearts on top.

Place the crème fraîche in the skillet, mix well to form a sauce then cook to reduce by half. Brush the veal pieces with the sauce and garnish with the truffle peel.

Instead of the veal cushion, you can use veal filet, also cut into small pieces.

Veal fricassee

FOR 4 PEOPLE
PREPARATION: 15 min
COOKING TIME: 55 min

> 1¾ lbs. veal shoulder, neck or brisket
> 1 large onion
> 3 tbsp. butter
> ½ cup all-purpose flour
> 4¼ cups veal broth or water
> 1 bouquet garni (SEE p. 576)
> 2 tbsp. crème fraîche (or sour cream)
> salt, freshly ground black pepper

Cut the veal into medium-sized pieces (approximately 2 ounces each). Peel and finely chop the onion.

In a skillet, melt the butter and cook the veal, without browning. Add the onion and cook gently for 5 minutes. Sprinkle in the flour and cook another 5 minutes while stirring.

Pour the broth or water in the skillet, add the bouquet garni and season with salt. Bring to a boil and cook for 45 minutes, covered.

Remove and drain the veal pieces and place them in a serving dish; keep warm.

Reduce the cooking juices by one-third, if needed, and add the crème fraîche; mix and bring to a boil while continuing to stir. Taste and adjust the seasoning as needed.

Strain the sauce then spoon it over the pieces of veal. Serve immediately.

make ahead recipe

Veal liver à l'anglaise

FOR 4 PEOPLE
PREPARATION: **5 min**
COOKING TIME:
5–10 min

> 4 slices veal liver,
  approximately 4½ oz.
  each
> 2 tbsp. butter
> 1 tbsp. peanut oil
> 4 slices lean, smoked
  bacon
> 1 tbsp. finely chopped
  parsley
> ½ lemon
> salt, freshly ground
  black pepper

Season the slices of veal liver with salt and pepper. Heat the butter and peanut oil in a skillet and cook the liver from 2 to 5 minutes on each side, according to their thickness and to the preferred level of doneness. Remove them to drain and place them on the serving plate; keep warm.

Sauté the 4 slices of bacon in the same skillet; place them on top of the liver slices and garnish with the chopped parsley.

Juice the lemon into the cooking fat still in the skillet, mix to incorporate and to loosen the cooked brown bits of meat on the bottom. Spoon the sauce onto the liver slices and serve immediately.

quick & easy · recipe ·

Tarragon chicken

FOR 4–6 PEOPLE
PREPARATION: **15 min**
COOKING TIME:
approximately 1 hour

> 2 cups chicken broth
> 2 bunches tarragon
> 1 whole chicken,
  approximately 4 lbs.
> ½ lemon
> 2 tbsp. all-purpose flour
> 1 tbsp. butter, room
  temperature
> salt, freshly ground
  black pepper

In a saucepan, heat the chicken broth and add 4 sprigs of the tarragon to it. Simmer very gently for approximately 10 minutes.

Prep the chicken and rub it with the cut side of the ½ lemon. Insert 4 sprigs of the tarragon into the cavity. Season the chicken with salt and pepper then truss it. Place the chicken in a stovetop-safe casserole dish and pour the infused chicken broth around it. Cover, bring to a boil and cook 45 to 50 minutes over gentle heat.

Remove and drain the chicken then place it, still hot, on a serving platter.

On a plate, mix the flour with the butter using a fork, just until all of the flour is absorbed and the mixture is smooth.

Chop the remaining tarragon sprigs.

Reduce the cooking juices by approximately one-third and add the butter/flour mixture, whisking vigorously. Taste and adjust the seasoning as needed then add the chopped tarragon. Brush the chicken with a little bit of the sauce then serve the remaining sauce on the side in a gravy dish.

Serve with cooked grains or pasta or with white button mushrooms sautéed in butter.

Lemon chicken

FOR 4–6 PEOPLE
PREPARATION: **15 min**
MARINADE: **1 hour**
COOKING TIME: **35 min**

> 1 chicken, 2½ to 3 lbs.
> 2 lemons
> 1 smidgen Cayenne
  pepper
> 2 tbsp. olive oil
> 2 sprigs of thyme
> ⅔ cup crème fraîche
  (or sour cream)
> salt, freshly ground
  black pepper

Cut up the chicken.

Remove the lemon zest in thin strips. Juice both of the lemons and mix the juice with salt and pepper and the smidgen Cayenne pepper. Pour the juice all over the chicken and marinate for at least 1 hour.

Drain the chicken pieces and pat them dry. In a stovetop-safe casserole dish, brown them in the olive oil over high heat. Lower the heat and sprinkle the chicken with crumbled pieces of the thyme. Cover and cook gently for 30 minutes.

Remove the chicken pieces and let drain; keep warm under a piece of aluminum foil.

Pour the chicken marinade along with the crème fraîche into the casserole dish. Heat, while stirring, to thicken the sauce. Taste and adjust the seasoning, as needed. Place the chicken pieces back into the casserole dish and cook for an additional 5 minutes. Serve in the casserole dish.

Baked chicken thighs with peaches

FOR 6 PEOPLE
PREPARATION: 10 min
COOKING TIME: 1 hour
15 min

> 6 chicken thighs
> 2 lbs. canned peaches in light syrup
> 3 sprigs of thyme
> 1 packet dehydrated onion soup
> salt, freshly ground black pepper

Preheat the oven to 300° F. Place the chicken thighs in a baking dish and season with salt and pepper. Drain the peaches and reserve the syrup. Distribute the peaches on top of the chicken thighs and add the thyme.

In a small bowl, mix together the peach syrup and the packet of dehydrated onion soup. Pour the mixture over the chicken and bake for approximately 1 hour 15 minutes, basting the chicken frequently with the cooking juices.

If necessary, use a fork to mash some of the peaches into the sauce toward the end of the cooking time to ensure they are well incorporated into the sauce.

Serve with couscous or steamed potatoes.

low calorie · recipe ·

Chicken en papillote with mustard

FOR 4 PEOPLE
PREPARATION: **10 min**
COOKING TIME:
20–25 min

> 4 chicken breast filets
> 4 tbsp. mustard
> 3 tbsp. crème fraîche
  (or sour cream)
> 2 sprigs of fresh thyme
> several leaves flat-leaf
  parsley
> 1 tsp. pink peppercorns
> 2 tbsp. olive oil
> salt, freshly ground
  black pepper

Preheat the oven to 350° F.

Cut out 4 square pieces of aluminum foil or parchment paper and place 1 chicken breast in the center of each (the square must be large enough to completely enclose the chicken breast).

In a small bowl, mix the mustard, the crème fraîche and the crumbled fresh thyme; season with salt and pepper. Brush each chicken breast with this mixture and sprinkle with finely chopped parsley and the peppercorns; drizzle with olive oil.

Close up the pieces of foil or parchment paper to completely enclose the chicken breasts. Place them on a baking sheet and bake for 20 to 25 minutes; serve while hot.

Curried turkey cutlets

FOR 4 PEOPLE
PREPARATION: **8 min**
COOKING TIME:
approximately 15 min

> 4 turkey breast cutlets
> 4 shallots
> 3½ tbsp. butter
> 1 cup heavy cream
> 1 tbsp. mild curry
> Cayenne pepper
> salt, freshly ground
  black pepper

Season the cutlets with salt and pepper. Peel and chop the shallots.

Heat the butter in a skillet and fry the cutlets for 5 minutes on each side; place them on a serving plate and keep warm.

Cook the shallots gently in the same skillet. When they have softened and become translucent, add the heavy cream and mix with a spatula while scraping the bottom of the skillet. Add the curry and just a touch of the Cayenne pepper; season with salt and pepper. Cook while stirring for another 4 to 5 minutes, just until the sauce becomes creamy. Add the juice that has released from the cooked cutlets. Taste and adjust the seasoning then top the cutlets with the sauce and serve.

The classic accompaniment with curry is creole rice (SEE p. 400). You can add dried raisins and cashews to the rice.

Chicken breasts and peppers

FOR 6 PEOPLE
PREPARATION: **20 min**
COOKING TIME:
approximately 30 min

> 5 red bell peppers
> 1 tbsp. olive oil
> 6 chicken breast filets
> 1 chicken bouillon cube
> 1 bunch cilantro
> 2 cups crème fraîche (or
  sour cream)
> salt, freshly ground
  black pepper

Clean the peppers by cutting them in half and removing their stems, seeds and the white membrane. Purée the peppers in a food processor. Heat the olive oil in a frying pan and add the purée then simmer for 20 to 25 minutes over gentle heat.

Meanwhile, prepare the chicken bouillon with 4¼ cups of water in a large saucepan and cook the chicken breasts in the broth for 20 minutes. Thinly slice the breasts and add them to the simmering pepper purée; season with salt and pepper. Store the dish refrigerated if you have prepared it in advance.

Wash and finely chop the cilantro.

Before serving, gently reheat the chicken and pepper purée. Add the crème fraîche and cilantro at the last minute. Serve very hot.

You can serve this dish with basmati rice on the side.

Spiced turkey cutlets en papillote

FOR 4 PEOPLE
PREPARATION: **20 min**
COOKING TIME: **15 min**

> 2 granny smith apples
> 2 bananas
> juice of 1 lemon
> ½ cup coconut milk
> 1 tsp. coriander seeds
> 1 tsp. cumin seeds
> 1 pinch ground cinnamon
> 1 pinch ground ginger
> 1 pinch saffron
> 4 turkey cutlets, each weighing approximately 5¼ oz.
> salt, freshly ground black pepper

Peel and core the apples then cut them into quarters. Peel the bananas and slice them into rounds. Immediately sprinkle the fruit with the lemon juice.

In a small bowl, mix the coconut milk, coriander seeds, cumin seeds, cinnamon, ginger and saffron. Lightly season with salt then season with pepper.

Preheat the oven to 400° F.

Place 4 pieces of parchment paper over a work surface (they must be large enough to completely enclose the turkey and fruit). Place 1 turkey cutlet in the center of each and distribute the banana and apple slices on top. Spoon an even amount of the spiced coconut milk over each cutlet.

Close up the pieces of parchment, folding the edges and tying the ends with cooking twine. Place them in a baking dish and bake for 15 minutes. Turn off the oven and let them rest for 5 minutes. Tear open the parchment paper and serve in the baking dish.

low calorie recipe

Squab with peas

FOR 4 PEOPLE
PREPARATION: **30 min**
COOKING TIME:
approximately 30 min

> 3⅓ lbs. small fresh peas
> 1 lettuce heart
> 20 small white onions (preferably grelots)
> 1 shallot
> 3½ tbsp. butter
> 1 tbsp. peanut oil
> 4 squab (domestic pigeon)
> just over ¾ cup white wine
> 2 oz. thick-cut bacon, cut into small cubes
> 1 pinch sugar
> salt, freshly ground black pepper

Shell the peas. Wash and thoroughly dry the lettuce heart then chop it. Peel the small onions. Peel and mince the shallot.

In a stovetop-safe casserole dish, melt 2 tablespoons of the butter with the peanut oil and sauté the shallot until soft, while stirring. Add the squab to the dish and brown them, turning them several times; season with salt and pepper. Add the wine, cover, and cook for 20 minutes.

Meanwhile, melt the remaining 1½ tablespoons of butter in a saucepan and brown the bacon. Add the peas, the lettuce heart and the small onions. Season with salt and add the pinch of sugar and 1 cup of water. Cover and cook for 15 minutes over medium heat.

Remove the squab from the casserole dish to drain them of excess fat. Place them in the saucepan gently nestled down into the peas and cook for another 5 minutes over gentle heat. Serve very hot.

Rabbit with prunes

FOR 4-6 PEOPLE
SOAKING: **2 hours**
PREPARATION: **20 min**
COOKING TIME:
approximately 50 min

> 1 large bowl of strongly brewed tea
> 12 oz. prunes
> 1 cleaned rabbit, approximately 3⅓ lbs., with the liver
> 2 shallots
> 2 tbsp. butter
> 2 tbsp. vegetable oil
> 1 sprig of thyme
> just over ¾ cup white wine
> 1 tbsp. vinegar
> salt, freshly ground black pepper

Prepare the tea then soak the prunes in the tea for 2 hours.

Cut up the rabbit and season the pieces with salt and pepper. Peel and mince the shallots.

Heat the butter and the vegetable oil in a stovetop-safe casserole dish and brown the rabbit pieces over high heat, turning them to brown them on all sides. Add the shallots, thyme and the white wine. Cover and simmer for 30 minutes.

Meanwhile, remove the pits from the prunes.

Process the rabbit liver in a food processor with the vinegar then add this mixture to the casserole dish along with the pitted prunes. Cook for an additional 20 minutes; serve very hot in the casserole dish.

Serve with fresh pasta or cooked whole grains.

Stewed fresh cod in cream sauce

FOR 4-6 PEOPLE
PREPARATION: **10 min**
COOKING TIME:
20-25 min

> 1¾ lbs. fresh cod fillets
> 2 onions
> 2 tbsp. butter
> just over ¾ cup white wine
> just over ¾ cup crème fraîche (or sour cream)
> salt, freshly ground black pepper

Place the cod fillets on paper towels and season with salt and pepper.

Peel and chop the onions. In a sauté pan, melt the butter and cook the onions for 10 to 15 minutes, stirring occasionally. When the onions have softened and become translucent, add the cod fillets and fry them quickly over high heat. Remove them from the pan with a slotted spoon or sturdy spatula and place them on a plate.

Pour the white wine into the sauté pan and reduce it by three-quarters. Add the crème fraîche, mix well, and cook for 5 minutes over high heat to reduce further.

Place the cod fillets back in the pan and cook for another 5 minutes.

Enjoy the cod with cooked whole grains (such as bulgur), puréed potatoes or sautéed mushrooms.

quick & easy · recipe ·

Fresh cod and shrimp en papillote

FOR 4 PEOPLE
PREPARATION: **15 min**
COOKING TIME: **10 min**

> 3 tbsp. olive oil
> 14 oz. frozen, julienned vegetables
> 1 tbsp. crème fraîche (or sour cream)
> 4 fresh boneless cod fillets (use the meatiest part of the fish)
> 4¼ oz. peeled shrimp
> 2 tsp. coriander seeds
> several sprigs of parsley
> salt, freshly ground black pepper

In a skillet, heat 1 tablespoon of the olive oil and cook the vegetables for 5 minutes over medium heat; season with salt and pepper then stir in the crème fraîche.

Preheat the oven to 400° F.

Cut out 4 square pieces of parchment paper (large enough to completely enclose the fish and vegetables) and place equal amounts of julienned vegetables in the center of each one. Place a cod fish fillet on top of the vegetables then add the shrimp along with crushed coriander seeds and a little parsley; season with salt and pepper then drizzle on the remaining 2 tablespoons of olive oil. Close the parchment paper squares completely, encasing the ingredients well.

Place on a baking sheet and bake for 10 minutes.

Serve with wild rice or basmati rice.

low calorie recipe

1 Prepare a large square piece of parchment paper and place all of the ingredients on top.

2 Seal the paper tightly, folding over and creasing the edges well all the way around, or use cooking twine to tie the paper together. The ingredients will cook slowly inside and will maintain their flavor.

3 Keep the parchment paper closed until ready to eat; eat immediately once opened.

Fried whiting fish

FOR 4 PEOPLE
PREPARATION: **15 min**
COOKING TIME:

6–8 min

> 4 whiting fish, whole and cleaned from the gills, approximately 7 oz. each
> 1 cup milk
> vegetable oil, for frying (enough to nearly immerse the fish)
> 3 tbsp. all-purpose flour
> salt, freshly ground black pepper

Clip the fins from the fish then wash the fish under cold, fresh water and pat them dry.

Pour the milk into a shallow dish and season with salt and pepper. Place the fish in the milk and soak for 2 or 3 minutes.

In a large, heavy-bottomed sauté pan, heat the vegetable oil to 350° F.

Remove the fish and let the liquid drain from them somewhat; roll them in the flour then gently tap them to remove the excess.

Place the fish in the hot oil (two at a time if necessary to prevent them from sticking together) and cook for 6 to 8 minutes, turning them over 2 or 3 times while cooking.

When well-browned and crispy, remove with a slotted spoon and place on paper towels to drain. Place the fish on serving plates and serve very hot, seasoned with salt and pepper. Serve immediately.

You can serve this dish with tartar sauce and a salad.

Baked sardines

FOR 4 PEOPLE
PREPARATION: **20 min**
COOKING TIME:
10–12 min

> 24 sardines
> 4 shallots
> several sprigs of parsley
> 3 tbsp. butter
> juice of 1 lemon
> ¼ cup white wine
> salt, freshly ground
  black pepper

Wash and clean the sardines, removing the entrails; season with salt and pepper.

Preheat the oven to 475° F.

Peel and mince the shallots. Wash and chop the parsley.

Butter a baking dish with 1 tablespoon of the butter and distribute the shallots over the bottom of the dish; season with salt. Place the sardines in the baking dish and drizzle them with a little bit of the lemon juice. Add the white wine to the dish along with the remaining 2 tablespoons of butter spread throughout in small pieces. Bake for 10 to 12 minutes.

Sprinkle the chopped parsley over the fish as soon as they come out of the oven; serve immediately.

Red mullet en papillote

FOR 4 PEOPLE
RESTING TIME: **20 min +
1 hour**
PREPARATION: **20 min**
COOKING TIME:
15–20 min

> 8 small red mullet fish,
  5¼ to 7 oz. each
> 5 slices white bread
> ½ cup milk
> 5–6 sprigs of parsley
> ¼ cup olive oil
> 2 lemons
> salt, freshly ground
  black pepper

For the anchovy butter

> 3½ tbsp. butter
> 3–4 salted anchovy
  fillets
> ½ lemon

Prepare the anchovy butter. Allow the butter to soften to room temperature. Place the anchovies in a bowl of cold water for 20 minutes to extract the salt. Purée the anchovies in a food processor or mash well with a fork. Add 1 teaspoon of lemon juice then mix them into the softened butter.

Clean and scale the red mullet fish.

Crumble the bread into a bowl and pour the milk over it then mix together. Wash and chop the parsley. Squeeze the milk from the bread then incorporate it and the chopped parsley into the anchovy butter.

Salt and pepper the fish on both sides. Using a small fork, stuff the anchovy butter into the fish. Place on a plate, brush with the olive oil and refrigerate for 1 hour.

Preheat the oven to 475° F.

Grease 4 rectangular sheets of parchment paper. Place 2 of the red mullet onto each square and fold up the parchment square to completely enclose the fish. Bake for approximately 15 to 20 minutes. Serve in the parchment paper with lemon slices.

Basque tuna

FOR 4–6 PEOPLE
PREPARATION: **20 min**
COOKING TIME:
approximately 1 hour

> 2 red bell peppers
> 1 eggplant
> 2 onions
> 1 garlic clove
> 4 tomatoes
> 2 tbsp. all-purpose flour
> 1 slab of red tuna, approximately 1¾ to 2¼ lbs.
> 2 tbsp. olive oil
> 1 sprig of thyme
> 1 bay leaf
> 1 smidgen Cayenne pepper
> salt

Cut the peppers in half and remove the seeds and the white membrane; slice each half into thin strips. Finely dice the eggplant; do not peel it. Peel and finely chop the onions and the garlic clove.

Immerse the tomatoes in boiling water for 20 seconds, then immediately put them in cold water; peel and chop them.

Sprinkle the flour over the tuna. Heat the olive oil in a stovetop-safe casserole dish and brown the tuna on both sides for 5 minutes then remove and set aside.

Place the peppers in the casserole dish and cook them for 3 minutes while stirring. Add the eggplant, the chopped garlic clove and the chopped onions and mix, then add the chopped tomato, thyme, bay leaf, salt and Cayenne pepper. Mix again and cook just until the mixture reaches a boil.

Place the tuna back in the casserole dish, cover, and lower the heat. Simmer for approximately 45 minutes. Serve very hot.

Enjoy with zucchini or steamed potatoes.

Tuna samosas

FOR 6 PEOPLE
(18 SAMOSAS)
PREPARATION: **30 min**
COOKING TIME:
approximately 1 hour

> 1 large potato
> 3½ oz. small peas
> 2 onions
> 2 tbsp. olive oil
> 1 tsp. curry paste
> 12 oz. canned tuna
> 9 sheets feuilles de brick
  (or phyllo dough)
> 1 tbsp. sesame seeds
> salt

Boil the potato for approximately 15 minutes in salted water. Remove the peel and cut it into cubes. Boil the peas for 10 minutes in salted water.

Peel and finely chop the onions. In a skillet, heat 1 tablespoon of the olive oil and sauté the onions along with the curry paste.

Preheat the oven to 400° F.

In a large bowl, add the drained tuna, onions, potato and peas. Mix well and adjust the seasoning as needed.

Cut the sheets of feuilles de brick in half to make 18 semicircles. For each semicircle, fold the edge of the rounded side over onto the edge of the straight side to create a long strip.

Spoon a small amount of the tuna stuffing (approximately 1 heaping tablespoon) onto one end of the strip and fold the dough over toward its edge to create the shape of a triangle. Keep folding back and forth to maintain the triangle shape until you reach the end of the strip. Place the samosa on a parchment-lined baking sheet. Brush each one with a little bit of oil and sprinkle with sesame seeds. Bake for approximately 25 to 30 minutes. Serve hot or at room temperature.

1 Mix all of the stuffing ingredients together then taste and adjust the seasoning as needed.

2 Fold over each feuille de brick sheet to form a straight strip. Fold over one of the ends to form the shape of a triangle and place 1 spoonful of stuffing in the formed pocket.

3 Make another fold, folding the triangle over again onto the strip. Fold it again, in the same way, two more times, until you arrive at the end of the strip. Tuck any over hanging piece into the inside of the triangle.

Fillet of sole with basil

FOR 4-6 PEOPLE
PREPARATION: **15 min**
COOKING TIME:
approximately 15 min

> 4 large sole,
  approximately 10½ oz.
  each
> 4 shallots
> 2 tbsp. chopped basil
> 1 tbsp. olive oil
> ¼ cup fish broth
> ¼ cup white wine
> 1 tomato
> 8 tbsp. (1 stick) butter
> juice of ½ lemon
> salt, freshly ground
  black pepper

Fillet the sole (SEE p. 571). Preheat the oven to 475° F.

Peel and mince the shallots. Mix them with 1 tablespoon of chopped basil and the olive oil. Pour this mixture into an oven-proof skillet.

Season the sole fillets with salt and pepper and place them in the skillet. Mix the fish broth and the white wine then pour on top of the fillets. Place the skillet on the stove top, bring the liquid to a boil then cover with a piece of aluminum foil and place in the oven for 5 minutes.

Remove the fillets from the skillet to let drain; keep warm. Place the skillet back on the stove top and reduce the liquid by one-third.

Immerse the tomatoes in boiling water for 20 seconds, then immediately put them in cold water. Peel them, remove and discard the seeds, then finely dice them.

Cut the butter into small pieces and whisk it into the reduced liquid; season with salt and pepper and add the lemon juice.

Distribute the diced tomato over the fillets, brush with the reduced sauce and garnish with the remaining chopped basil and serve.

Sea bream fillets with julienned vegetables

FOR 4–6 PEOPLE
PREPARATION: **30 min**
COOKING TIME:
15–20 min

> 2 leeks (white part only)
> 4 celery stalks
> ½ fennel bulb
> 2 small turnips (preferably spring turnips)
> 3½ tbsp. butter
> 1¾ lbs. sea bream fillets
> 1–2 lemons
> just over ¾ cup crème fraîche (or sour cream)
> salt, freshly ground black pepper

Peel, wash and cut all of the vegetables into thin sticks. Melt 3 tablespoons of the butter in a skillet or in a saucepan and cook the vegetables gently until softened; season with salt and pepper.

Preheat the oven to 425° F.

Butter a baking dish and distribute the vegetables over the bottom. Season the sea bream fillets with salt and pepper and place them in the dish on top of the vegetables.

Juice the lemons to obtain 2 tablespoons of juice. In a small bowl, mix the juice and the crème fraîche and pour this mixture on top of the fish.

Cover with aluminum foil and bake for 15 to 20 minutes. Serve in the baking dish.

VARIATION You can prepare other types of fish fillets in this way, such as fresh cod, or you can substitute lime juice for the lemon juice.

Oven-braised flat fish

FOR 4 PEOPLE
PREPARATION: 15 min
COOKING TIME:
approximately 35 min

> 1 carrelet fish, brill or small turbot weighing 4 to 4½ lbs.
> 2 shallots (preferably gray shallots)
> 3 tbsp. butter + 1 tbsp. for the pan
> just over ¾ cup dry white wine
> salt, freshly ground black pepper

Rinse the fish under cold, fresh water and pat it dry with paper towels. Peel and mince the shallots.

Preheat the oven to 400° F. Generously butter a shallow dripping pan or a shallow baking dish with the 1 tablespoon of butter; the pan should be large enough to accommodate the fish.

Sprinkle the minced shallots in the bottom of the pan or dish and place the fish on top; season with salt and pepper then pour in the wine. Bake for approximately 35 minutes.

Gently place the baked fish on a serving plate and remove the skin; keep it warm inside of the oven with the door propped open.

Collect the cooking juice in a small saucepan and reduce it slowly, bringing it to a boil for a few minutes over high heat. Remove the sauce from the heat and add the 3 tablespoons of butter in small pieces while whisking continuously.

Taste and adjust the seasoning as needed. Pour the sauce into a warmed gravy dish. Serve the fish immediately, with the sauce.

You can serve this dish with spinach or boiled potatoes.

Baked gurnard

FOR 4 PEOPLE
PREPARATION: 10 min
COOKING TIME: 20 min

> 3 shallots
> 1 garlic clove
> 4 tbsp. butter
> 2 gurnard fillets, cleaned and scaled, 14 oz. each
> just over ¾ cup white wine
> 1 sprig of thyme
> 1 bay leaf
> 4 tbsp. pastis liqueur
> salt, freshly ground black pepper

Peel and mince the shallots and the garlic clove.

Preheat the oven to 400° F.

Butter a baking dish with ½ tablespoon of the butter and distribute the minced shallots and garlic over the bottom.

Melt the butter in the microwave or in a small saucepan. Place the gurnard fillets in the baking dish and add the wine and melted butter over and around the fish; season with salt and pepper and add the thyme and bay leaf.

Bake for 20 minutes, basting the fish several times in the cooking juices.

Remove the baking dish from the oven and discard the thyme and the bay leaf. At the moment the dish is served, heat the pastis then pour it over the fish and light it to flambé it.

quick & easy
· recipe ·

Haddock with poached egg

FOR 4-6 PEOPLE
SOAKING: **30 min**
PREPARATION: **15 min**
COOKING TIME:
approximately 15 min

> 1¾ lbs. of haddock fillets
> 4¼ cups cold milk
> 1 bay leaf
> 4-6 eggs
> ½ cup white vinegar
> 8 tbsp. (1 stick) butter
> 1 lemon
> several sprigs of flat-leaf parsley
> freshly ground black pepper

In a large bowl, soak the haddock in the cold milk for approximately 30 minutes.

Remove the haddock then pour the milk into a large saucepan; add the bay leaf and bring to a boil. Immerse the haddock in the milk and reduce the heat to very low. Poach the haddock gently for no more than 10 minutes.

Meanwhile, poach the eggs. In a saucepan, bring 8½ cups of non-salted water and the vinegar to a gentle boil. Break an egg into a ladle and immerse it into the simmering water.

Remove the ladle out from under the egg and simmer for 3 minutes; do not boil. Repeat with the remaining eggs, placing each one on a paper towel to drain when done.

Cut the butter into pieces and melt it gently in the microwave or a small saucepan. Juice the lemon and mix it into the melted butter.

Remove the haddock and let drain. Place a poached egg next to each fillet and drizzle the fillet with the lemon butter; season with pepper and garnish with chopped parsley.

Serve with boiled or steamed potatoes.

Shrimp sautéed in cider

FOR 4–6 PEOPLE
PREPARATION: **10 min**
COOKING TIME:
approximately 5 min

> 1¾ lbs. very fresh, raw gray shrimp
> 2 tbsp. butter
> 1 tbsp. peanut oil
> ½ cup hard apple cider
> 1 tbsp. coarse-grained sel de mer (sea salt)
> freshly ground black pepper

Quickly wash the shrimp in cold water and pat them dry with a towel.

Heat the butter and the peanut oil in a large skillet. Add the shrimp to the skillet; stir, then cook, covered, for 3 minutes. Add the cider to the skillet and cook for another 2 minutes.

Drain the shrimp and place them in a serving dish. Add the sea salt, season well with the pepper and mix well; serve warm.

You can sauté the shrimp without the cider.

Sautéed shrimp with cucumber

FOR 4 PEOPLE
PREPARATION: **5 min**
COOKING TIME: **15 min**

> 3 apples (reinette, belle de Boskoop, or golden delicious)
> 1 cucumber
> 1 onion
> 2 tbsp. butter
> 1 tsp. ground cumin
> ½ cup heavy cream
> 14 oz. pre-cooked and peeled shrimp
> salt, freshly ground black pepper

Peel and dice the apples and the cucumber. Peel and thinly slice the onion.

Melt the butter in a skillet and cook the onions until they soften and become translucent. Add the diced apples and cucumber followed by the cumin; season with salt and pepper. Cook over medium heat for 5 minutes, stirring occasionally.

Add the heavy cream then the shrimp to the skillet. Lower the heat and simmer for 10 minutes. Serve immediately.

VARIATION For a more exotic version of this dish, replace the heavy cream with coconut milk, the cumin with turmeric, and sprinkle the plate with finely chopped cilantro.

Stuffed calamari provençal

FOR 4 PEOPLE
PREPARATION: **40 min**
COOKING TIME:

approximately 45 min

> 3 large onions
> 4 large calamari (squid), cleaned, with tentacles attached
> approximately 2⅓ cups (3½ oz.) stale bread crumbs, for stuffing
> ½ cup milk
> 4 garlic cloves
> 1 bunch of parsley
> 4 tbsp. olive oil
> 2 tomatoes, chopped
> 2 egg yolks
> ½ cup dry white wine
> 2–3 tbsp. bread crumbs
> salt, freshly ground black pepper

Chop 2 of the onions along with the calamari tentacles. Soak the stale bread crumbs in a little bit of the milk then wring out the milk with your hands and add the bread crumbs to the chopped onions and chopped tentacles.

Chop 3 of the garlic cloves and half of the parsley.

In a cast iron skillet or similar heavy earthenware pan, brown the chopped calamari mixture in 2 tablespoons of the olive oil. Add the chopped garlic, the parsley and the chopped tomatoes.

Remove the pan from the heat and add the egg yolks, mixing well.

Using a spoon, stuff the calamari with the mixture. Seal the opening of the calamari using very thin cooking twine and a needle.

Preheat the oven to 350° F. Grease a stovetop- and broiler-safe baking dish.

Chop the rest of the garlic, the onion and the parsley; season with salt and pepper.

Line the calamari up against each other in the baking dish and sprinkle on the chopped garlic, onion, and parsley; season with salt and pepper. Add the wine to the dish along with ⅔ cup of water.

Lightly grease a piece of aluminum foil and cover the dish. Place the dish on the stove over medium heat for 5 minutes, to start the cooking, then place it in the oven and bake for 30 minutes.

Remove the aluminum foil cover from the baking dish and place the dish back on the stove over high heat for 5 minutes to reduce the cooking liquid. Drizzle the calamari with olive oil, sprinkle the bread crumbs over the top then place the baking dish under the broiler for 3 minutes to lightly brown the bread crumbs. Serve immediately.

low calorie recipe

Calamari fricassee with olives

FOR 4 PEOPLE
PREPARATION: **30 min**
COOKING TIME:

approximately 1 hour

> 3 ⅓ lbs. fresh calamari, cleaned, or 2 ¼ lbs. frozen calamari
> ½ cup olive oil
> 6 tomatoes
> 1 onion
> 3 garlic cloves
> 1 cup white wine
> 3 sprigs of lemon thyme
> 4 ¼ oz. pitted black olives
> salt, freshly ground black pepper

Wash the calamari if you purchased them fresh or leave them to thaw in a colander set over a plate if purchased frozen. In a large skillet, add 1 tablespoon of olive oil and sauté the calamari for 3 minutes to release as much water as possible. Remove the calamari and place them in a colander to drain.

Immerse the tomatoes in boiling water for 20 seconds, then immediately put them in cold water. Peel them, remove and discard the seeds, then roughly chop them.

Peel and chop the onion and garlic cloves and sauté them for 5 minutes in ¼ cup (or approximately 4 tablespoons) of the olive oil in a stovetop-safe casserole dish. Add the chopped tomatoes, the white wine and the thyme; season with salt and pepper. Cook for 10 minutes over medium heat.

Add the calamari to a clean skillet and reheat them over high heat in the remaining olive oil. Place them in the casserole dish and cook over medium heat for 30 to 40 minutes, uncovered.

Add the olives approximately 10 minutes before the end of the cooking time; serve very hot.

You can replace the fresh tomatoes with 1¼ cups of canned tomato sauce.

Vegetables

Pesto soup

FOR 4-6 PEOPLE
SOAKING: 12 hours
PREPARATION: 1 hour
COOKING TIME: 1 hour
50 min

> 8½ oz. dried haricots blancs (white navy or kidney beans)
> 5 oz. dried red kidney beans
> 9 oz. large, flat haricots verts (string beans)
> 2–3 small zucchini
> 4 medium potatoes
> 5 garlic cloves
> 3 tomatoes
> 1 large bunch basil
> 4–5 tbsp. olive oil
> 2½ oz. grated, young parmesan cheese
> 5¼ oz. spaghetti
> salt, freshly ground black pepper

Soak the haricots blancs and the red kidney beans in water overnight (at least 12 hours); drain. String the haricots verts, cut off the ends, then cut them into sections. Peel the zucchini, the potatoes and the garlic cloves. Immerse the tomatoes in boiling water for 20 seconds, then immediately put them in cold water. Peel them, then remove and discard the seeds.

Boil 9½ cups of water in a Dutch oven and add all of the beans, the zucchini, the potatoes and 1 tomato. Cook for approximately 1 to 1½ hours, or until the beans and potatoes are cooked through; season with salt.

Meanwhile, prepare the pesto. Chop the remaining two tomatoes and set aside. Wash and dry the basil then coarsely chop it. In a large mortar bowl or similar heavy bowl, crush the garlic cloves, add salt, then add the chopped basil and continue to mash to a paste. Slowly drizzle in the olive oil while mixing, then fold in the chopped tomatoes and the parmesan cheese; season with pepper.

Using a slotted spoon, remove the potatoes and the zucchini and mash them with a fork; place them back in the Dutch oven.

Break the spaghetti into strands approximately 1 inch in length. Place them in the Dutch oven and cook for approximately 20 minutes. Taste the noodles; the soup is done when the noodles are cooked. Adjust the seasoning as needed.

Spoon the pesto into the hot soup but off the heat (the pesto should not boil). Mix well and serve immediately.

You can also make this soup using pork knuckle. Cook the chilled knuckle for 40 minutes and add the vegetables at the end.

Vegetable soup

FOR 4-6 PEOPLE
PREPARATION: **20 min**
COOKING TIME:
1 hour 30 min

> 2 carrots
> 1 small turnip
> 1 leek (white part only)
> 1 onion
> 2 celery stalks
> 4 tbsp. butter
> ⅛ head of cabbage
> 1 potato
> 1 cup small, frozen peas
> several sprigs of chervil or parsley
> salt, freshly ground black pepper

Peel the carrots, turnip, leek, onion and celery stalks and cut them into large dice.

In a large saucepan, melt 2 tablespoons of the butter and add the diced vegetables. Cook for 10 minutes, covered, over low heat. Add 6⅓ cups of water and bring to a boil.

Meanwhile, add water to a second large saucepan and bring to a boil. Cut the cabbage into small pieces and boil for 3 to 4 minutes; drain and rinse under fresh water. Add the cabbage to the first saucepan with the other vegetables and simmer for 1 hour.

Peel and dice the potato. Place it in the saucepan with the vegetables and cook for an additional 25 minutes.

Add the peas approximately 12 to 15 minutes before the end of the cooking time. Remove the saucepan from the heat and blend the soup with an immersion blender. Just before serving, add the remaining 2 tablespoons of butter, stir, then garnish with the chopped chervil or parsley.

This soup can also be served with croutons.

Golden carrot soup

FOR 8 PEOPLE
PREPARATION: **30 min**
COOKING TIME: **10 min**
REFRIGERATION:
at least 3 hours

> 2 chicken bouillon cubes
> 2¼ lbs. carrots
> 2 onions
> 3½ tbsp. butter
> 2 tsp. granulated sugar
> 8 juicing oranges
> 1 cup crème fraîche
> 1 bunch chives
> salt, freshly ground black pepper

Prepare the chicken broth by placing the bouillon cubes in 6⅓ cups boiling water.

Peel the carrots and slice them into rounds. Peel and thinly slice the onions. Melt the butter in a saucepan and cook the carrots and onions for 5 minutes, just until they are lightly browned. Add the chicken broth, sugar, and 1 pinch of salt to the saucepan. Let cool for approximately 15 minutes then blend with an immersion blender.

Juice the oranges and add the juice along with the crème fraîche to the saucepan. Place the soup in the refrigerator for at least 3 hours. Serve well chilled, sprinkled with chopped chives.

Just before serving, you can add a few drops of heavy cream onto the surface of the soup for decoration.

Parsnip and carrot soup

FOR 4–6 PEOPLE
PREPARATION: **15 min**
COOKING TIME: **30 min**

> 1 lb. parsnips
> 4 carrots
> 1 leek
> 1 tbsp. butter
> 1 tbsp. vegetable oil
> 1 tsp. coriander seeds, crushed
> 2 tbsp. crème fraîche (or sour cream)
> salt, freshly ground black pepper

Peel the parsnips and carrots then rinse and dice them. Peel the leek then carefully clean any sand or dirt from between the leaves; thinly slice it.

Heat the butter with the vegetable oil in a large saucepan and sauté the sliced leek just until soft and translucent. Add the diced carrots and parsnips and the crushed coriander seeds; mix well. Add just enough water to the saucepan to cover the vegetables; season with salt and pepper and bring to a boil. Lower the heat and simmer for 30 minutes.

Gently blend the soup using an immersion blender, ensuring that some large pieces of vegetables remain. Stir in the crème fraîche and serve very hot.

Creamy zucchini soup with mint and feta

FOR 4 PEOPLE
PREPARATION: **5 min**
COOKING TIME: **10 min**

> 3 zucchini
> 2 potatoes (preferably Bintje or Yukon gold)
> 5¼ oz. feta cheese
> 25 mint leaves
> salt, freshly ground black pepper

Cut off the ends of the zucchini then wash them and slice them into round sections. Peel and wash the potatoes then cut them in half.

Place the vegetables in a pressure cooker, cover with approximately 4 cups of water and add half the feta and the mint leaves; season with salt and pepper. Close the pressure cooker and cook the vegetables for 10 minutes once the valve begins to rotate.

Blend the soup using an immersion blender then crumble the remaining feta, along with some of the chopped mint, over the top; serve immediately.

VARIATION Replace the feta with fresh goat cheese and add several diced black olives.

Creamy asparagus soup with whipped black-pepper cream

FOR 4 PEOPLE
PREPARATION: **20 min**
COOKING TIME:

15–20 min

> 2¼ lbs. green asparagus
> ½ cup heavy cream
> 3 cups milk
> 2 pinches Cayenne
  pepper
> 1 pinch grated nutmeg
> 1 tsp. cornstarch
> 2 tsp. hazelnut oil
> salt, freshly ground black
  pepper

Cut off the tough bottom ends of the asparagus stalks. Peel the stalks using a vegetable peeler. Cut off the asparagus tips to approximiately 1½ inches in length and chop the stems into small rounds. Steam the asparagus tips for 4 to 5 minutes; set aside.

Put the heavy cream in a small bowl in the freezer for 10 minutes; the cream must be very cold.

In a saucepan, bring the milk to a boil with 1 pinch of salt. Add the asparagus stalk pieces and cook for 10 to 12 minutes until very tender; season with pepper, add the Cayenne and the nutmeg and blend for 2 to 3 minutes using an immersion blender until the mixture is very smooth. Use a fine-mesh strainer to strain the soup into a clean saucepan.

Mix the cornstarch thoroughly with 1 tablespoon of cold water and add the mixture to the soup. Bring the soup slowly to a boil and cook for 2 minutes while stirring; the soup should be smooth and creamy.

Remove the heavy cream from the freezer and whip it to firm peaks, seasoning it lightly with freshly ground black pepper.

Spoon the soup into 4 bowls and place the whipped black-pepper cream in large dollops on top. Garnish with the steamed asparagus tips and cracked black peppercorns. When serving, drizzle several drops of hazelnut oil over the top.

Onion soup gratinéed with cheese

FOR 4–6 PEOPLE
PREPARATION: **15 min**
COOKING TIME:
45–50 min

> 6⅓ cups beef broth
> 3 onions
> 2 tbsp. butter
> 1 rounded tbsp. all-purpose flour
> 2 tbsp. port or madeira wine
> 4–6 slices of country-style bread
> 2–3 oz. grated emmental cheese
> salt, freshly ground black pepper

Heat the beef broth in a saucepan. Peel and cut the onions into very thin, round slices.

Melt the butter in a second saucepan and lightly brown the onions over medium heat; they should not take on too much color. When nearly cooked but still slightly firm, sprinkle them with the flour. Continue cooking for several minutes, stirring with a silicone spatula or wooden spoon; stir in the beef broth. Add the port (or madeira) wine, season with salt and pepper then cook for 30 minutes over low heat.

Meanwhile, preheat the oven to 400° F. Place the bread slices on a baking sheet in the oven to dry them out slightly.

Preheat the oven broiler. Place the bread slices on the bottom of oven-proof bowls. Ladle the soup on top of the bread and sprinkle on the emmental. Place the bowls under the broiler for 5 to 10 minutes; serve piping hot.

Carrot and pumpkin soup with cumin

FOR 4 PEOPLE
PREPARATION: **10 min**
COOKING TIME: **20 min**

> 1 lb. carrots
> 1 small cooking pumpkin, approximately 1 lb.
> 1 potato (preferably Bintje or Yukon gold)
> 1 tbsp. olive oil
> 1 juicing orange
> 1 chicken bouillon cube
> 2 tsp. ground cumin
> salt, freshly ground black pepper

Peel the carrots, the pumpkin and the potato. Wash them then cut them into pieces.

Heat the oil in a pressure cooker and cook the vegetables for 2 minutes while stirring.

Juice the orange and add the juice to the pressure cooker along with 4 cups water, the crumbled bouillon cube and the ground cumin; season with salt and pepper.

Close the pressure cooker and cook for 15 minutes once the valve begins to rotate. Blend using an immersion blender and serve very hot.

VARIATION Replace the ground cumin with curry powder.

Cucumber and yogurt salad

FOR 4 PEOPLE
PREPARATION: 10 min
SALTING AND
DRAINING: 30 min

> 1 cucumber
> ½ bunch chives
> approximately ½ cup (4 oz.) plain yogurt
> 3 tbsp. crème fraîche (or sour cream)
> ½ lemon
> salt, freshly ground black pepper

Peel the cucumber, cut it in half and scrape out the seeds using a spoon. Thinly slice the flesh and place the slices in a shallow dish, salt them, then set them aside for 30 minutes to expel their juice.

Meanwhile, wash and chop the chives. Add the yogurt and crème fraîche to a large bowl; season with salt and pepper and add a good drizzle of lemon juice. Mix, then add the chopped chives.

Drain the cucumber slices in a colander and rinse them thoroughly under running water; pat them dry with a towel. Add the cucumbers to the bowl with the yogurt and crème fraîche and mix to coat evenly. Keep chilled until ready to serve.

Sautéed cucumbers

FOR 4 PEOPLE
PREPARATION: 10 min
COOKING TIME:
8–10 min

> 2 large cucumbers
> 1 carrot
> 2 tbsp. butter
> 1 tbsp. vinegar
> 1 level tbsp. powdered sugar
> salt, freshly ground black pepper

Peel the cucumbers, cut them in half and scrape out the seeds using a spoon. Slice the flesh into small, thin sticks approximately 2½ inches long. Peel and wash the carrot then slice it into small sticks of the same size.

Bring water to a boil in a medium saucepan. Immerse the julienned vegetables and blanch them for 2 minutes; remove and drain.

Melt the butter in a skillet and add the julienned vegetables, seasoned lightly with salt. Add a little black pepper and cook for 4 to 5 minutes over medium heat while stirring.

Increase the heat then drizzle the vegetables with the vinegar and sprinkle the sugar over the top. Mix, then turn out onto a serving plate; serve while hot.

This dish makes a nice accompaniment to fish, chicken, pork or veal.

Smoked duck breast and zucchini salad with mimolette cheese

FOR 4 PEOPLE
PREPARATION: 20 min

> 4 tbsp. balsamic vinegar
> 4 tbsp. olive oil
> 3 zucchini
> 2 oz. (just less than ½ cup) pine nuts
> 4¼ oz. aged mimolette cheese
> 20 slices smoked duck breast
> salt, freshly ground black pepper

In a small bowl, mix the balsamic vinegar with the olive oil; season with salt and pepper.

Wash the zucchini without peeling them. Using a vegetable peeler, peel them into long thin strips, stopping before reaching the core.

Toast the pine nuts in a dry skillet. Remove the rind from around the mimolette cheese and shave off thin strips of the cheese using a vegetable peeler or a knife. Cut away any fat from the duck breasts.

Place all of the ingredients in a large bowl and add the vinaigrette, tossing gently. Serve immediately.

Use small zucchini, which have fewer seeds and are more tender inside but firm. You can also grate them.

Spinach and bacon salad with poached egg

FOR 4 PEOPLE
PREPARATION: **30 min**
COOKING TIME:

approximately 15 min

> ¼ cup white vinegar
> 4 large eggs
> just over ¾ cup red wine
> ½ cup veal broth
> 3½ oz. thick-cut bacon, cut into small pieces
> 3 tbsp. vegetable oil
> ½ small baguette of bread
> 3½ oz. baby spinach
> white wine vinegar and olive oil for seasoning
> salt, freshly ground black pepper

Fill a saucepan half full with water and add the vinegar. Bring to a boil then lower the heat to a simmer. Break each egg into an individual ramekin or cup then gently turn the eggs out into the simmering water. Poach the eggs for 3 minutes then retrieve them using a slotted spoon; place on paper towels to drain.

In a small saucepan, reduce the wine by half, seasoned with salt and pepper. Add the veal broth and reduce slightly further.

Fry the bacon in a skillet with 1 tablespoon of the vegetable oil. Place the bacon pieces on paper towels to drain then add them to the reduced wine.

Make the croutons. Slice the bread then brown it in a skillet for 3 minutes using the remaining 2 tablespoons of vegetable oil.

Toss the spinach with a little vinegar and olive oil then divide it among the plates. Place one poached egg on top and spoon some of the wine and bacon sauce over the egg and spinach; garnish with the croutons and serve immediately.

To successfully poach eggs, you should never salt the water. The eggs must be very fresh, otherwise the egg white and the yolk will separate once placed in the water.

Marinated bell pepper salad

FOR 4 PEOPLE
PREPARATION: **30 min**
COOKING TIME: **10 min**
RESTING TIME: **at least
2 hours**

> 6 red bell peppers
> 2 garlic cloves
> juice of 1 lemon
> ⅓ cup olive oil
> 1 tsp. thyme leaves
> 12 anchovy fillets in oil
> 12 pitted black olives
> 1 tbsp. chopped parsley
> salt, freshly ground
  black pepper

Preheat the oven to 425° F.

Lightly oil the bell peppers then place them on a parchment-lined baking sheet and bake for 10 minutes, just until the skin has blistered; set aside to cool.

Meanwhile, peel and finely chop the garlic cloves.

Remove the blistered skin from the cooled peppers. Cut the peppers in half, remove the seeds, then cut them into strips and place them in a shallow bowl.

Mix the lemon juice with the olive oil, the garlic and the thyme leaves. Pat the anchovy fillets with a paper towel to remove excess oil.

Drizzle the peppers with the lemon juice mixture, toss lightly, then place them on a serving plate. Garnish the top with the anchovy fillets and the black olives. Sprinkle on the chopped parsley and chill for at least 2 hours before serving.

This salad will stay fresh for 2 or 3 days, refrigerated.

Mushroom and green bean salad

FOR 4 PEOPLE
PREPARATION: **20 min**
COOKING TIME:
8–10 min

> 9 oz. white button
>   mushrooms
> juice of ½ lemon
> 7 oz. haricots verts
>   (string beans)
> 1 shallot
> ½ bunch chervil
> 1 hard-boiled egg
> 3 tbsp. olive oil
> 1 tbsp. tarragon vinegar
> salt, freshly ground
>   black pepper

Clean and finely chop the mushrooms. Sprinkle them with the lemon juice.

Immerse the haricots verts in a saucepan of boiling water and cook for 8 to 10 minutes; drain and let cool.

Peel and chop the shallot then finely chop the chervil.

Peel the shell from the hard-boiled egg and cut the egg in half. Remove the yolk and crumble it into a large bowl. Add the chopped shallot, the olive oil and the vinegar then season with salt and pepper.

Add the mushrooms and haricots verts to the bowl. Toss lightly to coat with the oil and vinegar mixture. Garnish the salad with chopped egg white and the chopped chervil.

VARIATION You can replace the chervil with cilantro.

Mushrooms in cream

FOR 4 PEOPLE
PREPARATION: **10 min**
COOKING TIME:
approximately 15 min

> 1¾ lbs. white button
>   mushrooms
> 2 tbsp. butter
> juice of ½ lemon
> 1⅔ cups crème fraîche
> 2 tbsp. chopped chervil
> salt, freshly ground
>   black pepper

Clean then finely chop the mushrooms. Melt the butter in a skillet then add the mushrooms and the lemon juice; season with salt and pepper. Cook for approximately 10 minutes over low heat, uncovered, stirring often.

When the water from the mushrooms has evaporated, add the crème fraîche and stir. Cook for another 5 minutes to slightly reduce the cream. Add the chervil, then taste and adjust the seasoning as needed. Serve immediately in a warm serving dish.

Lentil and carrot salad

FOR 4 PEOPLE
PREPARATION: **15 min**
COOKING TIME: **4 min**

> 2 carrots
> several green lettuce leaves, such as green leaf or batavia
> 4 quail eggs
> 7 oz. cooked green lentils (cooled)
> 20 walnut halves
> several sprigs of parsley

For the vinaigrette
> 1 tbsp. white or red wine vinegar
> 2 tsp. mustard
> 1 tbsp. walnut oil
> 2 tbsp. peanut oil
> salt, freshly ground black pepper

Peel and wash the carrots then grate them using a grater with large holes. Wash the lettuce leaves and dry them thoroughly.

Boil the quail eggs for 4 minutes then peel them and cut them in half.

Prepare the vinaigrette. Add the vinegar to a salad bowl; season with salt and pepper. Whisk in the mustard and the walnut and peanut oil to create a good emulsion.

Add the lentils, the carrots, the quail eggs and the lettuce leaves, chopped. Sprinkle the walnut halves and parsley over the top, toss and serve immediately.

To make this salad even more interesting, serve with slices of cold or smoked ham on the side or add diced ham directly into the salad.

quick & easy · recipe ·

Vegetable tian

FOR 6 PEOPLE
PREPARATION: **15 min**
COOKING TIME:
1 hour 30 min

> 5 tomatoes
> 1 eggplant
> 2 zucchini
> 10 white button mushrooms
> 2 tbsp. olive oil
> 2 sprigs of thyme, fresh or dried
> 1 lemon
> salt, freshly ground black pepper

Preheat the oven to 300° F.

Wash the vegetables. Slice the tomatoes, eggplant and zucchini into rounds. Clean and finely chop the mushrooms.

Place the vegetable slices and the chopped mushrooms in alternating layers in a baking dish and season each layer with salt and pepper. Drizzle the olive oil over the top and sprinkle on the thyme leaves.

Juice the lemon and pour the juice over the vegetables.

Bake for 1 hour 30 min. Serve in the baking dish.

This dish is best with grilled fish or grilled meat.

You can also prepare this in individual ramekins or pastry rings.

Pan-fried porcini mushrooms

FOR 4 PEOPLE
PREPARATION: **20 min**
COOKING TIME: **7–8 min**

> 1¾ lbs. small porcini mushrooms
> 2 garlic cloves
> ½ cup peanut oil
> juice of ½ lemon
> 3 tbsp. chopped parsley
> salt, freshly ground black pepper

Gently wipe away any dirt from the mushrooms then cut off the tough bottom portion of the stems. Cut the mushrooms in half down the middle from top to bottom.

Peel and chop the garlic cloves. Heat 6 tablespoons of the peanut oil in a frying pan then add the mushrooms and the lemon juice; season with salt and pepper. Cover and cook for 5 minutes, stirring occasionally. Place the cooked mushrooms on a paper towel to drain.

Heat the remaining peanut oil (around 2 tablespoons) in a skillet and add the mushrooms and garlic; adjust the seasoning as needed. Sauté over high heat for 2 to 3 minutes.

Place the mushrooms on a serving plate, sprinkle with the chopped parsley and serve.

Chanterelles in cream and bacon

FOR 4 PEOPLE
PREPARATION: **15 min**
COOKING TIME:
approximately 15 min

> 1⅓ lbs. chanterelle mushrooms
> 1 bunch small onions
> 4½ oz. thick-cut bacon, cut into small pieces
> 3 tbsp. butter
> 1 cup white wine
> ½ cup crème fraîche (or sour cream)
> 1 tbsp. chopped parsley
> salt, freshly ground black pepper

Gently wipe away any dirt from the mushrooms then cut off the tough bottom portion of the stems. If the mushrooms are very dirty, rinse them very quickly under water.

Peel the onions and cut them in half. Sauté the bacon in a skillet until softened then add the onions and brown. Remove the bacon and onions to drain and pour off the fat from the skillet. Melt the butter in the skillet, place the onions and bacon back in the skillet along with the mushrooms and sauté for approximately 5 minutes.

Add the white wine and stir. Let the liquid reduce by half over high heat. Add the crème fraîche and further reduce for 2 to 3 minutes; season with salt and pepper.

Place on a serving dish then sprinkle with parsley and serve immediately.

Ratatouille niçoise

FOR 4-6 PEOPLE
PREPARATION: **30 min**
COOKING TIME:
approximately 40 min

> 6 zucchini
> 2 onions
> 3 green bell peppers
> 6 tomatoes
> 3 garlic cloves
> 6 eggplants
> ½ cup olive oil
> 1 bouquet garni (SEE p. 576)
> 1 sprig of thyme
> salt, freshly ground black pepper

Cut off the stems of the zucchini. Slice the zucchini into rounds, leaving the peel intact. Peel and mince the onions.

Cut the peppers in half and remove the seeds and the white membrane then slice each half into thin strips.

Immerse the tomatoes in boiling water for 20 seconds, then immediately put them in cold water. Peel them, remove and discard the seeds, then chop them into large dice.

Peel and crush the garlic cloves. Slice the eggplants into rounds.

Heat 6 tablespoons of olive oil in a Dutch oven. Add the eggplants then the bell peppers, tomatoes, onions, zucchini and crushed garlic.

Add the bouquet garni and the thyme; season with salt and pepper and cook for 30 minutes over low heat.

Add the remaining 2 tablespoons of olive oil then continue to cook until the vegetables are done to your liking.

Remove the bouquet garni and serve very hot.

Ratatouille niçoise typically accompanies roasted or sautéed poultry dishes, braised fish, or omelets. It can also be enjoyed as a cold dish.

Prepare the ratatouille in large batches as it is even better when reheated the next day.

Glazed baby carrots

FOR 4 PEOPLE
PREPARATION: **15 min**
COOKING TIME:
approximately 30 min

> 1¾ lbs. baby (or young) carrots
> 4 tbsp. butter
> 2 tbsp. sugar
> salt, freshly ground black pepper

Peel and rinse the carrots. Cut them into small sections, or cut them into thin rounds if the carrots are a little large.

In a frying pan, melt the butter over low heat. Add the carrots and stir with a silicone spatula or wooden spoon to coat the carrots with the butter. Add approximately 2 cups of water, just enough to cover the carrots; season with salt and pepper then bring to a boil. Lower the heat then cook, uncovered, for 20 to 30 minutes.

Use the point of a knife to test the doneness of the carrots. If too firm, add a little more water and cook a few minutes longer.

Sprinkle the carrots with the sugar and cook for 1 to 2 minutes more, stirring gently. Taste and adjust the seasoning, as needed. Serve immediately.

Serve with any roasted white-meat dish.

Carrots vichy

FOR 4 PEOPLE
PREPARATION: **20 min**
COOKING TIME:
approximately 30 min

> 1¾ lbs. baby (or young) carrots
> 1 tsp. salt
> 2 tsp. sugar
> 2 tbsp. butter
> 2 tbsp. chopped parsley

Peel the carrots and cut them into thin rounds.

Put the carrots in a frying pan and add just enough water to cover them. Add the salt and the sugar then stir. Cook over low heat, covered, until all of the water has evaporated.

Place the cooked carrots on a serving plate. Cut the butter into small pieces and distribute it on top of the carrots and sprinkle with parsley.

Purple artichoke salad

FOR 6 PEOPLE
PREPARATION: **20 min**
COOKING TIME:
approximately 1 hour

> 30 small artichokes
  (preferably violets de
  Provence)
> juice of 1 lemon
> 4 green tomatoes
> 2 ripe tomatoes
> 2 garlic cloves
> 2 small white onions
> 7 oz. thick-cut, lean
  bacon, cut into small
  cubes
> 5 tbsp. olive oil
> 1 sprig of thyme
> ½ bay leaf
> 10 basil leaves
> salt, freshly ground
  black pepper

Snip off the end of the leaves of each artichoke using scissors. Cut the artichokes in half and extract the choke (the fuzzy core) using a small paring knife or spoon then sprinkle all sides of the artichoke with lemon juice.

Wash the tomatoes and cut them into quarters. Peel and finely chop the garlic cloves and the onions.

Add the bacon to a skillet and brown. Remove and drain on a paper towel. Add the tomatoes and the garlic to the skillet and sauté for 5 minutes; season with salt and pepper then remove and let drain.

Put the artichokes and the onions in the same skillet. Drizzle them with the olive oil and cook while stirring. Crumble the thyme and bay leaf over the top.

After 10 minutes, add the tomatoes, the garlic and the bacon. Cover and let simmer for 20 minutes.

Chop the basil leaves into large pieces and add them to the skillet. Cook for another 10 minutes then serve.

This dish can be served with grilled lamb, lamb cutlets or lamb tournedos. It's also delicious chilled as an appetizer with an olive oil and lemon vinaigrette with a touch of garlic and tarragon added.

Cauliflower and broccoli gratin

FOR 4 PEOPLE
PREPARATION: **10 min**
COOKING TIME: **25 min**

> 1 lb. cauliflower florets
> 1 lb. broccoli florets
> 2 tbsp. butter
> 2 eggs
> 1 cup heavy cream
> 1½ oz. almond meal
> 1¾ oz. grated emmental cheese
> salt, freshly ground black pepper

Immerse the cauliflower and broccoli florets into boiling, salted water and cook for 10 minutes; drain carefully.

Preheat the oven to 400° F.

Butter a baking dish and place the vegetables inside.

Break the eggs into a bowl, add the heavy cream and almond meal and beat briefly with a fork to combine; season with salt and pepper. Pour the eggs over the vegetables, sprinkle on the grated emmental cheese and bake for 15 minutes.

This dish is a perfect accompaniment to sautéed turkey cutlets.

Carrot and celery root crumble

FOR 4 PEOPLE
PREPARATION: **30 min**
COOKING TIME:
30–35 min

> 12 oz. carrots
> 12 oz. celery root
> 2 tbsp. butter
> 1 tbsp. caraway seeds
> salt, freshly ground
  black pepper

For the crumble topping
> 4 tbsp. softened butter
> ½ cup (2 oz.) all-purpose
  flour
> 1 tbsp. caraway seeds
> 2½ oz. grated parmesan
  cheese

Peel the carrots and the celery root and cut them into small dice.

In a skillet, melt the butter and add the diced carrots and celery root and the tablespoon of caraway seeds then lightly brown; add just over ¾ cup of water then season with salt and pepper. Cover the vegetables (using the skillet lid set slightly askew or with a piece of parchment paper) and cook for 20 minutes over medium heat.

Meanwhile, preheat the oven to 400° F and prepare the crumble topping. In a large bowl, mix the butter with the flour, the caraway seeds and the parmesan cheese using a silicone spatula; the mixture should have a coarse, sandy texture.

Distribute the vegetables among individual gratin baking dishes (or ramekins). Crumble the topping over the vegetables and bake for 10 to 15 minutes. Serve immediately.

To give the vegetables a glazed appearance, add 1 tablespoon of granulated sugar in the skillet just before adding the water.

Eggplant au gratin toulouse-style

FOR 4 PEOPLE
PREPARATION: **15 min**
SALTING AND DRAINING:
30 min
COOKING TIME: **30 min**

> 4 eggplants
> 1¼ cups olive oil
> 5 tomatoes
> 2 garlic cloves
> approximately 1 cup (1¾ oz.) stale bread crumbs
> 1 tbsp. chopped parsley
> salt, freshly ground black pepper

Cut the eggplants into thick slices crosswise or lengthwise. Salt them and let them sit for 30 minutes to expel their juices then rinse and gently pat them dry.

Heat just over ¾ cup of the olive oil in a skillet and brown the eggplant slices, turning them often.

Cut the tomatoes in half and remove the seeds. Heat 3 tablespoons of the olive oil in a second skillet and sauté the tomatoes; season with salt and pepper.

Preheat the oven to 400° F.

Peel and chop the garlic cloves and mix them with the stale bread crumbs.

Grease a baking dish with olive oil and add alternating layers of the tomatoes, eggplant and the garlic/bread mixture. Drizzle the top with the remaining olive oil and bake for 10 to 15 minutes. Serve very hot.

Leek and potato gratin with cumin

FOR 4 PEOPLE
PREPARATION: **15 min**
COOKING TIME: **30 min**

> 1⅓ lbs. leeks
> 1 onion
> 2 tbsp. olive oil
> 2 level tsp. ground cumin
> 1 lb. firm potatoes
> just over ¾ cup milk
> 2 tbsp. butter
> 1¾ oz. grated comté cheese
> salt, freshly ground black pepper

Peel the leeks and wash them thoroughly between the leaves then finely chop them. Peel and finely chop the onion.

In a skillet, heat the olive oil and add the onion and leeks then sprinkle over half the ground cumin; season with salt and pepper. Cook for 10 minutes, stirring occasionally.

Meanwhile, peel and wash the potatoes then slice them into rounds. Place them in a saucepan, add the milk and the remaining ground cumin, then add just enough water to cover them; season with salt and pepper. Cook for approximately 10 minutes, then drain.

Preheat the oven to 400° F.

Generously butter a baking dish. Place a layer of onion and leek mixture on the bottom followed by a layer of the potatoes. Cover with the comté cheese and bake for 10 minutes. Serve very hot.

VARIATION Season the gratin with a sprig of thyme and a bay leaf in place of the cumin.

Potato and olive croquettes

quick & easy recipe

FOR 4 PEOPLE
PREPARATION: **10 min**
COOKING TIME:
10–12 min per batch

> 1 lb. leftover puréed potatoes
> 2½ oz. pitted black olives
> 2½ oz. pitted green olives
> 1 tbsp. herbes de Provence
> ½ cup (1¾ oz.) all-purpose flour
> 3 eggs
> 3½ tbsp. butter
> salt, freshly ground black pepper

In a large bowl, mix the puréed potatoes with the olives, the herbes de Provence, the flour and the eggs; season with salt and pepper.

Heat the butter in a large, nonstick skillet until the butter begins to foam. Place one heaping tablespoon of the potato mixture in the skillet then press it down with the back of a spoon to flatten it to approximately ¾ inch thick. Repeat with the remaining potato mixture and cook for approximately 5 to 6 minutes on each side, until a deep golden brown.

Once cooked, place the croquettes on paper towels to absorb the excess oil; season again with salt and pepper. Enjoy them with a salad of crispy lettuce.

Before making the croquettes, gently heat the potato purée in the microwave. This will make it easier to work with.

You can also make the croquettes with other puréed vegetables.

Potatoes gratin

FOR 4-6 PEOPLE
PREPARATION: **15 min**
COOKING TIME:
approximately 55 min

> 2¼ lbs. firm potatoes
> 2 garlic cloves
> 6 tbsp. butter
> 5¼ oz. grated emmental cheese
> 2 cups milk
> 1 cup crème fraîche
> salt, freshly ground black pepper, nutmeg

Peel the potatoes and thinly slice them into rounds. Peel and crush the garlic cloves.

Preheat the oven to 425° F.

Rub a baking dish with garlic then butter it generously. Distribute the potato slices in even layers in the dish, adding some grated emmental cheese, a little salt, and some pepper and nutmeg between each layer; you should end with a layer of cheese.

Boil the milk with the crème fraîche and add 1 level teaspoon of salt. Pour this mixture over the potatoes and distribute pieces of butter all over the top. Bake for 50 minutes, until the cheese is browned and bubbly. Serve very hot.

Spinach and goat cheese tart

FOR 4-6 PEOPLE
PREPARATION: **15 min**
COOKING TIME:
approximately 40 min

> 1 lb. fresh spinach
> 2 tbsp. butter
> 2 eggs
> ½ cup heavy cream
> 4¼ oz. petits-suisses cheese (or other soft, creamy cow's milk cheese)
> 2½ oz. grated comté or emmental cheese
> 1 pinch grated nutmeg
> 1 pre-prepared puff pastry sheet, approximately 8 oz.
> 3½ oz. fresh goat cheese
> 1¾ oz. (just less than ½ cup) pine nuts
> salt, freshly ground black pepper

Wash and dry the spinach leaves then cut off the stems. Melt the butter in a frying pan and add the spinach leaves for several minutes, just until they have released their water.

Preheat the oven to 350° F.

Using a fork, briefly beat the eggs then season them with salt and pepper. Stir in the heavy cream and the petits-suisses cheese then add the grated cheese and the nutmeg.

Roll out the puff pastry sheet to line a 9-inch tart pan (the pastry should be approximately ⅛ inch thick). Lightly prick the dough all over with a fork then distribute the spinach evenly over the bottom; pour in the heavy cream mixture. Slice the goat cheese into rounds and distribute them evenly over the top of the tart. Bake for approximately 30 minutes.

Sprinkle the tart with pine nuts and continue to bake for several minutes, just until the nuts are golden brown. Serve hot.

Instead of making a large tart, you can make 4 individual tartlets using 4-inch-round tart pans and reducing the cooking time to around 15 to 20 minutes.

Endive and citrus tatin

FOR 4 PEOPLE
PREPARATION: **20 min**
COOKING TIME:
approximately 50 min

> 6 large, white Belgian endives
> 1 organic orange
> 1 organic lemon
> 2 tbsp. lightly salted butter (such as demi-sel)
> 2 tbsp. honey (fluid)
> 1 pre-prepared puff pastry sheet, approximately 8 oz.
> just over ¾ cup crème fraîche
> 3 pinches grated nutmeg
> salt, freshly ground black pepper

Cut the Belgian endives in half lengthwise. Hollow out the core near the stem end. Remove the orange zest in thin strips. Juice the orange and lemon then strain the juice.

In a frying pan, heat the butter. Add the Belgian endives then the citrus juice; season with salt and pepper. Cook, covered, for 20 to 25 minutes, just until the endives become slightly tender.

Meanwhile, place the orange zest in cold water and bring to a boil. After 2 minutes, remove the zest to drain and rinse under cold water.

Remove the cover from the frying pan and ladle out ⅔ cup of the cooking liquid and set aside; let the remaining liquid cook away. Add the honey and cook the endives until translucent, turning them several times; take the pan off the heat to cool.

Preheat the oven to 400° F.

Cover the bottom of a 9-inch springform pan (or regular cake pan) with parchment paper (extending the paper up the sides). Arrange layers of the endive halves in a rosette pattern in the cake pan. Cover the top with a piece of puff pastry that has been cut into a circle large enough to cover the top of the endives; tuck the ends of the pastry down inside the edge of the cake pan. Bake for 25 minutes.

Just before the end of the cooking time, bring the crème fraîche mixed with the reserved ⅔ cup cooking liquid, the orange zest and the nutmeg to a boil; season with salt and pepper and boil for 3 minutes.

Remove the tatin from the oven then place a flat serving platter over the cake pan and carefully, but quickly, invert the pan to release the cake onto the platter; carefully lift off the cake pan (if using a spring form pan, release the sides from around the tatin).

Spread a little bit of the crème fraîche over the top. Serve hot with the remaining crème fraîche on the side.

Tomato tart

FOR 4 PEOPLE
PREPARATION: **10 min**
COOKING TIME: **25 min**

> 5 tomatoes
> 1 pre-prepared
  puff pastry sheet
  (approximately 8 oz.) or
  pre-prepared pie dough
> 2–3 tbsp. black olive
  tapenade
> 3 oz. emmental or comté
  cheese
> 1 tbsp. poppy seeds
> several arugula leaves
> salt, freshly ground
  black pepper

Preheat the oven to 400° F.

Wash the tomatoes, remove the seeds then slice the tomatoes into thin rounds.

Roll out the puff pastry sheet or pie crust to line a 10-inch tart pan (the dough should be approximately ⅛ inch thick).

Brush the tart dough with the tapenade and place the tomato slices on top. Add a moderate amount of salt and then some pepper; cover with thin slices of the cheese.

Sprinkle the poppy seeds over the top and bake the tart for approximately 25 minutes. Serve with a side of the arugula leaves.

Serve this flavorful tart with a salad made with broccoli, diced ham, corn and walnuts.

quick & easy recipe

Pumpkin and zucchini quiche

FOR 4-6 PEOPLE
PREPARATION: **20 min**
COOKING TIME:
approximately 1 hour

> 9 oz. pre-prepared pie dough
> 3 zucchini
> 7 oz. fresh pumpkin flesh, skin removed (approximately 9 oz. with skin)
> 4 eggs
> 1 cup heavy cream
> ⅔ cup milk
> 1 pinch grated nutmeg
> salt, freshly ground black pepper

Preheat the oven to 350° F.

Cover the bottom of a 10-inch springform pan (or regular cake pan) with parchment paper then transfer the rolled pie dough to the pan, extending the dough approximately 1 inch up the sides of the pan. Lightly prick the dough all over with a fork. Cover the top of the dough with parchment paper then place dried beans or pie weights on top; bake for 10 minutes. Remove from the oven to cool and carefully lift off the top piece of parchment.

Meanwhile, wash the zucchini and cut off the ends. Cut the zucchini and the pumpkin into small dice then place them in a saucepan of boiling, salted water and cook for approximately 15 minutes.

In a bowl, briefly beat the eggs with a fork with the heavy cream, milk and the nutmeg. Season with salt and pepper and stir to combine.

Drain the vegetables then add them to the bowl with the egg mixture and stir to combine. Pour the mixture into the tart pan over the prebaked crust. Bake for 40 minutes. Serve hot.

You can also make 4 individual quiches using 4-inch round tart pans. Reduce the cooking time to only 20 minutes.

Artichoke galette

FOR 4 PEOPLE
PREPARATION: **10 min**
COOKING TIME: **30 min**

> 1 pre-prepared
  puff pastry sheet,
  approximately 8 oz.
> 4–5 tbsp. canned,
  crushed tomatoes
> 12 small artichoke hearts,
  conserved in oil
> 12 black olives
> 1¾ oz. parmesan cheese
> salt, freshly ground black
  pepper

Preheat the oven to 350° F.

Using a 9-inch tart pan bottom as a guide, cut out a circle of dough from the puff pastry sheet. Place the circle of dough onto a baking sheet and cover with parchment paper. Place a smaller tart pan (approximately 8 inches) on top of the parchment paper to prevent the dough from puffing while baking. Bake for 10 minutes then remove from the oven and lift off the parchment.

Spread the crushed tomatoes over the prebaked crust. Cut the artichoke hearts in half or in quarters and place on top of the tomatoes; season moderately with salt then season with pepper. Distribute the olives around the top then add a generous amount of parmesan cheese. Bake for approximately 20 minutes. Serve warm.

You can also make 8 individual tartlets using 2½- to 3-inch-round tart pans. Bake for 8 to 10 minutes.

Pan-fried tofu and bean sprouts

FOR 4 PEOPLE
PREPARATION: **10 min**
COOKING TIME: **20 min**

> 14 oz. frozen haricots verts (string beans)
> 2 onions
> 2 garlic cloves
> 7 oz. firm tofu
> 3 tbsp. peanut oil
> 2 tsp. ground ginger
> 14 oz. fresh or canned mung bean sprouts ("soy bean sprouts")
> 2 tbsp. soy sauce
> salt, freshly ground black pepper

Boil the haricots verts in salted water for 5 to 7 minutes from the time the water has reached a full boil; drain.

Peel and thinly slice the onions and the garlic cloves. Cut the tofu into large dice. In a skillet, heat 1 tablespoon of the peanut oil and cook the onions and garlic until soft and translucent. Add the haricots verts, the tofu and the ground ginger. Cook for 5 minutes over medium heat.

Rinse the bean sprouts then let them drain. Add the remaining peanut oil in a second skillet and sauté the sprouts for 5 minutes; season with salt and pepper. Add the soy sauce followed by the haricots verts and the tofu. Cook for an additional 2 minutes. Serve immediately.

What are frequently called "soy bean sprouts" are not real soy but instead mung bean sprouts.

Fennel and tomato parmesan gratin

FOR 4 PEOPLE
PREPARATION: **15 min**
COOKING TIME: **1 hour**

> 2 large, ripe tomatoes
> 2 fennel bulbs
> 1 small jar of black olive tapenade (approximately 3½ oz.)
> 2 tsp. herbes de Provence
> ½ cup olive oil
> 1¾ oz. parmesan cheese
> salt, freshly ground black pepper

Preheat the oven to 350° F.

Wash the tomatoes then cut them into thick slices. Cut the fennel bulbs in half from top to bottom and place them along with the tomato slices in a large baking dish. Coat each bulb half with a thick layer of tapenade. Sprinkle on the herbes de Provence then season with salt and pepper. Drizzle olive oil over the top.

Grate the parmesan cheese and sprinkle it over the fennel and tomatoes. Bake for 1 hour. Serve very hot as a main dish or as a side dish with grilled meat.

VARIATION You can also make this dish using small eggplants or zucchini.

Zucchini mousseline

FOR 8 PEOPLE
PREPARATION: **15 min**
COOKING TIME: **10 min**

> 5 zucchini
> 2 garlic cloves
> 2 tbsp. butter
> ⅔ cup crème fraîche
> 1 tbsp. fresh chopped parsley
> salt, freshly ground black pepper

Wash and peel the zucchini then slice them into rounds. In a saucepan, boil the zucchini for 10 minutes in salted water. Drain them then purée them using a blender; season with salt and pepper.

Peel and chop the garlic cloves. In a saucepan, heat the butter over low heat, then add the garlic, the crème fraîche and the parsley. Add the puréed zucchini and mix. Adjust the seasoning, if needed, and serve immediately.

Quick zucchini provençal

FOR 4 PEOPLE
PREPARATION: **10 min**
COOKING TIME: **15 min**

> 4 zucchini
> 1 fennel bulb
> 3 tomatoes
> 2 garlic cloves
> 2 sprigs of thyme, crumbled
> 1 tbsp. powdered (or instant) chicken bouillon
> 3 tbsp. olive oil
> salt, freshly ground black pepper

Wash the zucchini but do not peel them; cut off the ends then slice the zucchini into rounds. Cut off the fennel bulb then wash and thinly slice it. Immerse the tomatoes in boiling water for 20 seconds, then immediately put them in cold water. Peel them, remove and discard the seeds then chop them.

Place all of the vegetables on a microwave-safe plate. Add the peeled and crushed garlic, the thyme and the powdered chicken bouillon; season with salt and pepper. Pour the olive oil over the top of the vegetables, cover, then microwave for 15 to 18 minutes on high, stirring halfway through the cooking time. Serve immediately.

This quick and easy dish is a perfect accompaniment to roast beef or baked fish.

Puréed potatoes

FOR 4-6 PEOPLE
PREPARATION: **10 min**
COOKING TIME: **20 min**

> 2¼ lbs. large, tender-flesh potatoes
> just over ¾ cup whole milk
> 5½ tbsp. butter
> ¼ tsp. grated nutmeg
> salt, freshly ground black pepper

Peel the potatoes and cut them into large pieces. Boil for 20 minutes in salted water. Heat the milk.

Drain the potatoes and transfer them to a potato ricer or food mill (using the fine-mesh plate). Add the hot milk and the butter, in pieces. Mix well to blend, season with salt and pepper and a little nutmeg. Serve hot.

VARIATION Depending on the main dish you serve, you can flavor the potatoes with olive oil and dried or fresh chopped herbs (chives, parsley or tarragon), with a tapenade and olive oil, or with coconut milk and curry.

Jerusalem artichoke purée with hazelnut oil

FOR 4-6 PEOPLE
PREPARATION: **15 min**
COOKING TIME:

35–40 min

> 5¼ oz. potatoes
> 1⅓ lbs. Jerusalem artichokes
> ⅓ cup milk
> 3½ tbsp. butter
> 4 tbsp. hazelnut oil
> 4 tbsp. (1¼ oz.) pine nuts
> 2 tbsp. sliced almonds
> salt, freshly ground black pepper

Peel the potatoes and the artichokes then cut them into pieces. Boil them together for 35 to 40 minutes in a large saucepan of salted water. Heat the milk and melt the butter.

Process the potatoes and the artichokes through a potato ricer or food mill (using the fine-mesh plate) then add the hot milk and the melted butter followed by the hazelnut oil. Stir vigorously with a silicone spatula or wooden spoon; season with salt and pepper.

Add the pine nuts and almonds to a dry skillet and lightly toast them. Sprinkle them on top of the purée. Serve with roasted chicken.

VARIATION You can also make this with artichoke hearts instead of Jerusalem artichokes.

Potatoes dauphine

FOR 6 PEOPLE
PREPARATION: 40 min
COOKING TIME:
approximately 40 min

> 1⅔ lbs. potatoes
> 3 tbsp. butter
> 3 egg yolks
> vegetable oil, for frying

For the pâte à choux
> 2 tbsp. butter
> ½ tsp. salt
> ½ cup (2 oz.) all-purpose
  flour
> 1 pinch nutmeg
> 2 small eggs
> salt, freshly ground
  black pepper

Peel and wash the potatoes then cut them into quarters. Boil them for 20 minutes in salted water. Meanwhile, preheat the oven to 475° F. Dry the boiled potatoes in the oven for 3 or 4 minutes just until they have lightened in color. Process them through a potato ricer or food mill (using the fine-mesh plate). Add the butter then incorporate the lightly beaten egg yolks a little at a time into the purée; season with salt.

Prepare the pâte à choux. In a saucepan, bring ½ cup water to a boil with the butter and salt. Lower the heat then add the flour all at once and mix vigorously with a spatula while scraping the sides of the pan just until the dough becomes somewhat dry and pulls away completely from the side of the pan. Remove the pan from the heat, add some pepper and the nutmeg then stir in the eggs one at a time.

Mix the pâte à choux with the puréed potatoes. In a heavy-bottomed saucepan, heat the vegetable oil to 350° F.

Using a spoon, scoop up the batter and form it into a ball with your hands. Gently drop the ball down into the hot oil. Continue forming and frying balls in this manner. When the balls are puffed and a deep golden brown, remove them and place them on paper towels to drain; lightly season with salt and serve very hot.

1 To make successful potatoes dauphine, choose a starchy potato variety, such as Bintje or Yukon gold.

2 Traditionally, the batter for potatoes dauphine is seasoned with nutmeg, but try using fresh herbs or spices instead.

3 Fry the potatoes dauphine in batches of 6, estimating 10 minutes between each batch.

Pastas, rice and grains

Ham and peas tagliatelle

FOR 4 PEOPLE
PREPARATION: 10 min
COOKING TIME: 15 min

> 5¼ oz. small, frozen peas
> 1 onion
> 2 tbsp. olive oil
> 5¼ oz. Parma ham (prosciutto) or other similar ham
> ⅔ cup heavy cream
> 10½ oz. fresh tagliatelle pasta
> 3 oz. parmesan cheese shavings
> salt, freshly ground black pepper

Boil the peas for 5 minutes in a large amount of salted water; drain. Peel and chop the onion.

Heat the oil in a skillet and cook the onion until soft. Add the peas, the Parma ham (cut into small strips), then the heavy cream; season with salt and pepper. Continue to cook over low heat for 3 to 5 minutes while stirring.

Meanwhile, boil the tagliatelle in a large amount of salted water until al dente. Drain and turn out onto a serving plate. Coat the pasta with the peas and prosciutto sauce then add the parmesan cheese shavings on top. Serve immediately.

Spaghetti carbonara

FOR 4 PEOPLE
PREPARATION: **15 min**
COOKING TIME:

12–15 min

> 14 oz. spaghetti
> 1 onion
> 2 tbsp. butter
> 7 oz. thick-cut smoked bacon, cut into small cubes
> ¼ cup white wine
> 1 egg + 2 egg yolks
> 2½ oz. grated parmesan cheese
> salt, freshly ground black pepper

Boil the spaghetti for 5 minutes in a large amount of salted water until al dente. Warm a serving dish over a simmering saucepan of water or in a low oven.

Peel and chop the onion. Melt the butter in a skillet and add the onion and bacon. Add the white wine and cook for 2 to 3 minutes; pour out onto the warmed serving dish.

In a small bowl, beat together the egg and egg yolks using a fork; season with salt and pepper then add the parmesan cheese and 2 tablespoons of the pasta water; stir to combine.

Drain the spaghetti and pour it out onto the serving dish on top of the bacon and onion; toss to coat the spaghetti.

Immediately pour the eggs and parmesan mixture on top and toss lightly. Serve very hot.

Walnut pasta

FOR 4 PEOPLE
PREPARATION: **10 min**
COOKING TIME:
approximately 20 min

> ⅓ cup (1¾ oz.) pine nuts
> ½ cup (1¾ oz.) walnut halves
> 2 garlic cloves
> ½ bunch flat-leaf parsley
> ⅔ cup olive oil
> 14 oz. fresh pasta (such as tagliatelle)
> salt, freshly ground black pepper

Lightly toast the pine nuts in a dry skillet for 3 minutes, stirring occasionally. Coarsely chop the walnuts.

Peel and chop the garlic cloves. Wash and chop the parsley.

Heat half of the olive oil in a skillet and add the garlic and parsley; cook for 3 to 4 minutes while stirring. Add the chopped walnuts and the toasted pine nuts and brown them for 2 minutes while stirring.

Remove the skillet from the heat and add the remaining olive oil with ½ cup of water. Whisk together well. Adjust the seasoning as needed and keep the sauce warm.

Boil the pasta in a large amount of salted water, drain, then pour out onto a serving plate and toss with the warmed sauce. Sprinkle with parsley and serve immediately.

Serve with an arugula salad tossed with a balsamic vinaigrette.

quick & easy
· recipe ·

Tagliatelle with oyster mushrooms

FOR 4 PEOPLE
PREPARATION: **10 min**
COOKING TIME:
approximately 20 min

> 10½ oz. tagliatelle pasta
> 4 tbsp. olive oil
> 14 oz. oyster mushrooms
> 2 garlic cloves
> 10 tarragon leaves
> salt, freshly ground
  black pepper

Boil the tagliatelle pasta for 8 minutes in a large amount of lightly salted water with 1 tablespoon of the olive oil; drain.

Meanwhile, clean and thinly slice the mushrooms. Peel and chop the garlic cloves. Wash and chop the tarragon.

Heat the remaining 3 tablespoons of olive oil in a large skillet. Add the chopped garlic and stir with a spatula for 2 minutes. Add the mushrooms and sauté for 7 to 8 minutes.

Add the tagliatelle and the chopped tarragon. Mix gently then lower the heat to warm the pasta, approximately 3 minutes. Season with pepper then divide the pasta among warmed serving plates and serve immediately.

You can use other types of mushrooms in this dish. You can also add 2 slices of chopped ham sautéed with the mushrooms.

quick & easy
· recipe ·

Summer vegetable fusilli salad

FOR 4 PEOPLE
PREPARATION: **15 min**
COOKING TIME:

6–12 min

> 9 oz. fusilli pasta (or other short pasta such as farfalle)
> ⅓ cup olive oil
> 4 very ripe, but firm, tomatoes
> 1 avocado
> juice of 1 lemon
> 1 small garlic clove
> 1 spring onion
> 2 oz. hearts of romaine lettuce

Boil the pasta for 6 to 12 minutes in a large amount of salted water just until al dente; drain then pour the pasta into a bowl. Add the olive oil, toss to coat, then set aside to cool.

Immerse the tomatoes in boiling water for 20 seconds, then immediately put them in cold water. Peel them, remove and discard the seeds, then chop them into small pieces.

Cut the avocado in half and remove the pit. Scoop out the flesh using a spoon then cut it into strips and sprinkle with the lemon juice. Peel and chop the garlic clove and the onion. Wash the romaine hearts, dry them thoroughly, then cut them into strips.

When the pasta has cooled, add all of the prepared ingredients on top and toss well to combine.

This salad can be served as a main dish or served on the side to accompany a cold meat dish.

Eggplant farfalle

FOR 4 PEOPLE
PREPARATION: **10 min**
COOKING TIME:
approximately 20 min

> 2 eggplants
> 1 garlic clove
> ½ can crushed tomatoes
  (7 oz. drained)
> 3 tsp. powdered (or
  instant) chicken bouillon
> 3 tbsp. olive oil
> 7 oz. farfalle pasta
> salt, freshly ground
  black pepper

Peel the eggplants and cut them into medium dice. Peel and thinly slice the garlic clove.

Place the eggplants and the drained crushed tomatoes on a microwave-safe plate. Add the sliced garlic, the powdered chicken bouillon and 2 tablespoons of the olive oil; season with salt and pepper. Cover and microwave on high for 12 to 15 minutes, stirring halfway through the cooking time.

Meanwhile, boil the farfalle in a large amount of salted water until al dente; drain. Add the eggplant and tomato mixture, toss well, then drizzle the remaining 1 tablespoon of olive oil over the top and serve.

VARIATION To make this dish au gratin, place round slices of mozzarella cheese on top of the pasta and place the dish in a very hot oven (425° F) for 10 minutes.

quick & easy · recipe ·

Macaroni gratin with gouda

FOR 4 PEOPLE
PREPARATION: **15 min**
COOKING TIME:
approximately 25 min

> 14 oz. macaroni pasta, such as ziti
> 5 oz. cumin-spiced gouda cheese
> 1 cup heavy cream
> 5¼ oz. thick-cut bacon, cut into small cubes
> salt, freshly ground black pepper

Boil the macaroni in a large amount of salted water for the time indicated on the package; drain, then rinse briefly under cold water.

Cut half of the gouda cheese into small pieces. In a saucepan, heat the heavy cream then add the chopped gouda to melt over low heat while stirring with a silicone spatula or a wooden spoon.

In a bowl, mix the cooked macaroni with the gouda and cream; season with salt and pepper.

Preheat the oven to 400° F.

In a dry skillet, brown the bacon then transfer it to paper towels to drain. Stir the bacon into the macaroni then pour out into a baking dish.

Grate the remaining gouda cheese and sprinkle it over the top of the macaroni. Bake for 15 minutes. Serve very hot.

For a softer texture to this dish, soak the cooked macaroni for 12 hours in milk.

Prosciutto and penne pasta

FOR 4 PEOPLE
PREPARATION: **20 min**
COOKING TIME:
approximately 20 min

> 1 lb. penne pasta
> 2 oz. sun-dried tomatoes
> 1 bunch basil
> 8 thin slices prosciutto (preferably from Parma)
> 1⅔ cups tomato sauce
> 20 black olives
> 3 oz. parmesan cheese shavings
> 3 tbsp. olive oil
> salt, freshly ground black pepper

Boil the pasta in a large amount of salted water for 8 to 10 minutes; drain, then rinse briefly under cold water.

Cut the sun-dried tomatoes into small dice. Chop the basil into small pieces then slice the prosciutto into strips.

In a large, wide sauté pan, boil the tomato sauce for 5 minutes. Add the sun-dried tomatoes and the olives then season with salt and pepper. Add the pasta and heat for 4 to 5 minutes over medium heat, stirring to evenly coat the pasta with the sauce.

Add the prosciutto at the last minute. Divide the pasta among the serving plates, sprinkle with the chopped basil, add shavings of parmesan cheese and a drizzle of olive oil on top.

VARIATION To add more aromatic seasoning to this dish, sauté 2 shallots and 2 chopped garlic cloves in 1 tablespoon of olive oil before adding the sauce to the skillet.

Spinach ravioli

FOR 4 PEOPLE
PREPARATION: 1 hour
REFRIGERATION: 1 hour
DRYING: 4 hours
COOKING TIME: 10 min

> 3½ oz. frozen spinach
> 1 onion
> 3½ oz. leftover ground beef
> 3½ oz. cold, cooked ham slices
> 3½ oz. veal
> ¼ cup vegetable oil
> thyme, 1 bay leaf
> ½ cup beef broth or white wine
> 2 tbsp. butter
> 1¾ oz. grated parmesan cheese

For the pasta

> 3½ cups (14 oz.) all-purpose flour
> 4 eggs
> salt, freshly ground black pepper

Prepare the ravioli. Sift the flour into a bowl, making a well in the center with your fingers. Break the eggs into the well and add 1 or 2 pinches of salt. Start mixing the flour and eggs together using a silicone spatula or wooden spoon, then add water a little at a time until it starts to form a dough. Knead the dough until it becomes somewhat firm and elastic. Shape the dough into a ball and wrap it in plastic wrap then refrigerate for at least 1 hour.

Cook the spinach, drain, then finely chop it. Peel and chop the onion. Finely chop the ground beef, the ham and the veal.

In a skillet, heat the vegetable oil and sauté the onions. Add the ground beef, ham, and veal, then add a little bit of thyme and the crumbled bay leaf; season with salt and pepper. Moisten the mixture by adding the beef broth or white wine and cook over low heat for 5 minutes, then add the spinach.

Cut the pasta into two equal portions and roll each portion out into a large rectangle, both of equal size and approximately ⅟₁₆ inch thick. Using a pastry bag, pipe the filling in small mounds of equal size on one of the rectangles, leaving approximately 1½ inches between them. Using a pastry brush, moisten the pasta with a small amount of water in the areas between the mounds. Place the second rectangular piece of pasta on top of the first and press it down gently between the mounds to adhere the two layers of pasta together. Cut out the ravioli using a scalloped-edge pastry wheel and chill them for 4 hours to dry.

Boil the ravioli for 8 to 10 minutes in salted water; drain and drizzle with melted butter. Serve the parmesan cheese on the side.

1 Ravioli pasta is the same type of pasta used for other stuffed pastas.

2 You can replace the meat with a mixture of ricotta and parmesan cheese.

3 After chilling and drying the pasta, the raviolis will keep for 5 or 6 days refrigerated.

Mini ravioli in spicy beurre blanc

FOR 4 PEOPLE
PREPARATION: **20 min**
COOKING TIME:
approximately 15 min

> 1 large shallot
> ½ small red chile pepper
> 8 tbsp. (1 stick) cold
  butter
> ½ cup white wine
> ½ cup heavy cream
> 3 sprigs cilantro
> 1 carrot
> 9 oz. ravioli de Royan
  (mini ravioli)
> salt, freshly ground
  black pepper

Prepare the beurre blanc. Mince the shallot and the pepper. Cut the butter into small pieces. In a saucepan, bring the white wine to a boil with the shallot and continue to boil until the liquid reduces by two-thirds. Add the heavy cream then continue to cook for another 5 minutes over medium heat to reduce again by half. Off the heat, add the cold pieces of butter and whisk continuously. Add a little bit of hot water if the beurre blanc becomes too thick.

Strain the beurre blanc through a fine-mesh strainer and add the chopped cilantro and the chile pepper. Keep the sauce hot without boiling.

Peel the carrot and cut it into small dice. Boil for 5 minutes in salted water then rinse quickly under cold water, drain, and add it to the beurre blanc.

Immerse the ravioli in simmering, salted water and cook for 2 minutes without boiling. Drain, then divide among shallow serving plates. Top with the beurre blanc and serve immediately.

VARIATION If you are short on time, prepare a quick cream sauce by boiling just over ¾ cup heavy cream for 5 minutes, seasoned with salt and pepper. Off the heat, add approximately 1 tablespoon of butter, the cilantro and the chile pepper. Use an immersion blender to mix the cream for 20 seconds, then serve.

Ham and cheese cannelloni

FOR 4 PEOPLE
PREPARATION: **45 min**
RESTING TIME: **2 hours**
COOKING TIME: **20 min**

> 10½ oz. cannelloni pasta or 12 rectangles of fresh, store-bought lasagna noodles
> 1 lb. ricotta cheese or drained fromage blanc (or plain yogurt)
> 2 eggs + 1 egg yolk
> 4 tbsp. chopped parsley
> 5 tbsp. grated parmesan cheese
> 2 tbsp. butter
> 12 slices dry-cured ham (prosciutto)
> 1¼ cups tomato sauce
> salt, freshly ground black pepper, nutmeg

For the pasta (if not using store-bought)

> 1¾ cups (7 oz.) all-purpose flour
> 2 eggs

If not using store-bought pasta, prepare the cannelloni pasta. Sift the flour into a bowl, making a well in the center with your fingers. Break the eggs into the well and add a large pinch of salt. Start mixing the flour and eggs together using a silicone spatula or wooden spoon, then add water a little at a time until it starts to form a dough. Knead the dough until it becomes somewhat firm and elastic. Shape the dough into a ball and wrap it in plastic wrap then refrigerate for at least 1 hour. Lightly flour a work surface and roll the pasta out to approximately ⅛ inch thick. Using a pastry wheel, cut out 12 rectangles measuring 2½ by 3 inches and set them aside to dry for 1 hour.

Boil the pasta (if using either handmade or store-bought) for 4 minutes in salted water. Drain, then immerse immediately in cold water; drain again and spread them out onto a damp towel.

In a mixing bowl, combine the ricotta (or the fromage blanc), the eggs and egg yolk, the parsley and 1 tablespoon of the grated parmesan cheese; season with salt and pepper and a little bit of grated nutmeg. Melt the butter.

Preheat the oven to 425° F.

Place a slice of the ham on top of each pasta rectangle then spread on a layer of the cheese filling. Roll the cannelloni and arrange them in a well-buttered baking dish.

Drizzle the melted butter over the top then top with the tomato sauce and sprinkle over the remaining parmesan cheese. Bake for 20 minutes or until bubbling and the cheese is lightly browned.

Lasagna bolognese

FOR 4–6 PEOPLE
PREPARATION: **25 min**
COOKING TIME: **2 hours**

> 1 lb. lasagna noodles
> 1 large onion
> 1 carrot
> 1 small celery stalk
> 1 garlic clove
> 2 tbsp. olive oil
> 9 oz. ground beef
> 7 oz. canned, crushed tomatoes
> 2½ cups beef broth
> ½ cup white wine
> 2 tbsp. butter
> ¼ cup (1 oz.) all-purpose flour
> 5¼ oz. grated parmesan cheese
> salt, freshly ground black pepper, nutmeg

Boil the lasagna noodles (3 or 4 at a time) in a large saucepan of salted water and cook for 1 minute or until the noodles float to the surface; remove the noodles and place them on a clean towel to drain.

Prepare the bolognese sauce. Peel and finely chop the onion, the carrot, the celery and the garlic clove. In a large sauté pan, heat the olive oil and cook the vegetables over gentle heat for 10 minutes. Add the ground beef and cook for 5 minutes then add the tomatoes and cook for another 10 minutes. Add 1¼ cups of the beef broth and all of the wine; season with salt and pepper. Cook the sauce for 1 hour over low heat, covered. Adjust the seasoning as needed.

Prepare the white sauce. Heat the remaining beef broth. In a saucepan, melt the butter then add the flour and stir vigorously to obtain a smooth mixture. Cook for 2 minutes without letting the mixture brown. Add the heated beef broth, whisk, and cook for 10 minutes over very low heat; season with salt and pepper and a little bit of grated nutmeg.

Preheat the oven to 475° F. Butter an 8-inch-square baking dish, spread a little bit of the bolognese sauce all along the bottom of the dish then add alternating layers of lasagna noodles, white sauce, bolognese sauce and a little bit of parmesan cheese. End with a layer of the lasagna noodles covered with white sauce. Sprinkle the remaining parmesan cheese on the top and bake for 30 minutes.

1 Spread the bottom of a buttered baking dish with bolognese sauce then a layer of lasagna noodles. The noodles can overlap based on the size of the baking dish.

2 Cover the noodles with a generous layer of white sauce.

3 Spread on a layer of the bolognese sauce and sprinkle with a little parmesan cheese. Continue adding layers until all of the sauce is used.

Creole rice

FOR 4 PEOPLE
PREPARATION: **2 min**
COOKING TIME:

12–18 min

> 1 cup (7 oz.) long-grain, basmati, or thai jasmine rice
> salt

Wash the rice several times then drain it and add it to a saucepan. Season with salt then cover it with three times the amount of its volume in water (approximately 3 cups). Cook, uncovered, at a rolling boil.

When the water level is no longer above the rice, cover and cook over very low heat, just until all of the water has evaporated but the rice remains slightly moist.

Cantonese rice

FOR 4 PEOPLE
PREPARATION: **30 min**
COOKING TIME:

approximately 15 min

> 1 cup (7 oz.) long-grain, basmati, or thai jasmine rice
> 3½ oz. dry-cured ham (prosciutto) or chinese sausage
> 4 eggs
> ¼ cup peanut oil
> 2 tbsp. chopped scallion
> salt, freshly ground black pepper

Make creole rice (**SEE** above).

Cut the ham or the sausage into small dice. In a small bowl, beat the eggs to combine; season with salt and pepper.

Heat 2 tablespoons of the peanut oil in a skillet and cook the eggs to make an omelet; cut the omelet into small pieces.

Heat the remaining peanut oil in a skillet and quickly sauté the rice. Add the diced ham or sausage, the chopped omelet and the scallion and mix carefully. Taste, adjust the seasoning as needed, and pour out onto a serving dish.

Rice pilaf

FOR 4 PEOPLE
PREPARATION: **15 min**
COOKING TIME: **25 min**

> 1⅔ cups (10½ oz.)
  basmati rice
> 1 large onion
> 3 tbsp. vegetable oil
> 3 cups chicken broth
> 1 tbsp. curry powder
> salt, freshly ground
  black pepper

Rinse then drain the rice. Peel and finely chop the onion.

In a frying pan, heat the vegetable oil over medium heat and cook the onion just until it begins to brown.

Add the rice and mix. After 2 or 3 minutes, when the rice has become translucent, add a ladle of chicken broth and continue to stir until the rice has absorbed all of the liquid. Add the curry powder and a little more broth; season lightly with salt then season with pepper. Continue to cook over low heat for 15 minutes, adding more broth as needed and stirring often.

While the rice is cooking, preheat the oven to 250° F. Butter a baking dish.

When the rice is done, pour it into the baking dish then bake for 6 to 8 minutes to remove the excess moisture.

Rice pilaf can be served alone as the main dish or as a side with chicken or roasted meat.

Indian rice

quick & easy recipe

FOR 4 PEOPLE
PREPARATION: 10 min
COOKING TIME: 20 min

> 2 onions
> 2 tbsp. peanut oil
> 2 tsp. ground turmeric
> 1½ cups (8½ oz.) white rice
> 1⅔ cups coconut milk
> 15 cashews
> 7 level tbsp. sliced almonds or pistachios
> 3 level tbsp. golden raisins
> salt, freshly ground black pepper

Peel and thinly slice the onions. In a large skillet, heat the peanut oil then add the onions with the turmeric and cook until the onions have softened. Add the rice and cook for 2 minutes over medium heat while stirring. Add the coconut milk and 1¼ cups of simmering water then bring the mixture to a boil. Season with salt and pepper then lower the heat and simmer for 15 to 20 minutes until the rice is cooked (add a little bit of simmering water to the rice during cooking if the rice starts to stick).

Meanwhile, toast the cashews and almonds in a small, dry, nonstick skillet.

When the rice is almost cooked, add the golden raisins and simmer for an additional 2 minutes. Sprinkle the cashews and almonds over the rice and serve.

This dish is a perfect accompaniment to roasted chicken thighs.

Bean and asparagus risotto

FOR 4 PEOPLE
PREPARATION: **10 min**
COOKING TIME: **25 min**

> 8 fresh or frozen green asparagus
> 7 oz. shelled fresh or frozen fava or broad beans
> 1 chicken bouillon cube
> 1 onion
> 2 tbsp. olive oil
> 4 tbsp. butter
> 1 cup (7 oz.) risotto rice, such as arborio, carnaroli, or maratelli
> ½ cup white wine
> 1½ oz. parmesan cheese
> salt, freshly ground black pepper

Boil the asparagus and the beans in salted water for 5 minutes; drain.

Dissolve the chicken bouillon cube in 3 cups of boiling water. Peel and thinly slice the onion.

Heat 2 tablespoons of the butter in a frying pan and brown the onions. Add the rice and brown for 2 minutes while stirring. Add the wine and allow it to evaporate completely, then add the simmering chicken bouillon, one ladle at a time, waiting until the liquid is almost fully absorbed before adding the next. Season with salt, if needed, then season with pepper; cook for 15 minutes.

Add the asparagus and the beans and cook for an additional 5 minutes. Add the remaining 2 tablespoons of butter in small pieces. Garnish with shavings of parmesan cheese and serve.

Saffron risotto

quick & easy
· recipe ·

FOR 4 PEOPLE
PREPARATION: 10 min
COOKING TIME: 20 min

> ¼ onion
> ½ carrot
> 2 tbsp. butter
> 1⅔ cups (10½ oz.) risotto rice, such as arborio or carnaroli
> ½ cup dry white wine
> 4¼ cups chicken or beef broth
> several strands of saffron
> grated parmesan cheese

Peel and chop the onion and the carrot. In a microwave- and stovetop-safe glass casserole dish, melt 1 tablespoon of the butter and cook the onion and carrot for 1 minute.

Add the rice and slowly add ¼ cup of the white wine. Cook for 1 minute just until the wine has evaporated. Add all of the broth, cover, and place in the microwave on high for 12 minutes. Be careful that the rice does not absorb all of the broth; if it does, it will be too dry.

Remove the dish from the microwave, add the saffron then transfer the rice to a frying pan or wok over medium heat and finish cooking for approximately 2 additional minutes; the broth must be completely evaporated but the rice should not be dry.

Add the remaining 1 tablespoon of butter and serve with grated parmesan cheese on the side.

If you do not have a glass stovetop-safe casserole dish, you can start the cooking in a frying pan or a wok then transfer the ingredients to a microwave-safe dish.

Risotto marinara

FOR 4–6 PEOPLE
PREPARATION: **20 min**
COOKING TIME:

approximately 25 min

> 8 red mullet fish fillets approximately 3½ oz. each, with skin but scaled
> 16 raw prawns
> 10½ oz. littleneck clams
> 2 shallots
> 1 garlic clove
> 2 tbsp. dry white wine
> 4 tbsp. olive oil
> 3½ oz. diced tomatoes
> 1 cup (7 oz.) risotto rice, such as arborio or carnaroli
> 2½ cups fish broth (fresh or store-bought)
> salt, freshly ground black pepper

Rinse the fish fillets and the prawns under cold water then carefully pat them dry. Rinse the clams several times in a bowl of water, changing the water frequently until it remains clear; drain.

Peel and thinly slice the shallots and the garlic clove.

Heat the wine in a saucepan, add the clams, cover and cook over high heat until the clams open up, shaking the pan often while cooking. Remove the clams with a slotted spoon and keep them warm in a bowl set over a saucepan of simmering water. Strain the cooking liquid and set aside.

Heat the olive oil in a frying pan and cook the red mullet fillets skin-side up over medium heat for 3 minutes. Gently remove them with a large slotted spoon or spatula and keep them warm on a plate set on top of a saucepan of simmering water; cover with a piece of aluminum foil.

In the same frying pan, cook the prawns for 1 minute on each side over high heat. Remove the shells and keep the prawns warm with the fillets.

Add the garlic and shallot to the frying pan and cook for 1 to 2 minutes then add the diced tomato and cook for an additional 1 to 2 minutes.

Add the rice to the frying pan and stir to combine. When the rice has become translucent, moisten it with the fish broth and the cooking liquid from the clams. Stir, then cover and cook gently for 15 to 20 minutes just until all of the liquid is absorbed; adjust the seasoning as needed.

Remove the shells from the clams, mix the clams with the rice then place the red mullet fillets and the prawns on top. Remove from the heat, cover, and let rest for 2 minutes before serving on warmed plates.

Paella

FOR 8 PEOPLE
PREPARATION: **50 min**
COOKING TIME: **40 min**

> 1 whole chicken, approximately 3½ lbs.
> 12 oz. clams
> 12 oz. cockles
> 16 mussels
> 14 oz. calamari (squid)
> 2 onions
> 2 bell peppers
> 6 tomatoes
> 2 garlic cloves
> 9 oz. haricots verts (string beans)
> 1 cup olive oil
> 16 crayfish (or large prawns)
> 1 pinch saffron
> 9 oz. fresh or frozen green peas
> 2 cups (14 oz.) long-grain white rice
> 1 pinch Cayenne pepper
> salt, freshly ground black pepper

Cut up the chicken into 8 pieces. Brush the clams, cockles and mussels under running water to clean them. Wash the calamari and cut them into rings.

Peel and chop the onions. Cut the bell peppers in half, remove the seeds and the white membrane then slice each half into strips. Cut the tomatoes into small dice. Peel and crush the garlic cloves. Cut the haricots verts into sections.

In a paella pan (or a stovetop- and oven-safe casserole dish or large sauté pan), heat the olive oil then add the crayfish to brown them; remove and set aside.

In the same pan, add the chicken pieces and brown them. Add the calamari followed by the onions, the bell peppers and the tomatoes. Sprinkle the saffron over the top then add the crushed garlic, the haricots verts, and the peas. Cook for approximately 15 minutes over low heat.

Preheat the oven to 425° F.

Bring 4 cups of water to a boil.

Add the rice to the paella pan, mix, then add the clams, cockles and mussels. Add the boiling water then season with salt and the Cayenne pepper. Bring to a boil again, cover, and bake for 25 minutes.

Remove the pan and place the crayfish on top of the paella. Let rest for 10 minutes before serving.

Pearled barley with tomatoes and basil

FOR 4-6 PEOPLE
PREPARATION: **15 min**
COOKING TIME:

approximately 50 min

> 1½ cups (10½ oz.) pre-cooked pearled barley
> 1 lb. cherry tomatoes
> 1 bunch basil
> 4 garlic cloves
> 5 shallots
> ½ cup olive oil
> 7 oz. pitted black olives
> 3½ oz. oil-packed sun-dried tomatoes, drained
> salt, freshly ground black pepper

Boil the pearled barley in a large amount of salted water for 30 minutes (or for the time indicated on the package).

Meanwhile, wash the cherry tomatoes. Wash the basil then remove the leaves from the stems. Peel and chop the garlic cloves and the shallots.

In a large sauté pan, heat the olive oil and sauté the garlic and the shallots for several minutes over high heat just until they begin to brown. Add the olives, the cherry tomatoes and the sun-dried tomatoes; cook for 5 minutes.

Drain the barley and add it to the pan; season with salt and pepper, cover, and cook for 20 minutes, stirring frequently to allow all of the ingredients to blend together. Serve very hot.

Serve this as a main dish or as a side with chicken or roasted pork.

You can also use this as a stuffing for bell peppers or tomatoes.

Sautéed quinoa with vegetables

FOR 4 PEOPLE
PREPARATION: 10 min
COOKING TIME: 40 min

> 1 cup (6 oz.) quinoa
> 2 eggplants
> 4 tomatoes or ½ can
  crushed tomatoes
  (7 oz. drained)
> 1 garlic clove
> 2 onions
> 2 tbsp. olive oil
> 1 cup vegetable broth
> salt, freshly ground
  black pepper

Rinse the quinoa, add it to a saucepan then add two times the amount of its volume in water (approximately 2 cups). Season with salt and bring to a boil; cook for 15 minutes over low heat.

Meanwhile, peel and dice the eggplants. Immerse the tomatoes in boiling water for 1 minute, then immediately put them in cold water. Peel them, remove and discard the seeds, then chop them into small dice.

Peel then thinly slice the garlic clove and the onions. In a skillet, heat the olive oil and cook the onions. Add the diced eggplants, tomatoes and garlic and cook for 5 minutes over medium heat.

Add the vegetable broth then simmer for 20 minutes. Add the drained quinoa, mix, and serve immediately.

VARIATION Make this dish au gratin: Add 1 or 2 beaten eggs, place all of the ingredients in a greased baking dish, sprinkle with your favorite grated cheese and bake for several minutes in a very hot over (425° F) until the cheese is browned and bubbly.

low calorie · recipe ·

Bulgur and dried fruit fricassee

FOR 4 PEOPLE
PREPARATION: 10 min
SOAKING: 30 min
COOKING TIME:
approximately 25 min

> approximately 1½ cups (9 oz.) bulgur
> 6 dried apricots
> 6 dates
> 2 tbsp. unsalted pistachios
> 4 shallots
> 3 tbsp. olive oil
> 1 tsp. cumin seeds
> 2 tbsp. raisins
> salt, freshly ground black pepper

Add the bulgur to a large bowl and pour water over it just until it is approximately 1 inch above the bulgur. Let the bulgur soak for 30 minutes at room temperature; the water must be completely absorbed.

Cut the apricots and the dates into small pieces. Crush the pistachios into large pieces. Peel and finely chop the shallots.

In a sauté pan, heat the olive oil over high heat and fry the shallots. Reduce the heat and cook them for 3 to 4 minutes over low heat while stirring. Add the cumin seeds, apricots, dates, raisins and pistachios. Mix and cook for several minutes then add the bulgur; season with salt and pepper. Simmer for 20 minutes, stirring occasionally. Serve very hot.

Serve this as a main dish or as a side with lamb chops or grilled merguez sausage.

VARIATION Replace the dried fruits with a mix of spices and diced fresh mango.

Vegetable couscous

FOR 4 PEOPLE
PREPARATION: 1 hour
COOKING TIME:
approximately 1½ hours

> approximately 2½ cups (1 lb.) couscous
> 5¼ oz. shelled fresh or frozen fava or broad beans
> 1 onion
> 2 turnips
> 2 carrots
> 2 tomatoes
> 2 zucchini
> 2 artichoke hearts, from a jar or frozen
> 1¾ oz. canned chickpeas (garbanzo beans)
> 7 tbsp. butter
> quatre-épices, allspice, or ras al-hanout spice blend
> salt, freshly ground black pepper

If using frozen beans, thaw them. Peel and thinly slice the onion. Peel the turnips and the carrots then cut them into large dice. Slice the tomatoes and zucchini into rounds and dice the artichoke hearts.

Add the vegetables to a large saucepan then add the chickpeas and season with salt. Add water or vegetable broth up to two-thirds the level of the vegetables, bring to a boil then simmer, covered, for 1 hour or until the vegetables are softened.

Meanwhile, prepare the couscous. Spread out the couscous into a large shallow dish (such as a 9 x 13-inch glass casserole dish) and pour boiling, salted water or vegetable broth over it. (The volume of the water or vegetable broth should be one and a half times the volume of the couscous, or approximately 3¾ cups.) Cover the dish with plastic wrap and set aside for approximately 5 minutes; the couscous should absorb all of the liquid.

Fluff the couscous with a fork, or using lightly oiled fingers, to break up any lumps that are present. Distribute small pieces of butter over the top and mix. Pour the couscous out into a shallow serving dish.

Drain the vegetables (reserving the broth) and place them on top of the couscous or in a separate dish served on the side.

Adjust the seasoning of the broth as needed, using cracked black pepper or other spices such as quatre-épices, allspice or ras al-hanout. Serve the broth on the side so that each person can drizzle it over the couscous and vegetables to taste.

low calorie recipe

Polenta

FOR 6 PEOPLE
PREPARATION: **5 min**
RESTING TIME: **1 hour**
COOKING TIME:

9-11 min

> 4¼ cups water (or chicken broth or milk)
> 3½ tbsp. butter
> 9 oz. pre-cooked (or instant) polenta flour
> salt, freshly ground black pepper

Add the liquid (water, chicken broth or milk) to a large saucepan. Season with salt (if using chicken broth, only add salt if needed) and bring to a boil over high heat. Lightly butter a half-sheet baking pan with sides or use a large, shallow platter.

Sprinkle the polenta flour into the boiling liquid. As soon as all of it is added, stir constantly with a silicone spatula or wooden spoon. Bring back to a boil then lower the heat and cook for approximately 5 minutes while stirring continuously.

When all of the liquid is absorbed, the polenta will detach from the sides of the pan. Turn off the heat then season with pepper.

Spread the polenta out in a thin layer on the buttered baking pan or platter, smoothing it to an even layer with a spatula; cool for 1 hour.

Melt the remaining butter over moderate heat in a large skillet. Cut out the cooled polenta in various shapes (using cookie cutters, if desired) and add to the skillet as soon as the butter begins to foam; brown for 4 to 6 minutes, turning them over once. Remove with a slotted spoon or spatula, allowing the fat to drip from them back into the skillet. Place on a serving plate and serve very hot.

Serve the polenta cakes with a green salad. You can also serve them with meat cooked in a sauce. Polenta cakes are the perfect accompaniment to stews and wild game dishes.

Main dishes

Filet mignon en croûte

FOR 6 PEOPLE
PREPARATION: **15 min**
RESTING TIME: **10 min**
COOKING TIME:
approximately 30 min

> 1 tbsp. olive oil
> 2¼ lbs. beef filet
> 1 pre-prepared
>   puff pastry sheet,
>   approximately 8 oz.
> 1 egg yolk
> salt, freshly ground
>   black pepper

In a frying pan, heat the olive oil and brown the beef filet on all sides for 3 to 4 minutes; season with salt and pepper. Take the pan off the heat and let the filet rest for 10 minutes.

Preheat the oven to 400° F.

Unroll the puff pastry sheet and place the filet in the center. Wrap the puff pastry sheet up around the filet on all sides to completely seal it inside. Brush water along the border to help adhere the pastry and keep it closed.

Lightly beat the egg yolk with a fork and brush it all over the surface of the pastry. Place the wrapped filet on a baking sheet and bake for 25 minutes.

Turn the oven off and prop the door open slightly; let the filet rest inside the oven for 5 minutes then slice it using an electric or serrated knife and arrange the slices on a warmed serving plate.

Serve with sautéed potatoes and a green salad.

Rib steak and spring vegetables

FOR 4 PEOPLE
PREPARATION: **40 min**
COOKING TIME:

approximately 30 min
RESTING TIME: **30 min**

> 2 bunches of small (spring) carrots
> 3 small turnips
> 3½ oz. haricots verts (string beans)
> 7 oz. cauliflower
> 10½ tbsp. (1 stick + 2½ tbsp.) butter
> 3½ oz. green peas
> 1 pinch sugar
> 3 sprigs of thyme
> 14 oz. small new potatoes, quartered
> 1 bone-in rib steak, weighing approximately 3½ lbs.
> ¼ cup beef broth
> salt, freshly ground black pepper

Wash all of the vegetables. Cook the carrots, turnips, haricots verts and cauliflower separately in boiling, salted water. Drain, then sauté them together in a skillet set over high heat with 3½ tablespoons of the butter.

Cook the green peas with ¼ cup water, ½ tablespoon of the butter, 1 pinch of sugar, 1 pinch of salt and the thyme. Cook the potatoes in a skillet with 3½ tablespoons of the butter; keep all of the vegetables warm.

Preheat the oven to 475° F.

Season the rib steak with salt and pepper, place it in an oven-proof skillet then drizzle the remaining 3 tablespoons of butter, melted, over the top and place it in the oven, estimating 18 minutes of cooking time per 2 pounds of steak.

Remove the steak from the skillet and let the excess fat drain from it. Turn off the oven and cover the steak with a piece of aluminum foil and let rest for 30 minutes inside the oven to allow the heat inside the steak to distribute evenly.

Meanwhile, heat the beef broth and pour it into the skillet. Set it over medium heat then scrape the cooked bits of meat off of the bottom using a silicone spatula or wooden spoon. Reduce the broth until it is somewhat thickened and smooth.

Place the steak on a serving plate and surround it with the cooked vegetables then brush it with the reduced broth.

You can also add 4 artichoke hearts to the vegetables.

Sirloin steak and shallots in red wine

FOR 4 PEOPLE
PREPARATION: **20 min**
COOKING TIME: **45 min**

> 16 small shallots
> just over ¾ cup
  sunflower oil
> 1 carrot
> 1 small celery stalk
  (approximately 1 oz.)
> 3 cups red wine
> 1 tbsp. light brown sugar
> 2 tbsp. butter
> 4 sirloin steaks, weighing
  approximately 6 oz. each
> salt, freshly ground
  black pepper

Peel the shallots then add them to a saucepan and pour in just enough of the sunflower oil to cover them; season with salt and pepper. Heat the oil over high heat until hot then reduce the heat to low and cook the shallots for 30 minutes; they must be soft but not browned. Let them cool while still in the oil then strain them.

Peel the carrot and cut it into small dice, thinly slice the celery stalk, then place the carrot and celery in a saucepan with the red wine. Reduce the wine by two-thirds over high heat then add the light brown sugar and cook for several minutes more until the sauce becomes syrupy.

Remove the pan from the heat and add the butter in small pieces while whisking continuously. Add the drained shallots to the sauce; set aside to keep warm.

In a skillet, heat 1 tablespoon of the sunflower oil and cook the steaks on each side over medium heat for 3 to 4 minutes; season with salt and pepper. Serve immediately with the shallot sauce.

Serve with a purée of Jerusalem artichoke or celery root.

Lamb's knuckle with sweet potato fries

FOR 4 PEOPLE
PREPARATION: 30 min
COOKING TIME: 1 hour
45 min

> 1 onion
> 4 lamb's knuckles
> 3 tbsp. olive oil
> 1 tbsp. + 2 pinches
  ground cinnamon
> 3 tbsp. honey (fluid)
> 1⅓ lbs. orange-fleshed
  sweet potatoes
> ⅔ cup sunflower oil
> salt, freshly ground
  black pepper

Peel and thinly slice the onion.

Tie the lamb's knuckles well using kitchen twine. In a large stovetop-safe casserole dish, heat the olive oil over high heat and brown the lamb's knuckles with the onion for 2 to 3 minutes. Sprinkle 1 tablespoon of the cinnamon over the meat then add the honey; season with salt and pepper. Let the meat cook until lightly caramelized.

Preheat the oven to 350° F.

Add 2 cups of water to the casserole dish. Cover and bake for 1½ hours, turning and basting the lamb's knuckles every 15 minutes.

Peel the sweet potatoes then cut them into long, thick sticks to make fries. Boil them for 5 minutes in salted water then rinse them under cold water and drain.

Just before serving, heat the sunflower oil in a skillet and fry the sweet potato sticks for 4 to 5 minutes. Place them on paper towels to drain, season with salt and pepper then sprinkle with the remaining 2 pinches of cinnamon. Serve immediately with the cooked lamb's knuckles and a little bit of the cooking liquid.

Did you know? There are two varieties of sweet potatoes, one with pale yellow flesh and the other with a dark orange flesh. The darker orange variety, used in this recipe, has a slightly sweeter taste.

Roasted leg of lamb with sage butter

FOR 4 PEOPLE
PREPARATION: **20 min**
COOKING TIME: **45 min**
RESTING TIME: **15 min**

> 12 sage leaves
> 1 cup (3 oz.) walnut halves
> 7 tbsp. lightly salted (demi-sel) butter
> 1¾ lbs. leg of lamb, boned but not trussed
> 1 tsp. fleur de sel (sea salt)
> salt, freshly ground black pepper

Preheat the oven to 350° F.

Chop the sage leaves and the walnut halves then mix them in a bowl along with the softened butter; season with salt and pepper.

Coat the inside of the leg of lamb with half of the sage and walnut butter. Tie the leg of lamb and place it in a baking dish and brush the remaining sage and walnut butter over the outside. Bake for 40 to 45 minutes, lightly basting it from time to time with the cooking juices.

Remove the leg of lamb from the oven then wrap it in a piece of aluminum foil and let it rest for 15 minutes. Just before serving, slice it and season it with the fleur de sel.

You can add 8 cleaned and cut-up potatoes around the leg of lamb before placing it in the oven.

VARIATION You can use a boned lamb shoulder instead of leg of lamb. In this case, reduce the cooking time by 10 minutes.

Rack of lamb niçoise

FOR 4 PEOPLE
PREPARATION: **30 min**
COOKING TIME:
15–20 min

> 3 zucchini
> 3 tomatoes
> 14 oz. small new
  potatoes
> ⅔ cup olive oil
> 1 rack of lamb weighing
  2½ lbs., clipped and
  trimmed
> 1 sprig of thyme
> 2 tbsp. small black olives
  (perferably niçoise)
> 8 to 10 sprigs of parsley
> salt, freshly ground
  black pepper

Peel the zucchini and cut it into large dice. Immerse the tomatoes in boiling water for 20 seconds, then immediately put them in cold water. Peel them, remove and discard the seeds, then chop them. Peel the potatoes.

Heat a few tablespoons of the olive oil in a skillet and brown the zucchini and the potatoes separately; set aside to drain.

Preheat the oven to 400° F.

In a stovetop-safe, stoneware casserole dish, heat the remaining olive oil and brown the rack of lamb on all sides. Remove the lamb then pour off the fat from the dish. Place the lamb back in the dish along with all of the vegetables; season with salt and pepper then add the sprig of thyme and bake for 15 to 20 minutes. Add the olives during the last 5 minutes of cooking.

Wash and chop the parsley. Serve the rack of lamb in the casserole dish with the parsley sprinkled over the top.

Rack of lamb bordelaise

FOR 4 PEOPLE
PREPARATION: **15 min**
COOKING TIME: **25 min**

> 14 oz. small potatoes
  (preferably charlotte)
> 14 oz. porcini mushrooms
> ⅔ cup olive oil
> 3 tbsp. butter
> 1 rack of lamb weighing
  2½ lbs., clipped and
  trimmed
> ¼ cup veal broth
> 1 tsp. tomato paste
> 1 garlic clove
> salt, freshly ground
  black pepper

Peel the potatoes then boil them for 10 minutes in salted water; drain.

Preheat the oven to 350° F.

Brush off any dirt from the porcini mushrooms. Heat ½ cup of the olive oil in a frying pan and brown the mushrooms; remove them to drain.

In a stovetop-safe casserole dish, melt the butter with the remaining olive oil and brown the rack of lamb on all sides. Add the mushrooms and the potatoes then season with salt and pepper. Cover and bake for 25 minutes.

Mix the veal broth with the tomato paste.

Several minutes before serving, peel and crush the garlic clove and add it to the casserole dish along with the veal broth mixture. Stir to combine and serve hot.

Veal filet à l'orange

FOR 4 PEOPLE
PREPARATION: **10 min**
COOKING TIME: **1 hour
30 min**

> 1 tbsp. peanut oil
> 1 veal filet weighing 1½ lbs.
> 2 organic oranges
> 1 tbsp. cognac
> 3 tbsp. crème fraîche (or sour cream)
> salt, freshly ground black pepper

In a stovetop-safe casserole dish or a large sauté pan, heat the peanut oil and brown the veal filet for 5 minutes on both sides.

Wash the oranges and remove the zest from one of them; finely chop the zest then juice both of the oranges.

Add the orange juice and the zest to the casserole dish. Cook for 5 minutes while stirring. Add the cognac then light it to flambé it; season with salt and pepper. Cover and simmer for 1½ hours.

If you have prepared this dish in advance, leave the filet in the covered casserole dish to prevent it from drying out; reheat it just before serving.

Just before serving, remove the filet and set it aside. Add the crème fraîche and stir to combine it with the cooking juices. Reduce until the liquid is creamy and somewhat thickened. Meanwhile, slice the filet. Serve very hot with the sauce on the side.

This dish is delicious with fresh pasta or steamed potatoes.

Veal filets with black trumpet mushrooms

FOR 4 PEOPLE
SOAKING: 1 hour
PREPARATION: 20 min
COOKING TIME:
approximately 25 min

> 4¼ oz. dried black trumpet (chanterelle) mushrooms
> 14 oz. fresh green peas (weighed without the pods)
> just over ¾ cup veal broth
> 8 barded veal filets, 3 oz. each (SEE p. 567)
> 3 tbsp. vegetable oil
> 2 sprigs of fresh thyme, leaves removed
> 3 tbsp. butter
> salt, freshly ground black pepper

Add the black trumpet mushrooms to a bowl with 2 cups of cold water and let them soak for 1 hour.

Boil the peas for 5 to 6 minutes in salted water. Drain them then rinse them under cold water.

Add the veal broth to a saucepan along with ½ cup of the water used to soak the mushrooms and reduce the liquid over medium heat; season with salt and pepper. Add the drained mushrooms then keep the mixture hot; do not boil.

Tie the veal filets so that they remain in a tight, rounded shape while cooking; season with salt and pepper. In a large skillet, heat the vegetable oil over high heat and brown the filets on both sides for 1 to 2 minutes. Lower the heat and cook for an additional 5 to 6 minutes on each side. Remove the filets from the skillet and wrap them in a piece of aluminum foil; let rest for 10 minutes.

Pour off the fat from the skillet. Add the mushroom sauce to the skillet along with the thyme leaves. Bring to a boil then add the butter in small pieces while whisking continuously. Just before serving, add the peas to the sauce to reheat them then serve immediately with the veal filets.

In season, use fresh black trumpet (chanterelle) mushrooms (estimating 4¼ ounces per person) or replace them with yellow chanterelle or small porcini mushrooms.

Veal sweetbread fricassee with asparagus and morel mushrooms

FOR 4 PEOPLE

SOAKING: **2 hours**

PREPARATION: **35 min**

COOKING TIME: **30 min**

> 1 oz. dried morel mushrooms
> 2 lbs. veal sweetbreads
> approximately 20 green asparagus
> ¼ cup all-purpose flour
> 6 tbsp. butter
> 1 tbsp. sunflower oil
> 2 cups heavy cream
> salt, freshly ground black pepper

Soak the mushrooms in just over ¾ cup warm water. At the same time, place the sweetbreads in a large container of cold water for 2 hours.

Immerse the sweetbreads for 10 minutes in boiling water; drain, then remove the white outer membrane; thinly slice the sweetbreads and keep them chilled.

Peel the asparagus and cut them off approximately 4 inches from the tips. Boil the tips in salted water for 6 to 8 minutes; they should remain somewhat crisp. Drain then rinse under cold water.

Drain the mushrooms then strain and reserve the soaking liquid. Preheat the oven to the warm setting or the lowest possible temperature.

Dredge the sweetbreads in the flour to lightly coat them. In a large skillet, add the butter with the sunflower oil over medium-high heat. When the butter has melted and begins to foam, add the sweetbreads and fry; season with salt and pepper and cook for 10 minutes over low heat, just until brown. Turn them over and brown them on the other side 5 to 10 minutes, basting them occasionally with the cooking juices. When well-browned and crispy, transfer to a serving plate and place them in the warm oven.

Add the asparagus tips and the morel mushrooms to the hot skillet and cook for 5 minutes. Set them aside to keep warm, along with the sweetbreads.

Add the strained soaking liquid from the mushrooms to the skillet and reduce by half. Add the heavy cream and reduce again by one-third to obtain a slightly thick sauce; season with salt and pepper. Place the sweetbreads and the asparagus and mushrooms on serving plates and top with the sauce; serve immediately.

A hot dish of morel mushrooms and asparagus makes a delicious accompaniment for special-occasion meals.

Veal kidney casserole

FOR 4 PEOPLE
PREPARATION: **15 min**
COOKING TIME:
approximately 15 min

> 2 veal kidneys
> 3 tbsp. butter
> ½ cup calvados (apple brandy) or cognac
> ½ bunch chives
> 1 cup crème fraîche
> 1 tsp. mustard
> salt, freshly ground black pepper

Pull open both of the kidneys and remove the membrane that covers them. Remove any filaments and white fat that remain. Cut each half into two or three pieces.

In a stovetop-safe casserole dish or large sauté pan, melt the butter but do not let it brown. Add the kidney pieces and cook over low heat for 5 to 6 minutes, turning them several times. Add the calvados or cognac, cover, then remove the dish from the heat; let rest for 10 minutes.

Meanwhile, wash and chop the chives.

Transfer the kidneys to a shallow dish; cover with a piece of aluminum foil.

Reduce the sauce by half; season with salt and pepper.

Add the crème fraîche to the casserole dish and boil, while stirring, until thickened.

In a small bowl, combine the mustard with 1 tablespoon of the sauce and add the mixture to the casserole dish. Mix well and spoon over the kidneys. Sprinkle with the chopped chives and serve immediately.

Venison with bacon and red cabbage

FOR 4-6 PEOPLE
MARINADE: 12 hours
PREPARATION: 25 min
COOKING TIME:
approximately 50 min

> 1 venison filet weighing 2¼ lbs.
> 1 small red cabbage
> 6 slices lean, smoked bacon or dry-cured ham such as prosciutto
> just over ¾ cup veal broth
> 5¼ oz. fresh or frozen blueberries
> 9 tbsp. (1 stick + 1 tbsp.) butter
> 3½ oz. raisins
> 2 tbsp. sunflower oil
> salt, freshly ground black pepper

For the marinade
> 1 carrot
> 1 large onion
> 2 garlic cloves
> 2 cups red wine
> 10 black peppercorns
> 2 sprigs of fresh thyme
> 2 bay leaves

The night before: Prepare the marinade. Peel and thinly slice the carrot and the onion. Crush and peel the garlic cloves. In a large bowl, combine the red wine, peppercorns, carrot, onion, thyme, garlic and bay leaves then add the venison filet; let marinate overnight, refrigerated.

The next day: Remove the venison filet from the marinade and let drain. Strain and reserve the marinade liquid.

Thinly slice the red cabbage. Wrap the venison filet in the slices of bacon and tie it with kitchen twine as if trussing a roast.

In a large saucepan, reduce the marinade by three-quarters, add the veal broth then reduce the mixture again by half over low heat. Add the blueberries then mix and lightly crush them into the sauce; season with salt and pepper and keep warm.

Melt 5½ tablespoons of the butter in a saucepan and quickly sauté the cabbage and the raisins over medium-high heat. Lower the heat then season with salt and pepper; cook for 30 minutes, covered.

Preheat the oven to 475° F.

In a large skillet, heat the remaining 3½ tablespoons of butter along with the sunflower oil. When the butter starts to foam, add the venison filet and fry over medium-high heat for 1 or 2 minutes on each side until browned. Transfer the filet to a baking dish, baste it with the butter and oil from the skillet and bake for 20 minutes. When finished, place a piece of aluminum foil over the top and let rest for 5 minutes. Slice it, top with the blueberry sauce, and serve with the cooked red cabbage.

VARIATION You can prepare venison haunch or leg (with or without the bone) in the same way. In this case, increase the cooking time by 15 to 20 minutes.

Chicken in salt crust

FOR 4–6 PEOPLE
PREPARATION: **15 min**
COOKING TIME: **1 hour
30 min**

> 1 chicken weighing 3½ to 4 lbs.
> 2 sprigs of tarragon or 1 sprig of thyme
> 3½ cups (2¼ lbs.) coarse-grained sel de mer (sea salt) or kosher salt
> 9 cups (2¼ lbs.) all-purpose flour

Stuff the chicken with the tarragon or thyme sprigs. In a large bowl, mix the salt with the flour. Add approximately 2 cups of water a little at a time and knead just until a supple and homogenous dough is formed.

Preheat the oven to 450° F.

Roll out the dough to approximately ½ inch thick. Place the chicken in the center of the dough and wrap the dough up around the chicken on all sides to completely seal it inside. Brush water along the border to help adhere the pastry and keep it closed.

Place the wrapped chicken on a half-sheet baking pan lined with parchment paper. Bake for 1½ hours.

Remove the chicken from the oven and break open the hardened dough using a small kitchen mallet. Carefully wipe down the chicken with a paper towel to remove excess moisture then place it on a serving platter. Serve immediately.

You can prepare other types of poultry or fish in this way.

low calorie · recipe ·

1 Do not roll the dough too thinly. To add more flavor, you can incorporate fresh or dried herbs into the dough.

2 Tightly seal the dough around the chicken to prevent it from drying out while cooking.

3 If the crust has become too hard once the cooking is complete, use a small kitchen mallet to break it open.

Quail with grapes

FOR 4 PEOPLE
PREPARATION: **10 min**
COOKING TIME: **25 min**

> 4 quails
> 4 tbsp. butter
> ⅔ cup white wine
> 2 tbsp. freshly-squeezed lemon juice
> 20 to 25 large red grapes
> 1 tbsp. sliced almonds
> salt, freshly ground black pepper

Season the inside of the quails with salt and pepper then truss them.

Heat the butter in a stovetop-safe casserole dish, place the quails in the dish and brown them on all sides. Add the white wine and the lemon juice. Lower the heat, cover, and let simmer for 15 minutes.

Wash and dry the grapes then peel them and remove the seeds. Add them to the casserole dish along with the almonds. Stir and cook for an additional 10 minutes. Serve immediately.

Serve the quails with a cooked grain or roasted sweet potatoes.

Quail with cherries

FOR 4 PEOPLE
PREPARATION: **10 min**
COOKING TIME: **35 min**

> 1 lb. morello cherries
> ⅔ cup sugar
> 1 tbsp. red currant jelly
> 4 barded quails (SEE p. 567)
> 2 tbsp. butter
> 1 tbsp. vegetable oil
> salt, freshly ground black pepper

Remove the stems and the pits from the cherries. Place them in a saucepan with the sugar and ¼ cup of water. Cook for 8 to 10 minutes. Add the red currant jelly and cook for an additional 5 minutes.

Preheat the oven to 400° F.

Place the quails in a baking dish with the butter and the vegetable oil; season with salt and pepper then bake for 15 minutes.

At the end of the cooking time, add the cherries and a little bit of the cherry juice to the baking dish and cook for an additional 2 minutes. Serve the quail surrounded with cherries.

Duck breast with chestnuts and spring onions

FOR 4 PEOPLE
PREPARATION: **15 min**
COOKING TIME: **35 min**

> 1 bunch small spring onions
> ½ bunch chervil
> 2 large (or 3 small) duck breasts
> 3 tbsp. honey (fluid)
> 15 oz. jar of chestnuts
> salt, freshly ground black pepper

Peel the spring onions and remove the green portion. Wash the chervil and tear off the leaves from the stems.

Cut away and wipe off any excess fat from the duck breasts. In a nonstick skillet, cook the breasts skin-side down over high heat for 1 minute, reduce the heat to low, then cook for an additional 5 to 10 minutes, according to the size of the breasts and to melt away nearly all of the fat; the skin must be golden brown and crisp. Season with salt and pepper, increase the heat to medium, then turn the breasts over on the flesh side and cook for 1 to 2 minutes more; season again with salt and pepper. Remove the breasts to drain them of excess fat then cover them with a piece of aluminum foil; let rest while preparing the spring onions and chestnuts.

Pour off most of the fat from the skillet then, using the same skillet but with a little bit of the hot duck fat remaining, cook the spring onions for 30 seconds until they begin to brown; add the honey then lower the heat and cook for an additional 10 to 15 minutes.

Meanwhile, preheat the oven to 300° F.

When the spring onions are cooked and well-caramelized from the honey, add the chestnuts and cook for an additional 5 minutes while stirring; season with salt and pepper.

Reheat the duck breasts, still wrapped in aluminum foil, on a baking sheet by placing them in the hot oven for 2 minutes. Thinly slice the breasts then transfer them to a serving platter surrounded by the cooked spring onions and chestnuts. Sprinkle with chervil and serve immediately.

Serve with a celery root purée.

Duck à l'orange

FOR 4–6 PEOPLE
PREPARATION: **35 min**
COOKING TIME:
**approximately 1 hour
15 min**

> 6 oranges
> 7 oz. kumquats
> 5 tbsp. butter
> 1 cleaned duck weighing
> 4½ lbs.
> ⅔ cup orange liqueur
> 1 tbsp. vinegar
> ⅔ cup veal broth
> 1 heaping tbsp. all-
> purpose flour
> salt, freshly ground
> black pepper

Remove the zest from 2 of the oranges and cut the zest into thin strips. Immerse the zest in boiling water for 5 minutes then drain and set aside.

Peel the remaining 4 oranges, completely removing the white membrane, then slice them. Slice the kumquats into thick rounds.

In a stovetop-safe casserole dish, melt 4 tablespoons of the butter then brown the duck over moderate heat; season with salt and pepper. Cover the dish, lower the heat then simmer for 40 minutes, turning the duck several times.

Add ½ cup of the orange liqueur and cook for an additional 5 minutes.

Remove the duck and let drain then cover with aluminum foil to keep warm.

Juice the zested oranges and add the juice to the casserole dish along with the sliced kumquats, the vinegar, the remaining orange liqueur and the veal broth. Simmer for 10 minutes then strain the sauce and skim off the fat.

On a plate, mix the remaining 1 tablespoon softened butter with the flour just until the flour is absorbed. Stir this mixture into the sauce.

Place the orange slices in a small saucepan along with 4 tablespoons of the sauce. As soon as the mixture begins to boil, remove the orange slices. Pour the liquid into the casserole dish.

Cut up the duck and transfer the pieces to a warmed serving plate. Reserve the juices from the duck that have collected in the aluminum foil and add them to the casserole dish. Reheat then strain the sauce.

Pour several spoonfuls of sauce over the duck then sprinkle on the orange zest and surround the duck with the orange slices. Serve the remaining sauce on the side.

Duck breast with peaches

FOR 4 PEOPLE
PREPARATION: **15 min**
COOKING TIME:

approximately 20 min

> 2 duck breasts, excess
  fat removed
> 4 large, white peaches
> 6 tbsp. butter
> 2 tbsp. powdered sugar
> 1 tsp. powdered (instant)
  chicken bouillon
> ¼ cup white wine
> salt, freshly ground
  black pepper

Using a small paring knife, make small incisions in the skin side of the duck breasts.

Immerse the peaches for 2 minutes in boiling water then rinse them under cold water. Peel them, cut them in half and remove the pits, then cut each half in two.

Heat 2 tablespoons of the butter in a skillet and brown the duck breasts skin-side down for 5 minutes over very high heat. Remove the breasts to allow the fat to drain then pour off the fat from the skillet. Place the duck breasts back in the skillet and season with salt and pepper. Continue to cook over medium heat for 5 minutes on each side.

Remove the breasts from the skillet, slice them, then place them on a warm serving plate.

Melt 2 tablespoons of the butter in the skillet, add the sugar, and cook the peach quarters for 5 to 7 minutes, turning them often. Add them to the plate surrounding the duck slices.

Mix the chicken broth with the white wine then pour this mixture into the skillet. Using a wooden spoon or silicone spatula, scrape the cooked bits of meat off the bottom of the skillet and reduce the liquid by approximately one-third. Off the heat, add the remaining 2 tablespoons of butter, whisking to combine, then spoon the sauce over the duck breasts. Serve very hot.

Warm foie gras with citrus

FOR 4 PEOPLE
PREPARATION: **10 min**
COOKING TIME:
approximately 15 min

> 1 orange
> 1 grapefruit
> 2 tbsp. butter
> 3 tbsp. honey
> ¼ cup floc de Gascogne
> fortified wine
> ½ cup chicken broth
> 1 lb. raw duck foie gras
> salt, freshly ground
> black pepper

Wash the orange and the grapefruit. Cut 4 thin slices from each of them then press the juice from the remaining portion and set aside.

Melt the butter in a skillet and brown the orange and grapefruit slices for 1 minute on each side then add 1 tablespoon of the honey to the skillet. Reduce the heat to low and let the slices lightly caramelize.

Add the remaining 2 tablespoons of honey to a small saucepan and cook to caramelize (it should thicken and turn darker). Add the reserved orange and grapefruit juice and the floc de Gascogne. Reduce for 5 minutes then add the chicken broth and reduce again until the sauce is slightly thickened and smooth; season with salt and pepper and set aside to keep warm.

Wash the foie gras and pat it dry; do not devein it. Cut it into 4 thick slices. Heat a dry skillet. Season the slices of foie gras with salt and pepper and place them in the skillet. Cook for 2 minutes over medium heat, carefully turning them once and cooking for 2 additional minutes on the other side; transfer them to paper towels to drain.

Distribute the foie gras slices and the orange and grapefruit slices among 4 plates and season well with freshly ground black pepper. Top with the sauce and serve immediately.

You can add orange and grapefruit segments into the sauce at the end of the cooking time. In this case, do not boil the sauce at the end.

Guinea fowl in cabbage

FOR 4 PEOPLE
PREPARATION: **30 min**
COOKING TIME:
approximately 1 hour

> 1 small green Savoy cabbage
> 9 oz. smoked bacon
> 1 tbsp. peanut oil
> 1 cleaned guinea fowl weighing 2¼ to 2½ lbs.
> 2 tbsp. butter
> salt, freshly ground black pepper

Cut the cabbage into quarters and discard any large outer leaves. Boil the cabbage for 5 to 6 minutes in salted water; drain.

Cut the bacon into large pieces and place in a stovetop-safe casserole dish then cook over medium heat while stirring; remove to drain.

Add the peanut oil to the casserole dish. Add the guinea fowl and brown it on all sides, turning it several times. Place the bacon back in the dish, add the cabbage quarters then season with pepper. Cover and cook gently for 45 to 50 minutes.

Remove the guinea fowl from the casserole dish, untie it (if trussed), then cut it up.

Remove the bacon pieces and the cabbage to drain, place them on a serving dish and arrange the pieces of guinea fowl on top; set aside to keep warm.

Strain the cooking liquid then add it back to the casserole dish and reduce by approximately one-third over high heat.

Off the heat, whisk in the butter. Taste and adjust the seasoning if needed. Serve the reduced sauce on the side in a gravy dish.

Roasted young turkey with chestnut stuffing

FOR 6 PEOPLE
PREPARATION: **30 min**
COOKING TIME: **1 hour 40 min**

> 1 small turkey weighing 5½ lbs. (preferably a young turkey)
> ¼ cup chicken broth
> 1⅓ lbs. canned or frozen whole chestnuts
> 3 oz. barding fat (SEE p. 567)
> salt, freshly ground black pepper

Clean and prepare the turkey for baking but do not truss it; season the inside with salt and pepper.

Heat the chicken broth in a saucepan and add the chestnuts; cook for 5 minutes.

Preheat the oven to 400° F.

Drain the chestnuts then place them inside the turkey and close up the opening.

Bard the turkey then truss it; season with salt and pepper. Place it in a baking dish with 2 or 3 tablespoons of water. Bake for approximately 50 to 55 minutes (estimating 20 minutes per pound if baked in the oven or 15 minutes per pound if roasting on a spit).

Approximately 15 minutes before the end of the cooking time, remove the barding fat to allow the turkey to brown on all sides; season with salt. Baste the turkey often while it cooks.

Strain the cooking liquid and serve it on the side in a gravy dish. Cut up the turkey and serve it with the chestnuts.

If you have the opportunity to use raw, unshelled chestnuts, you can cook them yourself. Using a paring knife, score the shell in the pattern of an X across the rounded end then immerse them for 10 minutes in boiling water. Peel them while still hot as you remove them in batches from the boiling water using a slotted spoon. Place them in boiling chicken or vegetable broth (just enough to cover them) along with 1 celery stalk and cook for 30 to 40 minutes; drain. You need approximately 2¼ lbs. of fresh chestnuts to obtain 1⅓ lbs. of cooked chestnuts.

Roasted herbed monkfish and cream of celery

FOR 4 PEOPLE
PREPARATION: **25 min**
COOKING TIME:
approximately 30 min

> 14 oz. peeled celery root
> 10½ tbsp. (1 stick + 2½ tbsp.) butter
> ½ cup heavy cream
> 1 bunch chervil
> 1 bunch cilantro
> 4 monkfish fillets, approximately 5½ oz. each
> 1 cup fish broth
> 3 tbsp. olive oil
> salt, freshly ground black pepper

Cut the celery root into medium dice and boil for 20 minutes in salted water, drain, then place in a food processor with 7 tablespoons of the butter and all of the heavy cream. Process for 2 minutes or until smooth and creamy; keep warm.

Wash and chop the chervil and the cilantro.

Cut a deep slit through the thickest part of the monkfish fillets to form a pocket. Place half of the chopped herbs inside the pocket, season with salt and pepper, then close the pocket and tie the fillets by wrapping them in kitchen twine as if tying a roast.

In a small saucepan, reduce the fish broth by half. Add the remaining butter in pieces and boil for 2 minutes. Off the heat, add the remaining herbs and blend the sauce until smooth using an immersion blender.

In a large skillet, heat the olive oil and cook the monkfish fillets over high heat for 1 to 2 minutes. Lower the heat and cook for 6 to 8 minutes, turning them frequently.

Serve the cooked monkfish in bowls with the cream of celery, topped with the herb sauce.

Do not cook the monkfish fillets too long as they may become rubbery.

Salmon en croûte

FOR 6–8 PEOPLE
PREPARATION: **30 min**
REFRIGERATION: **30 min**
COOKING TIME: **45 min**

> 1 whole salmon weighing
  2 to 2¼ lbs.
> 2 eggs
> 14 oz. pre-prepared puff
  pastry
> salt, freshly ground
  black pepper

Scale and clean the salmon (do not remove the head); carefully wash the inside.

Boil 8 cups of water. Place the salmon on a grilling rack and place the rack in a shallow pan. Pour the boiling water over the entire salmon (except the head) and lift off the skin. Turn the salmon over and repeat this step. Carefully pat the salmon dry using paper towels; season the inside with salt and pepper.

Line a baking sheet with parchment paper.

Lightly flour a work surface.

In a small bowl, beat the eggs with a fork. Roll out two-thirds of the puff pastry into a rectangle measuring 14 inches by 5½ inches and approximately ⅛ inch thick.

Place the puff pastry rectangle on the baking sheet then place the salmon on top of the puff pastry; season with salt and pepper. Fold in the edge of the puff pastry by approximately 1 inch all the way around then lightly brush the folded edges with some of the beaten egg.

Roll out the last third of the puff pastry into a rectangle measuring 12 inches by 4 inches and approximately ⅛ inch thick. Place the rectangle over the salmon and press the bottom and top portions of the pastry together to completely encase the salmon (the egg wash on the bottom folded edges will help adhere the pastry together). Trim off any excess pastry all the way around, following the natural shape of the fish. Using the point of a knife, lightly draw the form of the head, the tail and the scales in the pastry; brush the pastry all over with the egg wash.

Place the baking sheet in the refrigerator for 30 minutes.

Preheat the oven to 350° F. Brush the pastry all over again with the egg wash then bake for 45 minutes.

Remove the baking sheet from the oven and let the salmon rest for 10 minutes. Transfer to a serving platter and serve very hot.

Salmon gravlax

FOR 8 PEOPLE
PREPARATION: **15 min**
(beginning 3 days in advance)

> 2 very fresh salmon fillets, each weighing 1 lb.
> 2 bunches of dill
> 4 tbsp. powdered sugar
> 4 tbsp. white pepper
> 4 tbsp. kosher salt

For the sauce
> 1 bunch dill
> 2 tsp. mustard
> 2 tsp. powdered sugar
> 2 tsp. white wine vinegar
> 1 egg yolk
> ½ cup crème fraîche (or sour cream)
> salt, freshly ground black pepper

Three days ahead: Run your fingers in both directions along the flesh of the salmon. If any bones are present, remove them with tweezers. Wash the dill and roughly chop it. In a small bowl, mix the dill with the powdered sugar, the white pepper and the kosher salt.

Line a large plate approximately the size of the fillets with plastic wrap, leaving plenty of overhang along the sides. Place one of the fillets on the plate skin-side down and distribute half of the dill mixture over the top. Place the second fillet skin-side down on a work surface and distribute the remaining dill mixture on top. Place this second fillet skin-side up on top of the first fillet. Wrap the ends of the plastic wrap over the top of the fillets. You can also wrap the fish again in a piece of aluminum foil to keep out odors.

Place a plank on top of the wrapped fillets and add a weight on top to press them (such as a couple of heavy canned goods or a carton of milk). Place in the refrigerator to marinate for 3 days, taking care to turn the entire package over once each day.

The fourth day: Prepare the sauce. Wash and chop the remaining 1 bunch dill. Mix it in a bowl with the rest of the ingredients.

Separate the two salmon fillets and slice them very thinly. Arrange them on a serving plate and serve with the chilled sauce on the side.

Place the whole salmon in the freezer for 2 hours before slicing it. This will make it firmer and easier to slice. Serve with warm steamed potatoes.

make ahead recipe

Salmon koulibiac

FOR 6 PEOPLE
PREPARATION: **40 min**
COOKING TIME:
approximately 1 hour

> ½ cup (3½ oz.) white rice
> 4 eggs
> 3 tbsp. couscous
> 1⅓ lbs. salmon fillets
> ½ cup white wine
> 1 bouquet garni (SEE p. 576)
> 1 tbsp. paprika
> 3 shallots
> 12 oz. white button mushrooms
> 11 tbsp. (1 stick + 3 tbsp.) butter
> 1 lb. pre-prepared puff pastry
> salt, freshly ground black pepper

Rinse the rice and boil it in a large quantity of salted water for 15 minutes. Hard boil three of the eggs.

Spread out the couscous on a shallow plate and pour boiling, salted water over it (the volume of the water should be one and a half times the volume of the couscous, or approximately ¼ cup).

Wash the salmon fillets and pat them dry with paper towels. Boil 6⅓ cups of salted water with the wine, the bouquet garni and the paprika. Add the salmon fillets and lower the heat and simmer gently for 10 minutes. Let the salmon cool in the water then drain.

Chop the shallots and the mushrooms and brown them in a saucepan with ½ tablespoon of the butter; season with salt and pepper.

Peel the boiled eggs and cut them into quarters.

Preheat the oven to 450° F.

Line a baking sheet with parchment paper. Lightly flour a work surface and roll out two-thirds of the puff pastry sheet to a ⅛-inch-thick rectangle. Even up the edges then place it on the baking sheet.

Spread layers of the rice, salmon (crumbled), mushrooms, couscous and the egg quarters onto the puff pastry rectangle, leaving a 1-inch border all the way around.

Fold the edges of the pastry over onto the filling then roll out the remaining portion of the puff pastry sheet and place it on top of the filling. Pinch the edges of the dough closed all the way around to completely seal the filling inside.

Use left over pieces of the puff pastry to create a decorative pattern on top then brush the pastry all over with the remaining egg, beaten lightly with a fork. Bake for 30 minutes. Serve very hot with the remaining butter, melted, served on the side.

Salmon in sorrel

FOR 4 PEOPLE
PREPARATION: 15 min
COOKING TIME:
approximately 10 min

> 3½ oz. sorrel
> 2 shallots
> 4 salmon fillets weighing 4¼ oz. each, cut from the meatiest part of the fish
> ⅓ cup white wine
> ⅓ cup fish broth
> 2 tbsp. vermouth
> 1¼ cups crème fraîche
> juice of ¼ lemon
> salt, freshly ground black pepper

Quickly rinse the sorrel under running water and break off the stems. Peel and chop the shallots.

Place the salmon fillets between two pieces of lightly oiled parchment paper and gently pound them flat using a kitchen mallet or the bottom of a small saucepan. Season only one side of the fillets with salt and pepper.

Pour the white wine, fish broth and vermouth into a saucepan then add the shallots. Reduce the liquid over medium heat just until almost all of the liquid has evaporated.

Add the crème fraîche and boil to obtain a creamy consistency; add the sorrel to the cream. Remove the saucepan from the heat after 2 minutes; season with salt and pepper then add the lemon juice.

While the sauce is reducing, heat a dry nonstick skillet and cook the salmon fillets for 30 seconds on the side without the seasoning then carefully turn the fillets over and cook for 20 seconds.

Divide the sorrel cream sauce among 4 warmed plates and place the salmon fillets on top. Serve immediately.

quick & easy · recipe ·

Poached turbot with hollandaise sauce

FOR 4 PEOPLE
PREPARATION: **20 min**
COOKING TIME:
approximately 30 min

> 1 turbot fish weighing approximately 4½ lbs., head removed, cleaned, scaled and cut into 4 pieces (3 from the back and 1 from the underbelly)
> several sprigs of curly-leaf parsley

For the milk-based court-bouillon

> 1 onion
> 1 garlic clove
> 1 carrot
> 1 bouquet garni (SEE p. 576)
> 2⅓ tsp. (½ oz.) kosher salt
> 4¼ cups milk
> freshly ground black pepper

For the hollandaise sauce

> 18 tbsp. (2 sticks + 2 tbsp.) butter
> 1 tbsp. white wine vinegar
> 1 tsp. lightly crushed white and black peppercorns
> 4 egg yolks
> juice of ½ lemon
> 1 pinch of salt

Rinse each piece of turbot and pat dry with paper towels.

Prepare the court-bouillon. Peel the onion and the garlic clove. Peel the carrot and cut it into rounds. In a large saucepan, add the onion, garlic clove and carrot and the bouquet garni along with 4¼ cups of water, the salt and the milk; season with pepper. Bring the mixture to a boil then simmer gently for 15 minutes, skimming any film from the surface during this time; set aside to cool.

Carefully immerse the pieces of turbot in the cooled court-bouillon. Bring just to a boil and simmer gently for 15 minutes.

Meanwhile, prepare the hollandaise sauce. Cut the butter into small pieces. Prepare a bain-marie by heating water in a saucepan approximately ⅓ full. In a smaller saucepan, heat the vinegar with the crushed peppercorns and boil for several minutes on the stovetop to reduce the liquid somewhat. Add the egg yolks and 1 tablespoon of cold water to the vinegar mixture while whisking gently to emulsify. Place the small saucepan over the larger saucepan of simmering water and whisk continuously. When the mixture has started to thicken, add the butter piece-by-piece while whisking continuously. Taste and adjust the seasoning if needed. Whisk in a little bit of lemon juice and set aside to keep warm.

Carefully remove the pieces of turbot from the court-bouillon using a slotted spoon or spatula. Remove the skin then place the turbot on warm plates. Surround the fish with the sprigs of parsley.

Serve the hollandaise sauce on the side in a warm gravy dish.

Sea bream royale with preserved lemons

quick & easy · recipe ·

FOR 4-6 PEOPLE
PREPARATION: **5 min**
COOKING TIME: **30 min**

> 1 sea bream fish weighing 3½ lbs.
> 5 tbsp. olive oil
> 15 slices of salt-preserved (pickled) lemons
> 1 tbsp. coriander seeds
> juice of 1 or 2 lemons (for 2 tbsp. juice)
> salt, freshly ground black pepper

Scale and clean the sea bream. Using a knife, make shallow X-shaped incisions across the back.

Preheat the oven to 450° F. Lightly oil a baking dish using 1 tablespoon of the olive oil and line the bottom with 9 slices of the salt-preserved lemons. Place the sea bream on top and season with salt and pepper; sprinkle the coriander seeds over the top.

Place the remaining 6 slices of salt-preserved lemons on top of the sea bream and drizzle on 2 tablespoons of lemon juice and the remaining 4 tablespoons of olive oil.

Bake for 30 minutes, basting with the cooking juices several times.

Monkfish medallions with mango

FOR 4 PEOPLE
PREPARATION: **15 min**
COOKING TIME: **6-8 min**

> 4 monkfish medallions, approximately 7 oz. each
> 1 mango
> juice of 1 lime
> 1 tsp. olive oil
> ½ cup (3½ oz.) crème fraîche
> 1 pinch Cayenne pepper
> salt, freshly ground black pepper

Rinse the monkfish medallions and pat them dry with paper towels; season with salt and pepper. Peel the mango, cut off the flesh from around the pit and cut it into medium dice; drizzle it with some of the lime juice.

Heat a skillet lightly coated with oil over medium heat. Cook the monkfish medallions 3 to 4 minutes on each side, according to the thickness, turning them carefully with a spatula.

Meanwhile, using a standing or immersion blender, blend the mango with the remaining lime juice and the crème fraîche. Add the Cayenne pepper then season with salt and pepper. Pour this mixture into a small saucepan and heat gently while stirring.

Spoon a little bit of the mango sauce onto 4 warmed serving plates and place a monkfish medallion on top of the sauce. Serve the remaining mango sauce in a warmed gravy dish. Serve immediately.

quick & easy · recipe ·

Scallop and leek beggar's purse

FOR 4 PEOPLE
PREPARATION: **20 min**
COOKING TIME:
approximately **20 min**

> 2 small leeks
> 4 tbsp. butter
> 2 tbsp. olive oil
> 12 or 16 cleaned scallops (without the roe)
> 4 buckwheat or plain wheat crêpes
> 2 sprigs of thyme
> salt, freshly ground black pepper

Cut off the rough ends of the green section of each leek as well as the beard from the root end and discard; remove any rough outer leaves. Julienne the leeks then rinse them well to remove any sediment. Heat 2 tablespoons of the butter in a skillet and cook the leeks for 6 to 8 minutes until softened.

In a second skillet, heat the olive oil and cook the scallops quickly over high heat for 1 minute on each side.

Preheat the oven to 350° F and line a baking sheet with parchment paper.

Divide the cooked leeks among the crêpes, placing them in the center. Add 3 or 4 scallops on top. Sprinkle with thyme leaves, season with salt and pepper, then place a small piece of the remaining butter in each crêpe.

Carefully fold up each crêpe into a purse shape or simply fold them over the filling, using toothpicks to keep them closed. Place the crêpe purses on the baking sheet and bake for 6 to 8 minutes.

VARIATION You can add julienned fresh truffle on top of the leeks after they are cooked.

1 Cut the leeks into a very fine julienne.

2 To make closing the purses easier, fold the crêpes in from the left and right sides toward the center to give them an elongated shape.

3 To keep the purses closed, lift up the ends and gather them carefully toward the center and pierce with a toothpick.

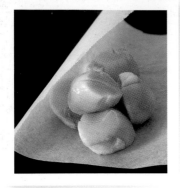

Scallop and leek crumble

FOR 6 PEOPLE
PREPARATION: **15 min**
COOKING TIME: **55 min**

> 20 fresh or frozen cleaned scallops
> 1 tbsp. olive oil
> 1 lb. leeks (white part only)
> 2 onions
> 2 tbsp. butter
> 1 bunch chives
> juice of 1 lemon
> 1 cup crème fraîche
> salt, freshly ground black pepper

For the crumble topping

> 3 tbsp. softened butter
> 2 oz. grated, aged mimolette cheese
> 1 oz. grated parmesan cheese
> 1 cup (3½ oz.) all-purpose flour

Thaw the scallops if frozen. In a skillet, heat the olive oil and cook the scallops quickly over high heat for approximately 5 minutes without letting them brown; set aside.

Thoroughly wash the leeks to remove any sediment between the leaves and cut them into rounds. Peel and thinly slice the onions. In a skillet, heat the butter, add the leeks and the onions and cook for 10 minutes over medium heat, stirring occasionally.

Preheat the oven to 300° F.

Wash and chop the chives. Place the sautéed leeks and onions in a baking dish or in individual baking dishes (4 or 5 inches in diameter). Add the scallops and season with salt and pepper. In a small bowl, mix the lemon juice with the chopped chives and the crème fraîche; pour this mixture on top of the scallops.

Prepare the crumble topping. Using your fingertips, mix the butter, mimolette, parmesan and flour just until the mixture comes together and has a sandy texture. Sprinkle this mixture over the scallops.

Bake for 40 minutes. Serve hot in the baking dish.

This dish is sufficient served alone, but you can add a side of plain rice for a heartier meal.

Mussels with saffron

FOR 4-6 PEOPLE
PREPARATION: 1 hour
COOKING TIME:
approximately 20 min

> 6½ to 7½ lbs. mussels
> 1 cup white wine
> 8 garlic cloves
> 10½ tbsp. (1 stick + 2½ tbsp.) butter
> 1 dozen sprigs of parsley
> several saffron strands or 1 pinch ground saffron
> just over ¾ cup crème fraîche
> 1 tsp. cornstarch

Carefully clean and wash the mussels. Place them in a large Dutch oven and add the white wine. Cook over high heat until the mussels have opened, approximately 5 to 10 minutes, stirring often or shaking the pan from time to time. Remove the mussels to drain, reserving the cooking liquid. Remove any empty shells and place the mussels on the half shell on a serving plate; keep warm.

Peel and chop the garlic cloves. Cut the butter into small pieces. Wash and chop the parsley to obtain 2 tablespoons.

Strain the cooking liquid through a strainer lined with a paper towel. Heat the liquid in a saucepan but do not let it boil. Add the garlic and the parsley, followed by the butter, stirring well with a silicone spatula or wooden spoon, then add the saffron. When the butter has melted, add the crème fraîche.

Increase the heat and bring to a gentle boil. Dissolve the cornstarch in a little cold water then add this to the saucepan while continuing to stir. Pour the saffron sauce over the mussels, mix gently, then serve immediately.

VARIATION You can replace the saffron with 1 teaspoon of curry powder and the cornstarch and water mixture with 1 egg yolk mixed with cream, added off the heat.

Crab and potato stacks with caraway

FOR 4 PEOPLE
PREPARATION: **20 min**
COOKING TIME:

approximately 35 min

> 14 oz. potatoes
> ⅔ cup milk
> 3 tbsp. butter
> 1 tbsp. crème fraîche (or sour cream)
> 1 tbsp. caraway seeds
> 1 large bunch of mixed herbs (chervil, chives, tarragon, parsley)
> 10½ oz. crab meat
> 3 tbsp. olive oil
> ¼ cup (1 oz.) bread crumbs
> balsamic vinegar and olive oil to season the herbs
> salt, freshly ground black pepper

Peel the potatoes and chop them then boil them in salted water for 20 minutes. Drain, then process through a potato ricer or food mill (using the fine-mesh plate).

Heat the milk in a saucepan with 2 tablespoons of the butter then pour this mixture over the potatoes. Add the crème fraîche and the caraway seeds and season with salt and pepper. Stir until creamy and slightly thick.

Wash and chop the mixed herbs. Crumble the crab meat in a skillet set over high heat, add the olive oil and cook for 3 to 4 minutes. Off the heat, add half the chopped herbs then season with salt and pepper.

Preheat the oven to 350° F.

Place 4 pastry rings (or cookie cutters) approximately 3 to 3½ inches in diameter on a baking sheet lined with parchment paper. Grease them with the remaining butter and fill them three-quarters full of the potato purée. Add a layer of crab meat to each ring then top them with the remaining potato purée. Sprinkle the top with the bread crumbs and add several small pieces of butter on top. Bake for 10 to 15 minutes until the the tops are nicely browned.

Just before the end of the cooking time, toss the remaining chopped herbs with a little bit of olive oil and balsamic vinegar. Remove the crab stacks from the oven and transfer them, using a spatula, onto serving plates. Carefully lift off the metal rings, running a thin knife blade around the edges between the cakes and the rings to loosen them. Arrange a few herbs on top and serve immediately.

For this recipe, do not use canned crab meat, which is too crumbly. You can find high-quality frozen crab meat in large pieces with both the flesh and the leg meat combined.

Seafood and leek gratin

FOR 4 PEOPLE
PREPARATION: **30 min**
COOKING TIME:

approximately 40 min

> 3 ½ tbsp. butter
> ½ cup (2 oz.) all-purpose flour
> 1 ¼ cups milk
> ⅔ cup fish broth
> 1 large leek
> 3 tbsp. olive oil
> 1 ¾ lbs. frozen mixed seafood
> 1 ¾ oz. grated emmental cheese
> ½ cup (2 oz.) bread crumbs
> salt, freshly ground black pepper

Melt 2 tablespoons of the butter in a saucepan. Add the flour and cook for 2 minutes over medium heat then pour in the milk. Bring to a boil and boil for 5 minutes while whisking to create a thick béchamel sauce. Add the fish broth, whisk to combine, then season with salt and pepper.

Cut off the beard from the root end of the leek as well as any rough green portion. Thoroughly wash the leek between the leaves then thinly slice it. In a saucepan, melt the remaining 1½ tablespoons of butter and sauté the leek for 8 to 10 minutes until soft; season with salt and pepper.

Preheat the oven to 400° F.

In a large skillet, heat the olive oil and cook the seafood (still frozen) over high heat for 1 to 2 minutes. Season with salt and pepper and cook for an additional 6 to 8 minutes over high heat then strain.

Stir the cooked seafood into the béchamel sauce. Place a little bit of the cooked leeks on the bottom of each of four individual baking dishes or ramekins (4 or 5 inches in diameter) and add the seafood béchamel sauce on top. Sprinkle the top with the grated emmental then the bread crumbs. Bake for 15 to 20 minutes until the cheese is melted and bubbly and the bread crumbs golden brown. Serve immediately.

If you use fresh seafood for this dish (cockles, mussels, shrimp, calamari), combine them with the béchamel sauce using the liquid from the mussels or cockles in place of the fish broth.

Flavors from afar

Chili con carne

make ahead recipe

FOR 6-8 PEOPLE
PREPARATION: 15 min
COOKING TIME: 2½ hours
30 min

> 4 large onions
> 3 garlic cloves
> 3⅓ lbs. top round of beef, in chunks or slices
> 4 tbsp. corn oil or peanut oil
> 3 tsp. chili powder
> 1 tsp. cumin seeds
> 1 tsp. dried oregano
> Tabasco sauce
> 2 cups beef broth
> 14 oz. canned, peeled tomatoes
> 2 cans plain red kidney beans (approximately 1¾ lbs.)
> 3½ oz. cheddar cheese
> salt, freshly ground black pepper

Peel and chop 2 of the onions and all of the garlic cloves. Chop the beef into either very small dice or into large pieces, according to your preference.

Heat the oil in a large stovetop-safe casserole dish or large sauté pan and brown the chopped onions and garlic. After 10 minutes, add the meat and cook uncovered for 5 or 6 minutes while stirring. Add the chili powder, cumin, oregano, and several drops of Tabasco sauce; season with salt and pepper. Stir well to combine then reduce the heat to low and add the beef broth and stir.

Drain the tomatoes and add them to the casserole dish. Mix well and simmer, covered, between 1 hour and 1 hour 10 minutes.

Drain the red kidney beans and add them to the casserole dish and cook for an additional 1 hour.

Peel and finely chop the remaining 2 onions and place them in a small serving bowl. Grate the cheddar and place it in a separate serving bowl.

Serve the chili very hot with the onions and grated cheddar on the side as a garnish.

Mexican fajitas

FOR 4 PEOPLE
PREPARATION: **20 min**
COOKING TIME:
approximately 35 min

For the tortillas
> 1¾ cups (7 oz.) all-
  purpose flour
> 1½ tsp. baking powder
> ½ cup vegetable oil +
  3 tbsp. for frying

For the topping
> 1 onion
> 2 garlic cloves
> 1 red chile pepper
> 1 red or yellow bell
  pepper
> 2 tbsp. vegetable oil
> 14 oz. ground beef
> 1 tsp. ground Cayenne
  pepper
> 1 tsp. ground cumin
> ½ cup tomato sauce
  or canned, crushed
  tomatoes
> salt, freshly ground
  black pepper

Prepare the tortillas. In a large bowl, mix the flour with the baking powder, the ½ cup vegetable oil, just over ¾ cup of warm water and salt. Mix into a smooth dough then divide the dough into 8 equal portions and roll each one into a thin circle approximately 6 to 8 inches in diameter.

Heat the remaining 3 tablespoons of vegetable oil in a skillet and cook each tortilla for 1 to 2 minutes on both sides.

Prepare the toppings. Peel and chop the onion and garlic cloves. Chop the chile pepper then wash the bell pepper and cut it in half. Remove the seeds and the white membrane then slice it into thin strips.

Heat the 2 tablespoons of vegetable oil in a skillet and cook the bell pepper strips for 3 minutes. Add the ground beef, onion, garlic and chile pepper. Cook for 10 minutes over high heat while stirring. Add the Cayenne pepper, cumin, and tomato sauce; season with salt and pepper and cook for an additional 10 minutes over medium heat.

Just before serving, add the toppings on top of each tortilla then roll them carefully and serve immediately.

VARIATION Replace the beef with chicken or top the tortillas with only grilled, spiced vegetables for a vegetarian option.

Harira

FOR 4 PEOPLE
SOAKING : **12 hours**
PREPARATION: **30 min**
COOKING TIME:
1½ hours

> 4¼ oz. dried chickpeas
  (garbanzo beans)
> 2 large potatoes
> 2 large carrots
> 1 celery stalk
> 1 onion
> 2 garlic cloves
> 12 oz. beef for boiling
  (any cut)
> 3 tbsp. vegetable oil
> 1 tsp. turmeric
> 1 tbsp. harissa paste
  (or hot chile sauce)
> 8 cups beef broth
> 2 tomatoes
> ½ cup (3 oz.) long-grain
  white rice
> salt, freshly ground
  black pepper

The day before: Soak the chickpeas for 12 hours in a bowl of cold water.

The next day: Peel the potatoes and carrots then dice them. Thinly slice the celery stalk then peel and chop the onion and garlic cloves. Cut up the meat into small pieces.

Heat the vegetable oil in a large saucepan and cook the meat along with the onions and garlic over high heat for 2 to 3 minutes. Add the turmeric and the harissa paste and cook for 2 additional minutes. Pour in the beef broth then add the chickpeas and the vegetables and season with salt and pepper. Cook for 1 hour over medium heat.

Chop the tomatoes. Add them to the saucepan along with the rice and cook for an additional 30 minutes. Serve very hot with pieces of bread.

VARIATION Replace the rice with red lentils, which cook very quickly. If you are short on time, use canned chickpeas. To make the soup thicker, you can use a little bit of potato starch dissolved in a little cold water and added at the end of the cooking time.

make ahead recipe

Marinated lamb chops, tomatoes stuffed with couscous and preserved lemon

FOR 4 PEOPLE
PREPARATION: **35 min**
MARINADE: **1 hour**
COOKING TIME:
approximately 20 min

> 1 bunch cilantro
> 12 lamb loin chops
> 3 tbsp. olive oil
> 2 tbsp. curry powder

For the tomato filling
> approximately ½ cup (2½ oz.) couscous
> 1 salt-preserved (pickled) lemon
> 4 tomatoes
> 1 tbsp. olive oil
> 2 level tsp. curry powder
> salt, freshly ground black pepper

Wash and coarsely chop the cilantro. Marinate the lamb chops in the olive oil, cilantro and the curry powder for 1 hour.

Meanwhile, prepare the stuffed tomatoes. Place the couscous in a large bowl then add warm water to approximately ½ inch above the top of the couscous and let soak for 15 to 20 minutes.

Remove the zest from the perserved lemon and finely chop it. Wash the tomatoes and slice off the top portion near the stem end. Hollow out each tomato using a spoon, removing all of the seeds.

Preheat the oven to 350° F.

When the couscous has absorbed the water, season it with salt and pepper then stir in the olive oil, curry powder and the chopped lemon zest.

Stuff each tomato with the couscous mixture then place them in a lightly oiled baking dish and replace the tops. Bake for 20 minutes.

Meanwhile, thread 3 lamb chops onto each of four wooden or metal skewers. Cook them over high heat for 5 minutes on each side either in a skillet, on a grill or under the broiler.

When the tomatoes are finished, serve them immediately with the lamb skewers.

VARIATION Prepare a seafood version of this dish using prawns.

Moussaka

FOR 4–6 PEOPLE
PREPARATION: **30 min**
COOKING TIME: **1 hour
40 min**

> 5 eggplants
> 2 cups olive oil
> 1 lb. tomatoes
> 1 garlic clove
> 1 onion
> 2 sprigs of thyme
> 1 bay leaf
> 1 tsp. sugar
> 10 mint leaves
> 10 sprigs of parsley
> 1⅔ lbs. ground beef
> salt, freshly ground
   black pepper

Slice the eggplants lengthwise into long, flat strips. Add 1¼ cups of the olive oil to a skillet and fry the eggplants until browned. Transfer them to paper towels and let them drain for 30 minutes while preparing the tomato sauce, changing the paper towels two or three times.

Meanwhile, immerse the tomatoes in boiling water for 20 seconds, then immediately put them in cold water. Peel them then coarsely chop them. Peel and crush the garlic clove then peel and chop the onion. In a skillet, heat 2 tablespoons of the olive oil and brown the onion for 2 to 3 minutes over medium heat. Add the chopped tomatoes, the garlic, the thyme and the bay leaf then season with salt and pepper and add the sugar. Mix well then cook for 20 to 35 minutes over gentle heat just until the sauce has thickened and come together.

Wash and chop the mint and parsley.

In a bowl, mix the ground beef, tomato sauce, mint, parsley and the remaining olive oil (reserve 2 tablespoons of the olive oil for the baking dish); season with salt and pepper.

Preheat the oven to 350° F.

Lightly oil a baking dish with the reserved 2 tablespoons of olive oil and line it with the eggplant slices, then continue by adding alternating layers of the ground beef mixture and the eggplant, ending with a layer of the beef mixture on top.

Place the baking dish in a larger stovetop-safe baking dish or roasting pan filled with water (the water should only go halfway up the sides of the smaller baking dish) to make a bain-marie. Set on the stovetop and bring to a boil. Place the baking dish still in the bain-marie in the oven and bake for 1 hour.

Turn off the oven and prop open the door; let the moussaka sit in the oven for 15 minutes. Unmold the moussaka from the baking dish and serve.

Moroccan beef keftas

FOR 4 PEOPLE
PREPARATION: **20 min**
COOKING TIME: **10 min**

> 1 red onion
> 5½ oz. feta cheese
> 14 oz. ground beef
> 2 tbsp. cumin seeds
> 1 tsp. ground cumin
> 2 tbsp. all-purpose flour
> 3 tbsp. peanut oil or rapeseed oil
> salt, freshly ground black pepper

Peel and finely chop the onion. Cut the feta into small pieces. In a large bowl, mix the ground beef with the onion, cumin seeds, ground cumin and feta; season with salt and pepper.

Using your hands, form the kefta mixture around small wooden skewers then roll them in the flour.

In a skillet, heat the peanut or rapeseed oil and cook the skewers for 8 to 10 minutes, turning them often. Transfer them to paper towels to drain. Serve immediately with a green salad.

VARIATION Replace the beef with veal. In this case, add an additional 1 tablespoon of flour to the kefta mixture.

Stir-fried spicy beef with vegetable and noodle sauté

FOR 4 PEOPLE
PREPARATION: **30 min**
MARINADE: **3 hours**
COOKING TIME: **15 min**

> 1½ lbs. skirt steak
> 9 oz. chinese noodles
> 2 carrots
> 1 zucchini
> 3 tbsp. olive oil
> 3 tbsp. peanut oil or rapeseed oil
> salt, freshly ground black pepper

For the marinade
> ½ cup Asian chile sauce
> 2 tbsp. oyster sauce
> 3 tbsp. strong soy sauce
> 1 red chile pepper, minced

Cut up the skirt steak and place it in a large bowl.

Prepare the marinade. In a small bowl, mix the chile sauce, oyster sauce, soy sauce, minced chile pepper and some freshly ground black pepper. Pour the marinade over the steak and mix to coat the meat completely. Cover the bowl with plastic wrap and refrigerate for 3 hours.

Boil the noodles in a large amount of salted water for 2 minutes; drain, then rinse them under cold water.

Peel the carrots and wash the zucchini. Cut both the carrots and the zucchini into thin strips. In a large skillet, heat the olive oil and cook the carrot and zucchini strips for 3 to 4 minutes. Add the noodles and sauté over high heat while stirring.

Drain the marinated steak, reserving the marinade liquid. Heat the peanut oil in a wok and sear the steak for 1 minute on each side.

Add approximately ⅓ cup of water to the marinade. When the meat is seared, pour the marinade into the wok and cook for 3 to 4 minutes over high heat while stirring.

Serve immediately with the sautéed noodles and vegetables.

You can add 2 tablespoons golden sesame seeds browned in the wok at the end of the cooking time. You can also add 3½ ounces soy bean sprouts to the sautéed noodles.

The ingredients that make up the marinade in this dish are easily found in the International foods section of most supermarkets.

Stir-fried pork in coconut milk

FOR 4 PEOPLE
PREPARATION: **10 min**
COOKING TIME: **20 min**

> 2 onions
> 2 garlic cloves
> 1 lb. pork (filet or shoulder)
> 2 tbsp. peanut oil
> 2 tsp. curry powder
> 1 pinch ground red pepper
> 1 tsp. ground ginger
> just over ¾ cup coconut milk
> ½ cup (4½ oz.) extra-creamy plain yogurt or ½ cup crème fraîche
> salt, freshly ground black pepper

Peel and finely slice the onions and the garlic cloves. Cut the pork into strips.

Heat the peanut oil in a wok and cook the onion and the pork strips over high heat until the meat is well-browned. Sprinkle the curry powder, ground red pepper and ground ginger into the wok then add the garlic cloves.

Pour in the coconut milk and add the yogurt then season with salt and pepper. Simmer over gentle heat for 15 minutes. Serve very hot.

As a side dish, serve rice noodles or minced chinese cabbage briefly sautéed over high heat.

quick & easy · recipe ·

Caribbean pork

FOR 6 PEOPLE
PREPARATION: **20 min**
MARINADE: **30 min**
COOKING TIME: **55 min**

> 2 ½ lbs. pork loin
> 2 spring onions
> 1 green mango
> 3 medium eggplants
> 3 potatoes
> 3 tbsp. peanut oil
> 3 tbsp. colombo spice
>   blend (Caribbean curry
>   powder)
> juice of 1 lemon

For the marinade
> 2 garlic cloves
> 1 small chile pepper
> 3 tbsp. vinegar
> salt, freshly ground
>   black pepper

Prepare the marinade. Peel and crush the garlic cloves or finely chop them. Mince the chile pepper. Mix the garlic and the chile pepper in a shallow dish with the vinegar then season with salt and pepper.

Cut up the meat into medium dice and place it in the marinade, stirring well to ensure it is completely coated; marinate for 30 minutes.

Meanwhile, peel the spring onions and thinly slice them. Peel the mango then cut it in half to remove the pit; dice the flesh. Peel the eggplants and the potatoes, rinse, then dice them.

In a stovetop-safe casserole dish or large sauté pan, heat the peanut oil over medium heat. Remove the pork and let some of the marinade drain from it. Add the pork to the casserole dish along with the diced mango and the sliced onions. Gently cook for approximately 5 minutes while stirring, until the ingredients are browned.

Mix the colombo spice blend with a little bit of water then pour it into the casserole dish. Add the eggplants and the potatoes; season with salt and pepper and mix. Add just enough water to cover the contents then bring to a boil. Lower the heat and cook, covered, for 50 minutes.

Approximately 5 minutes before the end of the cooking time, add the lemon juice. Taste, adjust the seasoning as needed, then transfer to a serving dish.

Serve very hot with creole rice (SEE p. 400).

Crispy pork spring rolls

**FOR 4 PEOPLE
(APPROXIMATELY 16
SPRING ROLLS)
PREPARATION: 40 min
COOKING TIME: 10 min**

> 3 oz. dried Chinese
  black mushrooms
> ½ cup (1¾ oz.) vermicelli
  rice noodles
> 2 onions
> 3 garlic cloves
> 1 carrot
> 1½ lbs. ground pork
> 2 eggs + 1 egg white
> 3 tbsp. nuoc-mâm sauce
  (Vietnamese fish sauce)
  plus more for dipping
> 16 spring roll wrappers
  or rice paper wrappers
> vegetable oil, for frying
> lettuce leaves for
  serving
> salt, freshly ground
  black pepper

Place the dried mushrooms and vermicelli rice noodles in a bowl and pour boiling water over them. Let soak for 15 minutes to reconsitute.

Peel and chop the onions and the garlic cloves.

Drain the mushrooms and the vermicelli then chop them into large pieces or cut them up using scissors. Peel and finely grate the carrot.

In a large bowl, mix the ground pork with the 2 eggs, mushrooms, vermicelli, carrot, onions, garlic, and the nuoc-mâm sauce; season with salt and pepper.

Lay out the spring roll wrappers. Spoon a small portion of the pork filling in the center of each wrapper then fold the wrapper in over the filling from the left and right sides. Roll it up tightly starting from the bottom end. Lightly beat the egg white and use it to brush the seam of the roll to seal it closed. Complete the remainder of the spring rolls in this way.

Place enough vegetable oil in a heavy-bottomed saucepan to cover the spring rolls; heat the oil to 350° F. Immerse the spring rolls in the oil and fry them until golden brown and crispy. Transfer to paper towels to drain briefly then serve immediately on lettuce leaves. Serve the nuoc-mâm sauce on the side mixed with a little sugar and salt and topped with a few grated carrots.

You can prepare the spring rolls in advance. Once fried, set them on paper towels to drain, then just before serving reheat them for several minutes in a very hot oven.

make ahead · recipe

Five-spice pork shoulder

FOR 4–6 PEOPLE
PREPARATION: **5 min**
COOKING TIME:
approximately 1 hour

> 3 garlic cloves
> 4 shallots
> 1 tbsp. powdered sugar
> 1 tbsp. nuoc-mâm sauce (Vietnamese fish sauce)
> 1 tbsp. soy sauce
> 1 tbsp. Chinese five-spice powder
> 1 roast pork shoulder weighing 2¼ lbs.
> just over ¾ cup white broth (such as chicken, veal or vegetable broth)
> salt, freshly ground black pepper

Peel and chop the garlic cloves and the shallots. Crush them in a mortar bowl (or use a blender) along with the powdered sugar, nuoc-mâm sauce, soy sauce, Chinese five-spice powder and freshly ground black pepper (approximately 3 turns of a pepper mill).

In a stovetop-safe casserole dish, add the pork shoulder with the rind still attached and brown for 10 minutes; add the mixed spices.

Pour in the white broth, cover, and cook for 50 minutes over gentle heat, turning the pork over halfway through the cooking time.

Just before removing the pork shoulder, roll it over several times in the casserole dish to coat it in the cooking juices. Remove it from the dish then slice it and place it on a serving platter; drizzle with more of the cooking juices.

Serve with chinese noodles or with mango pan-fried with shallot and coconut milk.

Lamb couscous with carrots and raisins

FOR 4 PEOPLE
PREPARATION: **15 min**
COOKING TIME:

approximately 3 hours

> 1 onion
> 1 garlic clove
> 14 oz. carrots
> 3 tbsp. olive oil
> 2¼ lbs. lamb's shoulder, boned
> ½ cup port wine
> 6⅓ cups veal broth
> 2 sprigs of thyme
> 1 sprig of rosemary
> approximately 1½ cups (9 oz.) couscous
> 4¼ oz. raisins
> salt, freshly ground black pepper

Peel and thinly slice the onion and the garlic clove. Peel the carrots and cut them into sections. In a stovetop-safe casserole dish, heat the olive oil over high heat then sear the lamb shoulder. Add the sliced onion and garlic and cook for 5 minutes then add the port. Season with salt and pepper, boil for 5 minutes, and add the veal broth followed by the carrots, thyme and rosemary.

Cover the dish and cook for 2 hours 30 minutes over low heat, turning the lamb shoulder frequently until cooked all the way around. Add a little water from time to time to keep the meat covered well with liquid.

Remove the casserole dish from the heat and let the lamb cool while still in the cooking liquid. Remove the lamb and the carrots from the dish and shred the lamb into pieces; reserve the cooking liquid.

In a bowl, pour approximately ½ cup cold, salted water over the couscous and let soak for 5 minutes. Add the couscous to a pressure cooker and cook for 5 to 8 minutes once the valve begins to rotate. Remove the couscous then use a fork to fluff it and break up any lumps.

Reheat the cooking liquid and add the raisins and cook over gentle heat for 10 minutes. Add the lamb pieces and the carrots back to the dish to gently reheat them. Remove the lamb to drain then take out the carrots and raisins and place them on a serving platter. Spoon the couscous next to the lamb and vegetables and serve along with the cooking liquid on the side in a gravy dish.

make ahead recipe

You can make the couscous in advance. In a bowl, mix the couscous with 3 tablespoons of olive oil and a little salt. Pour boiling water just up to the level of the couscous and cover the bowl with a towel and let soak. Quickly reheat it in the microwave just before serving.

Lamb tagine with lemon and olive

FOR 8 PEOPLE
PREPARATION: **20 min**
COOKING TIME: **2 hours**

> 1 large onion
> 2 garlic cloves
> 1¾ lbs. lamb saddle (or loin)
> 2 salt-preserved (pickled) lemons
> 2 tbsp. olive oil
> 1 tsp. ground turmeric
> 1 tsp. ground coriander
> 1 tsp. coriander seeds
> 1 pinch ground cinnamon
> 1 tsp. quatre-épices (or allspice)
> 1¼ cups chicken broth
> 1 bunch cilantro
> 1 small can (approximately 2 to 3 oz.) green olives
> salt, freshly ground black pepper

Peel and chop the onion then peel and crush the garlic cloves. Cut up the lamb into large dice. Cut the lemons into quarters and remove the seeds.

Heat the olive oil in the base of a tagine dish or in a sauté pan. Add the onion and the crushed garlic and cook over gentle heat (they should not brown). Add the lamb, turmeric, ground coriander, corinader seeds, cinnamon, quatre-épices, the chicken broth and the quartered lemons; season with salt and pepper. Place the top on the tagine dish (or place the lid on the sauté pan) and cook over low heat for 2 hours.

Wash and chop the cilantro.

Approximately 10 minutes before the end of the cooking time, add the green olives to heat them. Scatter the chopped cilantro over the top and serve.

Serve this with couscous with dried currants. Prepare the couscous in advance and reheat it in the microwave just before serving.

Lamb curry

FOR 4-6 PEOPLE
MACERATION: 1 hour
PREPARATION: 40 min
COOKING TIME: 40 min

> 1 tbsp. grated fresh ginger
> 1 pinch saffron
> 5 tbsp. peanut oil
> 1 large pinch Cayenne pepper
> 3⅓ lbs. lamb collar or shoulder, cut into pieces
> 3 large tomatoes
> 4 large onions
> 3 garlic cloves
> 1 tbsp. curry powder
> 1 bouquet garni (SEE p. 576)
> 1 granny smith apple
> ⅔ cup coconut milk
> 1⅔ cups (10½ oz.) basmati or thai jasmine rice
> 2 or 3 slices fresh (or canned) pineapple
> 1 banana
> juice of ½ lemon
> ⅓ cup (2 oz.) cashews
> 3 tbsp. (1 oz.) golden raisins
> salt, freshly ground black pepper

Mix together the grated fresh ginger, saffron, 2 tablespoons of the peanut oil, and the Cayenne pepper then season with salt and pepper. Roll the pieces of lamb in the mixture and let macerate for 1 hour.

Blanch the tomatoes by immersing them in boiling water for 20 seconds, then immediately put them in cold water; peel and chop them. Peel and slice the onions into rounds then peel and chop the garlic cloves.

In a stovetop-safe casserole dish, heat the remaining peanut oil and brown the lamb; remove and set aside. Add the onions and cook for 5 minutes, then add the tomatoes, the curry powder, the garlic and the bouquet garni.

Peel and grate the apple then add it to the casserole dish and cook, while stirring, for 2 to 3 minutes. Place the lamb back in the dish, stir, then add the coconut milk. Cover and simmer for 40 minutes.

While the curry is cooking, wash the rice several times then drain it and add it to a saucepan. Season with salt then cover it with three times its volume in water (approximately 5 cups). Cook at a rolling boil, uncovered. When the level of the water is no longer above the rice, cover the pan and cook on low heat, just until all of the water is evaporated but the rice remains moist.

Taste and adjust the seasoning. Cut the pineapple slices into small dice. Slice the banana into rounds and toss it with the lemon juice. Serve the lamb curry with the rice and place the cashews, raisins, the diced pineapple and the banana in small serving bowls so that each person can add to the dish as desired.

Vegetable chop suey

FOR 6 PEOPLE
PREPARATION: **30 min**
COOKING TIME:
approximately 8 min

> 4 small carrots
> 3 small zucchini
> 3 small leeks
> 1 green bell pepper
> 2 tbsp. peanut oil
> ½ bunch small spring onions
> 5¼ oz. mung bean sprouts ("soy bean sprouts")
> 1 garlic clove
> 2 tomatoes
> 1 tbsp. soy sauce
> 1 tsp. sesame oil
> salt, freshly ground black pepper

Peel and wash the carrots, zucchini, leeks and green bell pepper then cut each into thin strips.

Heat the peanut oil in a frying pan then add the vegetables and stir. Cover and let steam over gentle heat for 4 to 5 minutes.

Cut the onion greens into short, thin strips and chop the onion bulbs.

Blanch the bean sprouts by immersing them in boiling water for 20 seconds. Immediately put them in cold water then drain them. Peel and chop the garlic clove.

Immerse the tomatoes in boiling water for 20 seconds, then immediately put them in cold water. Peel them then chop them into small dice.

Add the bean sprouts to the frying pan, mix, then cook for 1 minute. Add the tomatoes, onions, garlic, soy sauce and the sesame oil then season with salt and pepper. Mix and cook for 1 minute longer. Serve immediately.

Chicken tagine with potatoes and olives

FOR 4 PEOPLE
PREPARATION: **20 min**
COOKING TIME:
approximately 1½ hours

> 1 large onion
> 8 potatoes
> 3 tbsp. olive oil
> 1 whole chicken, cut up
into 8 pieces
> 3 tbsp. honey
> 4¼ oz. green olives
> 1 tsp. saffron strands
> salt, freshly ground
black pepper

Peel and thinly slice the onion. Brush the dirt from the potatoes then wash them and cut them into quarters.

In a large stovetop-safe casserole dish, a large sauté pan or tagine dish, heat the olive oil and brown the pieces of chicken. Add the onion and cook for 5 minutes over medium heat then add the honey and let it lightly caramelize. Add the potatoes, olives, and the saffron and season with salt and pepper.

Add 2 cups of water to the casserole dish, sauté pan or tagine dish. If using a casserole dish or sauté pan, set the lid on top slightly askew (if using a tagine dish, set the lid on top but do not set it askew) and cook for 1 hour and 15 minutes over low heat, just until the pieces of chicken have cooked down very well. Add a little water during the cooking time if necessary. Serve very hot.

If available, the poulet des Landes (Landes chicken) is preferred for this dish due to its yellowish color that is accentuated by the saffron. Although this type of chicken requires a longer cooking time, the flavor is better.

Moroccan chicken pastilla with saffron

FOR 4–6 PEOPLE
PREPARATION: **40 min**
COOKING TIME:
1½ hours

> 3 tbsp. olive oil
> 1 whole chicken, approximately 2½ lbs., cut up
> 1 level tsp. saffron strands
> 1 cube chicken bouillon
> 2 red onions
> 3 tbsp. butter, melted
> 8 sheets of feuilles de brick (or phyllo dough)
> 1 tsp. ground cinnamon
> 2 tbsp. powdered sugar
> salt, freshly ground black pepper

In a stovetop-safe casserole dish or large sauté pan, heat half the olive oil and sear the chicken pieces; season with salt and pepper. Cover the chicken with water then add the saffron and the bouillon cube; season with salt and pepper and cook for 1 hour 10 minutes over medium heat.

Peel and thinly slice the onions then add them to a skillet and cook for 15 minutes until soft and translucent.

When the chicken has finished cooking, bone each piece completely and chop the meat into large pieces and mix with the onions.

Preheat the oven to 350° F.

Brush the bottom of a cake pan (approximately 11 inches in diameter or of a size to accommodate the sheets of dough) with melted butter then line the bottom with 2 sheets of the feuilles de brick, also brushed with melted butter. Spoon one-third of the chicken mixture into the cake pan and spread it out evenly. Sprinkle with a little bit of cinnamon and powdered sugar. Cover the layer with 2 more sheets of feuilles de brick brushed with butter then add half of the remaining chicken mixture followed by more cinnamon and sugar. Continue in this way one more time, finishing with the last two sheets of feuilles de brick on top. Neatly tuck the edges of the feuilles de brick down into the inside of the cake pan.

Brush the top with butter then sprinkle on the remaining cinnamon and sugar. Bake for 20 minutes.

Carefully unmold the pastilla and slice it using a serrated knife. Serve immediately.

1 Do not remove the feuilles de brick (or phyllo dough) from the package too soon as once exposed to air it dries out quickly and becomes brittle.

2 The chicken can be replaced with lamb or veal instead, but traditional Moroccan pastilla is made with squab.

3 Be sure to tuck the edges of the last layer of the feuilles de brick snugly inside the cake pan to ensure a perfectly made pastilla.

Tandoori chicken

FOR 4 PEOPLE
PREPARATION: **30 min**
MARINADE: **24 hours**
COOKING TIME:

1½ hours

> 1 chicken, approximately
  2½ lbs.
> 1 cup (9 oz.) plain yogurt
> ½ cup lime juice
> 2 rounded tbsp. tandoori
  powder
> 2 tbsp. red wine vinegar
> 3 tbsp. peanut oil
> 1 lime, quartered, for
  garnish
> salt, freshly ground
  black pepper

The night before: Cut up the chicken into quarters then cut each quarter in half. Remove the skin and, using the point of a knife, make deep incisions in the flesh in several places going all the way down to the bone.

In a small bowl, mix the yogurt with the lime juice, the tandoori powder, the vinegar and the peanut oil; season with salt and pepper. Place the pieces of chicken in a large bowl and coat them with the yogurt marinade. Cover the bowl with plastic wrap and refrigerate for 24 hours.

The next day: Preheat the oven to 300° F.

Remove the chicken pieces, keeping them thickly coated with the marinade. Place them on a baking sheet lined with parchment paper. Bake for approximately 1 hour 30 minutes without moving the pieces, just until they are well-browned. Serve with lime quarters.

Serve with raisin and cinnamon rice.

To shorten the preparation time, marinate the chicken for 2 hours in lemon juice with a little salt, then for 12 hours in the plain yogurt mixed with the remaining ingredients.

Curried chicken

FOR 4–6 PEOPLE
PREPARATION: **20 min**
COOKING TIME:

45–50 min

> 1 chicken, approximately 3 lbs.
> 3 onions
> 2 bananas
> juice of ½ lemon
> 2 apples (such as Jonagold or McIntosh)
> 2 tomatoes
> 2 tbsp. peanut oil
> 3 tbsp. curry powder
> just over ¾ cup coconut milk
> 1 cup to 1⅔ cups (7 oz. to 10½ oz.) basmati or Thai jasmine rice
> ½ cup (4½ oz.) plain yogurt
> salt

Clean the chicken and cut it into pieces.

Peel and chop the onions. Cut the bananas into thick rounds and place them in a bowl and drizzle them with the lemon juice. Peel and dice the apples then add them to the bowl.

Immerse the tomatoes in boiling water for 20 seconds, then immediately put them in cold water. Peel them then chop them into large pieces.

Heat the peanut oil in a stovetop-safe casserole dish or large sauté pan and brown the chicken pieces with the onions. Sprinkle over 1 tablespoon of the curry powder, mix, and cook for 5 minutes while stirring.

Drain the bananas and the apples and add them to the casserole dish with the remaining curry powder and the tomatoes.

Pour in the coconut milk then mix and season with salt. Cover and cook over low heat for approximately 35 minutes.

Meanwhile, wash the rice several times, drain, and add it to a saucepan. Season with salt then add three times its volume in water to the pan (between 3 and 5 cups depending on the amount of rice used). Cook at a rolling boil, uncovered. When the level of the water is no longer above the rice, cover the dish and cook on low heat, just until all of the water is evaporated but the rice remains moist.

Transfer the pieces of chicken from the casserole dish to a serving plate and keep warm.

Add the yogurt to the casserole dish, stir, and cook for 5 to 10 minutes until the sauce has thickened. Taste and adjust the seasoning as needed then spoon the sauce over the pieces of chicken. Serve the rice on the side.

Yakitori

FOR 4 PEOPLE
PREPARATION: **20 min**
MARINADE: **2 hours**
COOKING TIME: **8 min**

> 3 tbsp. strong soy sauce
> 3 tbsp. sake
> 1 tsp. freshly ground black pepper
> 1 tbsp. powdered sugar
> 4 small chicken breasts

In a small bowl, mix the soy sauce, sake, the freshly ground black pepper and the powdered sugar. Dice the chicken breasts and thread them onto wooden skewers, keeping the pieces pressed tightly together. Place the skewers on a plate and pour the soy sauce marinade on top. Cover with plastic wrap and let marinate refrigerated for 2 hours.

Remove the skewers from the marinade and let some of the excess marinade drain from them. Pour the marinade into a small saucepan and reduce it by two-thirds over high heat until thick and syrupy.

In a nonstick skillet, cook the skewers for 6 to 8 minutes over medium heat, turning them frequently. Dip them into the reduced marinade to coat them and serve immediately.

You can replace the chicken with guinea fowl, which is more flavorful and unique.

Serve with white rice or puréed potatoes.

Chicken teriyaki

FOR 4 PEOPLE
PREPARATION: **15 min**
MARINADE: **4 hours**
COOKING TIME: **50 min**

> 4 chicken thighs
> ⅓ cup strong soy sauce
> 3 tbsp. sesame oil
> 3 tbsp. rice vinegar
> 1 tbsp. grated fresh ginger
> 1 tbsp. powdered sugar
> juice of 2 lemons
> freshly ground black pepper

Cut off and wipe away any excess fat from the chicken thighs. Using the point of a knife, make shallow incisions in several places in the flesh.

In a small bowl, whisk together the soy sauce, sesame oil, vinegar, ginger, powdered sugar and lemon juice; season with pepper but do not add salt (the soy sauce already contains salt).

Arrange the chicken thighs on a baking sheet with sides, keeping them close together. Pour the marinade over the top and coat the thighs well. Cover the baking sheet with plastic wrap and refrigerate for 4 hours.

Preheat the oven to 300° F.

Transfer the chicken thighs to a baking dish lined with parchment paper. Drizzle them with additional marinade then bake for 50 minutes to 1 hour, basting them frequently but not turning them. Serve immediately.

Serve with almond rice.

You can add 2 or 3 tablespoons of sake to the marinade. If fresh ginger is not available, use ground ginger.

Fish tikka skewers

FOR 4 PEOPLE
PREPARATION: **30 min**
MARINADE: **4 hours**
COOKING TIME: **10 min**

> 1⅓ lbs. fresh cod or perch fillet
> 1 red onion
> 3 oz. cucumber
> ¼ bunch cilantro
> ½ cup (4½ oz.) plain yogurt
> 1 lime, for garnish
> salt, freshly ground black pepper

For the marinade
> 2 garlic cloves
> 1 cup (9 oz.) plain yogurt
> ½ red onion, chopped
> 1 tbsp. grated fresh ginger
> juice of 2 limes
> 1 tbsp. garam masala spice blend
> 1 tbsp. ground chile pepper

Prepare the marinade. Peel and chop the garlic cloves. In a small bowl, mix the yogurt, the chopped half red onion, ginger, chopped garlic cloves, lime juice, garam masala, and chile pepper; season with salt and pepper.

Cut the fish fillets into medium dice. Peel the red onion and slice it into medium pieces.

Thread the skewers with alternating pieces of fish and onion. Place the skewers on a plate and pour the marinade over them, turning them over several times to coat them well. Cover the plate with plastic wrap and refrigerate for 4 hours.

Preheat the oven to 400° F.

Peel the cucumber and cut it into small dice. Wash and chop the cilantro. In a small bowl, mix the cucumber and the cilantro with the ½ cup yogurt then season with salt and pepper.

Place the skewers on a baking sheet lined with parchment paper and bake for 10 minutes.

Serve the tikka skewers with the yogurt and cucumber sauce and lime quarters.

You can create skewers combining your favorite fish such as salmon, tuna, swordfish, etc.

Surimi sushi

FOR 4 PEOPLE
PREPARATION: **30 min**
REFRIGERATION: **15 min**
COOKING TIME:
approximately 15 min

> ⅔ cup (5¼ oz.) sushi rice
> 1 tsp. salt
> 3 tsp. powdered sugar
> 1 small avocado
> 4 long strips of imitation crab meat (surimi)
> 4 sheets dried seaweed (nori), approximately 4 to 6 inches long
> 3 tbsp. rice vinegar
> soy sauce for serving

Rinse the rice in cold water then place it in a saucepan covered with one and a half times its volume in water (approximately 1 cup). Add the salt and the powdered sugar then bring to a boil and cook for 12 to 15 minutes; let cool.

Cut the avocado in half, remove the pit, scoop out the flesh with a spoon and slice into long strips. Cut the imitation crab meat into long, thin sticks.

Cut out 4 rectangles of plastic wrap and place the dried seaweed sheets on top. Using a pastry brush, rehydrate them by brushing them with the rice vinegar. Spread the rice over the top half of the dried seaweed sheets then place the strips of avocado and crab meat on top of the rice. Delicately roll up each of the composed portions, using the plastic wrap as a guide, and without rolling too tightly. Refrigerate for 15 minutes then slice each roll into ¾-inch-thick sections. Serve with the soy sauce for dipping.

You can use very fresh salmon or shrimp in place of the imitation crab meat for more variety.

You can find sheets of dried seaweed (nori) in natural foods supermarkets or in the International foods aisle of larger supermarkets.

low calorie recipe

1 After placing the crab meat and avocado on the rice, press down lightly to adhere them so that they stay secured when rolled.

2 Start by rolling the sushi using your finger tips and by using the plastic wrap to help guide you and keep the roll together and somewhat tight.

3 Use a very sharp knife to cut through the sushi easily without crushing it.

Seared sesame tuna

FOR 4 PEOPLE
PREPARATION: **25 min**
MARINADE: **6 hours**
COOKING TIME: **5–6 min**

> 4 slices of tuna approximately 5¼ oz. each
> approximately ¾ cup (3 oz.) golden sesame seeds
> 3 tbsp. sesame oil or another vegetable oil
> soy sauce and wasabi for serving

For the marinade

> 1 oz. fresh ginger root
> ½ cup soy sauce
> 3 tbsp. saté seasoning
> 1 level tsp. powdered sugar
> ½ tsp. ground Cayenne pepper

Prepare the marinade. Peel and finely grate the ginger and mix it in a small bowl with the soy sauce, saté seasoning, powdered sugar and the ground Cayenne pepper.

Place the tuna slices on a plate. Pour the marinade over the top then cover them with plastic wrap. Marinate for 6 hours, refrigerated, turning the tuna over once after 3 hours.

Remove the tuna slices and drain the excess marinade from them. Roll them in the sesame seeds, pressing down lightly so that the seeds adhere well.

Heat the sesame oil in a skillet and cook the tuna slices for 2 to 3 minutes on each side over medium heat. Transfer them to a plate and let them rest for 3 minutes before carefully slicing them. Serve with the soy sauce on the side mixed with a small portion of wasabi.

Serve this with cilantro tempura. Mix 1 cup (3½ ounces) all-purpose flour with ½ teaspoon of baking soda and ⅔ cup to ¾ cup ice water to make a slightly liquid batter. Dredge large, fresh cilantro leaves in the batter and deep fry them for several seconds in very hot oil.

Sea bream and zucchini tagine

FOR 4 PEOPLE
PREPARATION: **15 min**
COOKING TIME: **35 min**

> 14 oz. zucchini
> 2 shallots
> ½ cup olive oil
> 1 level tbsp. turmeric
> 4 sea bream fillets weighing approximately 5½ oz. each, cut into pieces
> salt, freshly ground black pepper

Wash the zucchini and cut them in half lengthwise then cut each half into thick slices. Peel and chop the shallots. In a skillet, heat half of the olive oil and cook the shallots over medium heat for 5 minutes until soft but not browned. Add the zucchini and half of the turmeric, then season with salt and pepper. Cook for 15 minutes, stirring frequently.

Preheat the oven to 400° F.

Distribute the zucchini in the bottom of a tagine dish or in a baking dish. Place the pieces of sea bream on top, sprinkle with the remaining turmeric and drizzle with the remaining olive oil.

Cover the dish with a piece of aluminum foil and bake for 15 minutes. Serve as soon as the dish is removed from the oven.

VARIATION Make this dish with red mullet fillets instead and replace the turmeric with 1 rounded tablespoon of fennel or cumin seeds.

Creole-style curried monkfish

FOR 4–6 PEOPLE
PREPARATION: **15 min**
COOKING TIME:
approximately 1 hour

> 1 cleaned monkfish fillet, weighing approximately 3 lbs.
> 3 onions
> 3 tomatoes
> 2 garlic cloves
> 1 organic orange
> ½ cup peanut oil
> 1 pinch saffron
> 1 tbsp. grated fresh ginger or 1 tsp. ground ginger
> 1 bouquet garni (SEE p. 576)
> 1 tsp. curry powder
> 1 smidgen Cayenne pepper
> salt, freshly ground black pepper

Cut the monkfish fillet into pieces. Peel and finely chop the onions.

Blanch the tomatoes in boiling water for 20 seconds then immediately put them in cold water. Peel them, remove and discard the seeds, then chop them. Peel and finely chop the garlic cloves. Zest the orange in long strips.

Heat the peanut oil in a stovetop-safe casserole dish or large sauté pan and brown the pieces of monkfish; remove them using a slotted spoon or spatula.

In the same casserole dish and without pouring off the fat, brown the onions for 5 minutes then add the tomatoes and mix.

Add the saffron, ginger, chopped garlic cloves, bouquet garni, orange zest and curry powder and cook for 5 to 6 minutes over medium heat, stirring continuously.

Add 1 cup of hot water to the casserole dish then add the Cayenne pepper and season with salt and pepper. Cover and simmer for 20 minutes.

Place the monkfish pieces back in the casserole dish, cover, and cook gently for 30 minutes. Remove the bouquet garni and the orange zest.

Serve with creole rice (SEE p. 400).

make ahead · recipe ·

Indian-style cod fillets

FOR 4–6 PEOPLE
PREPARATION: **15 min**
COOKING TIME: **45 min**

> 2 fresh cod fillets weighing 7 to 8 oz. each
> 1 red onion
> 2 large yellow onions
> 5 tomatoes
> 2 garlic cloves
> 1 small bunch parsley
> ⅓ cup peanut oil
> 1 heaping tbsp. curry powder
> just over ¾ cup dry white wine
> 3 or 4 sprigs cilantro
> salt, freshly ground black pepper

Season the cod fillets with salt and pepper.

Peel and chop the red and yellow onions. Immerse the tomatoes in boiling water for 20 seconds, then immediately put them in cold water. Peel then chop them. Peel and chop the garlic cloves then chop the parsley.

Heat 4 tablespoons of the peanut oil in a stovetop- and oven-safe casserole dish and add the onions and tomatoes and cook for several minutes over high heat. Cover and cook down further, without browning, for 20 minutes.

Add the chopped garlic cloves and the parsley to the casserole dish, season with salt and pepper and cook for an additional 10 minutes.

Preheat the oven to 425° F.

Place the cod fillets in the casserole dish on top of the vegetables, sprinkle on the curry powder then drizzle in the remaining 2 tablespoons of peanut oil and pour in the white wine. Bring the mixture to a boil on the stovetop then place the dish in the oven for 15 minutes, basting the fish 3 or 4 times during this time with the cooking juices. Scatter the chopped cilantro over the top and serve very hot.

Accompany this dish with basmati or Thai jasmine rice.

Curried monkfish with bananas

FOR 4 PEOPLE
PREPARATION: **20 min**
COOKING TIME:
30–35 min

> 1⅓ lbs. monkfish (1 whole piece)
> 1 lb. bananas

For the sauce

> 3½ oz. small onions
> 1 garlic clove
> 1 tbsp. olive oil
> 1 tbsp. grated coconut
> 1 rounded tbsp. mild curry powder
> 7 oz. canned, crushed tomatoes
> salt, freshly ground black pepper

Prepare the sauce. Peel and thinly slice the onions. Peel and crush the garlic.

Heat the olive oil in an enameled, cast-iron casserole dish or in a frying pan and brown the onions for 5 minutes over low heat, stirring often. Add the garlic, grated coconut, curry powder and the crushed tomatoes. Cover and simmer for 15 minutes over low heat; season with salt and pepper.

Meanwhile, cut the monkfish into 8 pieces. Peel the bananas then slice them into thick rounds.

When the sauce is finished, add the fish and the bananas to the dish. Cover and cook for an additional 10 to 15 minutes over low heat. Serve very hot.

Serve with basmati rice cooked in water with 1 pinch of saffron to give it a beautiful yellow color.

make ahead recipe

Asian-style fish fillets

FOR 4 PEOPLE
PREPARATION: **10 min**
COOKING TIME: **20 min**

> 4 white fish fillets, such as fresh cod or halibut
> 2 onions
> ¾-inch piece of fresh ginger root
> 4 limes
> 3 tbsp. soy sauce
> 5 tbsp. olive oil
> 1 bunch cilantro
> salt, freshly ground black pepper

Preheat the oven to 425° F.

Wash the fish fillets then pat them dry using paper towels. Place them in a lightly oiled baking dish.

Peel the onions and the ginger root and finely chop them. Spread this mixture on top of the fish fillets.

Juice the limes and sprinkle the fish fillets generously with the soy sauce, some of the lime juice and the olive oil. Lightly season with salt (the soy sauce already contains salt) then season with pepper and bake for 15 to 20 minutes.

Wash and chop the cilantro. Remove the fish fillets from the oven and sprinkle the cilantro over the top. Serve immediately.

Serve with plain basmati rice which can be drizzled with soy sauce.

Curried shrimp

FOR 4 PEOPLE
PREPARATION: **30 min**
COOKING TIME:
approximately 20 min

> 14 oz. frozen large
  shelled shrimp
> 1 large onion
> 2 fresh lemongrass stalks
> 1-inch piece of fresh
  ginger root
> 2 tomatoes
> 2 small red chile peppers
> 2 tbsp. sunflower oil
> 1 tbsp. ground cumin
> 1 tbsp. nuoc-mâm sauce
  (Vietnamese fish sauce)
> 1 cup coconut milk
> 1 tsp. powdered sugar
> juice of 1 lime
> 1 bunch cilantro

Thaw the shrimp.

Chop the onion and finely chop the lemongrass stalks. Grate the ginger and dice the tomatoes. Mince the chile peppers, removing any seeds, and set aside.

Heat the sunflower oil in a wok or a deep skillet. Cook the onions just until they begin to develop color. Add the lemongrass, ginger, ground cumin and the minced chile peppers. Cook for an additional 2 minutes while stirring.

Add the nuoc-mâm sauce and the coconut milk to the wok. Mix well then add the diced tomatoes. Cook over low heat just until the tomatoes have softened and all of the flavors in the sauce have developed. If you are preparing the dish in advance, stop at this point then complete the dish 10 minutes prior to serving, reheating the sauce first.

Add the shrimp to the mixture, pushing them down into the sauce, and simmer over low heat for 5 minutes, just until pink and tender. Add the powdered sugar and the lime juice then cook for 1 minute more; pour out onto a serving dish.

Serve immediately, generously distributing cilantro leaves over the top.

This dish goes very well with white rice with sautéed green, red or yellow bell peppers.

make ahead
· recipe ·

Thai shrimp

FOR 4 PEOPLE
PREPARATION: 25 min
COOKING TIME: 10 min

> 2 garlic cloves
> 1 white onion
> 1 lime
> 1 small red chile pepper
> 3 tbsp. peanut oil or rapeseed oil
> 1 rounded tbsp. curry powder
> 1⅓ lbs. pink shrimp, shelled
> ½ cup tomato purée
> just over ¾ cup coconut cream
> 2 sprigs cilantro
> salt, freshly ground black pepper

Peel and chop the garlic cloves and the onion. Wash the lime, zest it, then juice it. Mince the chile pepper.

In a skillet, heat the oil and cook the garlic and the onion for 3 minutes. Sprinkle over the curry powder and cook for 5 minutes over medium heat to ensure they are well-cooked. Add the shrimp and the minced chile pepper and brown them. Pour in the tomato purée and the coconut cream; season with salt and pepper and cook for 8 to 10 minutes over medium heat. Add a little water to the skillet if the sauce begins to thicken too much. At the end of the cooking time, add the lime zest and juice then cook for 1 minute more while stirring.

Divide the shrimp and the sauce among serving plates, scatter the cilantro leaves over the top and serve immediately.

For an extra spicy kick, add 1 teaspoon of red chile powder along with the curry powder.

Prawn and bacon skewers

FOR 4 PEOPLE
PREPARATION: **30 min**
MARINADE: **2 hours**
COOKING TIME: **8 min**

> 1 smidgen harissa paste
>   (or hot chile sauce)
> 3 tbsp. olive oil
> 1 tsp. ground sweet (or
>   mild) red chile pepper
> juice of ½ lemon
> 12 large prawns
> 6 large slices of lean,
>   smoked bacon
> salt, freshly ground
>   black pepper

In a small bowl, mix the harissa paste with the olive oil, the ground chile pepper and the lemon juice; season with salt and pepper.

Carefully shell the prawns, leaving the end of the tails intact. Cut the slices of bacon in half lengthwise. Wrap each piece of bacon around one prawn, but do not wrap too tightly.

Thread 3 prawns onto each of 4 skewers. Arrange them on a plate then pour the harissa paste mixture on top. Cover with plastic wrap and marinate, refrigerated, for at least 2 hours.

Just before serving, grill the skewers for 3 to 4 minutes on each side either on a grilling plank or in a skillet. Serve immediately.

Serve with flavored rice or a mixed green salad.

You can replace the lean, smoked bacon with thin slices of regular, fattier smoked bacon. For a less spicy dish, replace the ground sweet chile pepper with a milder chile pepper such as Espelette.

Stir-fried crayfish with lemongrass

FOR 4 PEOPLE
PREPARATION: 30 min
COOKING TIME: 6-8 min

> 3⅓ lbs. raw crayfish (or use prawns)
> 1 fresh lemongrass stalk
> 1-inch piece of fresh ginger root
> 2 garlic cloves
> 10½ oz. snow peas
> 3 oz. mung bean sprouts ("soy bean sprouts")
> ½ tsp. chile pepper purée (or any chile pepper sauce)
> 1 tbsp. soy sauce
> 1 tbsp. rice vinegar
> 1 tbsp. peanut oil
> 1 tsp. sesame oil
> freshly ground black pepper

Shell the crayfish. Remove the heads. Using a small pair of sharp scissors, cut each shell open down the center and back, just until you reach the tail. Slit open the flesh down the back and remove the black vein. Rinse the crayfish then carefully pat them dry using paper towels.

Remove any outside leaves from the lemongrass stalk then thinly slice it into rounds. Peel and finely chop the ginger root and the garlic cloves.

Wash and dry the snow peas and the bean sprouts. In a cup, mix the chile pepper purée, the soy sauce and the rice vinegar.

Place a wok (or a large skillet) over very high heat. Add the peanut oil. Once the oil is very hot (it should be shimmering), add the chopped garlic cloves, lemongrass, and the ginger root and cook for 15 seconds. Add the crayfish and cook for 1 to 2 minutes. Remove the crayfish from the wok using a slotted spoon or a spatula and keep them warm on a plate placed on top of a saucepan of simmering water.

With the wok still on medium heat, add the snow peas and bean sprouts and cook for 4 to 5 minutes, stirring often.

Place the crayfish back in the wok, add the soy sauce mixture and toss carefully, cooking for 1 minute more.

Pour out onto a warm serving plate and serve immediately, drizzled with sesame oil.

Cooking class

SAUCES, TECHNIQUES AND TIPS

Mayonnaise

FOR 8 PEOPLE (OR
APPROXIMATELY
2 CUPS)

PREPARATION: 10 min

> 2 egg yolks
> 2 tsp. strong mustard
> 2 tbsp. red or white wine
  vinegar or lemon juice
> 2 cups rapeseed or
  sunflower oil
> salt, freshly ground
  black pepper

1 Bring all of the ingredients to room
temperature by setting them out
approximately 1 hour ahead. Break the
eggs and separate the yolks from the
whites. Store the whites in the
refrigerator, covered, and keep them for
another use. Place the egg yolks in a large
bowl.

2 Add the mustard and the vinegar to
the bowl with the egg yolks, season
with salt and pepper then whisk together
vigorously.

3 Continue to whisk vigorously while
adding the oil drop by drop at first
and then in thin streams, whisking
vigorously between each addition, until
the mixture thickens.

4 Incorporate the remaining oil in
thin streams while whisking
vigorously so that the mixture forms a
thick mayonnaise. The mayonnise will thin
out if more oil is added. You can also use
a food processor to bring the mixture
together more quickly, slowly drizzling in
the oil while the machine is running.

How to fix a "broken" mayonnaise

Vigorously whisk together
1 tablespoon of cold water with
1 tablespoon of the mayonnaise
then incorporate the remaining
mayonnaise into this mixture a
little at a time while whisking
continuously.

Another approach is to add an
egg yolk to a separate bowl and
to start the process from the
beginning, replacing the oil with
the broken mayonnaise.

Saffron Mayonnaise

Start with 1 egg yolk, just over
¾ cup rapeseed or sunflower oil,
½ cup to ⅔ cup heavy cream,
1 tbsp. mild paprika, 1 pinch saffron,
a smidgen Cayenne pepper, salt
and 2 tsp. strong mustard. Prepare
a mayonnaise with the egg yolk,
vinegar and the oil as indicated
above; the mustard is optional.
Add the paprika, the saffron, and
the Cayenne pepper, then season
with salt. In a second bowl, whip
the very cold heavy cream to
medium-stiff peaks then gently
fold it into the mayonnaise. Serve
with shellfish or cold fish dishes.

Vinaigrette

FOR 6 PEOPLE (OR APPROXIMATELY ¼ CUP)

PREPARATION: 5 min

> 1 tbsp. vinegar
> 1 pinch salt
> 3 tbsp. vegetable oil
> freshly ground black pepper

1 Place the vinegar and salt in a bowl.

2 Vigorously whisk the mixture until the salt is completely dissolved. Add the oil in a thin stream while whisking continuously so that the mixture becomes well-emulsified.

3 Season with freshly ground black pepper according to taste. Add several dried or fresh herbs depending on the flavors of the main dish being served.

Making a successful vinaigrette

The flavor of the vinaigrette depends on the proportion of the ingredients that make it up. As a rule of thumb, the proportion is three times the amount of oil to vinegar but this will change based on the addition of other ingredients, such as strong mustard, lemon juice (in place of the vinegar), etc. When using lemon juice instead of vinegar, use 1 tablespoon of lemon juice for every 4 or 5 tablespoons of oil. The amount of mustard to add depends on its strength: In general, use 1 teaspoon for every 4 tablespoons of oil.

Avocado vinaigrette

Mix the flesh of one half avocado with the juice of one half lime then season with salt. Add ⅓ cup oil and a pinch of Cayenne pepper. Serve with fish or cold meat.

Hazelnut vinaigrette

Prepare a vinaigrette with raspberry vinegar and hazelnut oil. Add 1 tablespoon of finely chopped chervil and 1 tablespoon of finely chopped hazelnuts. This vinaigrette is delicious with a red cabbage and spinach salad.

Thai vinaigrette

Prepare a vinaigrette with 1 tablespoon of rice vinegar and 3 tablespoons of sunflower oil. Add 1 tablespoon chopped cilantro, 1 tablespoon chopped lemongrass, 1 tablespoon sesame seeds, ½ teaspoon of soy sauce and ½ teaspoon of nuoc-mâm sauce. Serve with shrimp.

Béchamel sauce

MAKES 2 CUPS

PREPARATION: 5 min

COOKING TIME:
approximately 15 min

> 3 ½ tbsp. (1 ¾ oz.) butter
> ½ cup (1 ¾ oz.)
  all-purpose flour
> 2 cups milk
> 1 large pinch grated
  nutmeg (optional)
> salt, freshly ground
  black pepper

1 Cut the butter into pieces and place it in a heavy-bottomed saucepan over low heat to melt completely but without browning.

2 Add the flour all at once while whisking vigorously. Cook gently for 2 minutes while stirring continuously with the whisk, just until the mixture forms a smooth, white paste.

3 Remove the pan from the heat and slowly pour in the milk while the mixture is still very hot. Whisk continuously to ensure the milk is well-incorporated.

4 When the mixture is smooth and homogenous, place it back over low heat and cook, without boiling, for approximately 12 minutes while continuing to stir. Season with salt and freshly ground black pepper then stir in the pinch of grated nutmeg. If you are not using the sauce immediately, melt a piece of butter on the surface of the hot sauce to prevent a skin from forming.

Making a successful béchamel sauce
The milk must be added slowly into the butter and flour mixture (a.k.a. the roux) while stirring continuously to prevent lumps. If the milk is cold, the roux must be very hot when you incorporate the milk. If the milk is hot, let the roux cool before incorporating it. If the sauce is too thick, add a little more milk.

Hollandaise sauce

MAKES 1 CUP TO 1¼ CUPS

PREPARATION: 15 min

COOKING TIME: 10 min

> 2 sticks + 2 tbsp. (9 oz.)
  cold butter
> 1 tbsp. vinegar
> 1 pinch freshly
  ground black pepper
> 4 egg yolks
> 1 pinch salt
> juice of ½ lemon

1 Cut up the butter into small cubes and place it in the refrigerator. Heat water in a saucepan to prepare a bain-marie. In a second saucepan, heat 2 tablespoons of water with the vinegar and the pepper; reduce the mixture somewhat by bringing it to a boil. Add the egg yolks in a third saucepan and add the water and vinegar mixture to it while whisking gently.

2 Place the saucepan with the yolks on top of the saucepan with the hot water (the water must be simmering).

3 Whisk the mixture just until it begins to thicken. Incorporate the cold butter a piece at a time while continuing to whisk; season with salt.

4 Remove the top saucepan off the bain-marie. Add a drizzle of lemon juice then taste and adjust the seasoning as needed. Serve with fish cooked in a court-bouillon or with steamed vegetables.

Did you know?
Just as with other emulsifed sauces, hollandaise is not very stable, which is why it is important to serve it as soon as it is made. If you keep it warm on top of the bain-marie, it will keep for approximately 30 minutes.

Mousseline sauce
Measure out just over ¾ cup hollandaise sauce and ½ cup heavy cream. Make the hollandaise sauce and whip the cream to medium-stiff peaks. Off the heat, add the whipped cream to the sauce, whisking continuously but gently. Taste and adjust the seasoning as needed. Use this sauce in the same way as the hollandaise sauce.

Beurre blanc

MAKES 1 CUP

PREPARATION: 10 min

COOKING TIME: 10 min

> 1 stick + 6 tbsp. (7 oz.) butter
> 4 shallots (preferably gray shallots)
> 3 tbsp. white wine vinegar
> ⅓ cup dry white wine
> salt, ground white pepper

1 Cut up the butter into small cubes and place it in the refrigerator. Peel and finely chop the shallots then place them in a small, heavy-bottomed saucepan with the vinegar and white wine. Mix well and heat slowly to a boil.

2 Cook the shallots over medium heat, uncovered, stirring occasionally until the majority of the liquid has evaporated; there should only be a thick mixture remaining but it should still be very moist. Strain the thickened liquid and set aside 2 tablespoons full.

3 Place the saucepan back over low heat and add the 2 tablespoons of reduced liquid and bring to a boil. Add the pieces of butter one at a time. Whisk continuously while incorporating the butter so that the mixture is thick and creamy.

4 Cook the sauce for several more minutes over low heat while continuing to whisk until the sauce is very hot. Season with salt and pepper then pour the liquid into a warmed gravy dish and serve immediately. Serve with fish cooked in a court-bouillon, such as pike or shad.

Making a successful beurre blanc

Pay close attention to the temperature of the mixture as soon as you start to incorporate the butter. If the sauce is too hot it will "break" immediately. The boiling liquid helps to incorporate the butter. As long as the liquid has not evaporated, the sauce will stay together. The gravy dish used to serve the beurre blanc should be just slightly warm to ensure the sauce stays creamy; rinse it in hot water then dry it thoroughly. Always make beurre blanc in small quantities. Never make a batch that contains more than approximately 9 ounces of butter.

Béarnaise sauce

MAKES APPROXIMATELY
1 CUP

PREPARATION: 15 min

COOKING TIME: 10-15 min

> 3 shallots
> 3 tbsp. chopped tarragon
> 1 tbsp. chopped chervil
> 3 or 4 tbsp. tarragon vinegar
> 2 tbsp. white wine
> 1 pinch salt
> 2 pinches crushed white and black peppercorns
> 3 egg yolks
> 1 stick + 1 tbsp. (4½ oz.) softened butter

1 In a heavy-bottomed saucepan, add the chopped shallots and some of the chopped tarragon and chervil. Add the tarragon vinegar and the white wine then add the salt and peppercorns. Reduce the mixture by two-thirds over low heat. Strain and remove from the heat and let cool.

2 Add the egg yolks and a little bit of water into the cooled, reduced sauce and whisk vigorously. Place the saucepan with the sauce on top of another saucepan of simmering water set over low heat to make a bain-marie.

3 Add the softened butter in pieces, a little at a time, while whisking.

4 When the sauce becomes creamy, add the remaining chopped tarragon and chervil. Taste and adjust the seasoning as needed. Serve with meat dishes or grilled fish.

How to fix a "broken" béarnaise sauce
If the béarnaise sauce has lost its emulsification, whisk in 1 tablespoon of hot water a little at a time if the sauce has cooled, or whisk in 1 tablespoon of cold water if the sauce is hot.

Tomato béarnaise sauce
Add 1 teaspoon of tomato paste to just over ¾ cup béarnaise sauce. This is traditionally referred to as a Choron sauce.

Tomato sauce

FOR 6 PEOPLE

PREPARATION: 20 min

COOKING TIME: 20-40 min

> 3⅓ lbs. very ripe tomatoes (or 2¼ lbs. canned, diced tomatoes)
> 1 large onion
> 4 tbsp. olive oil
> 1 bouquet garni (made with 1 bay leaf, 2 sprigs of thyme, and several sprigs of flat-leaf parsley; SEE p. 576)
> salt, freshly ground black pepper

1. If you are using fresh, ripe tomatoes, immerse them for 20 to 30 seconds in boiling water then immediately place them in a bowl of ice water.

2. Remove them to drain then peel them. Cut them in half then squeeze them gently to eliminate the seeds and the juice; cut the flesh into small dice. If you are using canned, diced tomatoes, skip this step.

3. Peel and finely chop the onion. In a saucepan, gently heat the olive oil and add the onion and cook over very low heat for 5 to 10 minutes, stirring frequently, just until the onions become translucent.

4. Add the diced tomatoes to the saucepan then add the bouquet garni; season with salt and pepper. Mix well then bring to a boil. Cook over very low heat, stirring occassionally until the liquid has completely evaporated, 20 to 40 minutes depending on the amount of liquid in the tomatoes. When the mixture has cooked down to a thickened sauce, turn off the heat. Remove the bouquet garni and taste and adjust the seasoning as needed.

Did you know?

When tomatoes are very ripe, the sauce, in general, will not be acidic. To lessen the acidity of a tomato sauce, sprinkle in 1 teaspoon of powdered sugar. To create a more concentrated tomato flavor, add 1 tablespoon of tomato paste.

Skimming fat from stock or broth

Did you know?
Once the fat has been removed from a stock, the remaining liquid is an excellent base for a soup or stew. If you do not have enough time to allow the stock to cool, remove as much of the fat as possible using a ladle then use a paper towel to skim the surface of the liquid to absorb any remaining fat.

1 Pour the stock (or broth) through a strainer lined with cheesecloth or muslin. Let the strained liquid cool then place it in the refrigerator.

2 When the fat has collected on the surface, remove it using a large spoon or a skimming ladle.

Deglazing a pan

1 After removing all of the cooked ingredients from the pan, pour in the deglazing liquid (such as heavy cream, broth, wine, etc.), with the pan still on the heat, to cover all of the browned and caramelized bits of food on the bottom. Scrape up the cooked bits using a spatula or wooden spoon so that they become mixed into the liquid.

2 Continue to cook for 3 or 4 minutes, while stirring, to reduce the liquid. Taste and adjust the seasoning as needed. Once reduced, you can strain the liquid to make it completely smooth.

Did you know?
To lighten the sauce, you can skim off or soak up some of the fat from the pan before adding the deglazing liquid.

Coating with bread crumbs

1 Break 1 egg onto a plate with a little salt and pepper and 1 tablespoon of vegetable oil and beat lightly with a fork. On a second plate, distribute 1⅓ cups all-purpose flour. On a third plate distribute 1¼ cups of bread crumbs.

2 Using a paper towel, pat dry the food you want to coat (such as meat cutlets or fish fillets). Dredge both sides in the flour and then the beaten egg.

3 Immediately coat both sides with the bread crumbs, pressing down lightly to help the bread crumbs adhere.

Trussing poultry

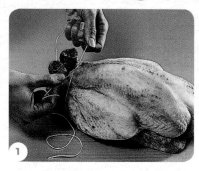

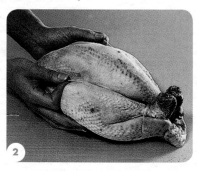

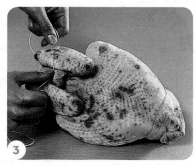

1 Cut a piece of kitchen twine long enough to wrap twice around the poultry lengthwise. Turn the poultry over on its back. Wrap the twine underneath the tail end then bring the ends up and wrap them around the ends of the drumsticks.

2 Bring the ends of the twine forward against the side of the poultry and up over the thighs.

3 Turn the poultry over on its side and pull the neck skin down between the wings. Wrap the twine around the wings and pull the string tight and tie a firm knot.

Barding meat or poultry

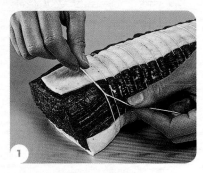

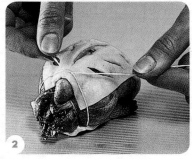

Barding fat is cut from the fatty part of pork and is used to protect the meat from intense heat that could dry it out while it cooks. In place of traditional barding fat, in certain recipes, you can use thin slices of pork breast (or bacon) that will not only protect the meat but also add flavor.

1 Wrap the barding fat all around the meat or place a large piece over the top and a second large piece on the bottom. Tie the fat to the meat using kitchen twine spaced evenly apart. Remove the barding fat at the end of the cooking time.

2 For poultry, tie the wings down first then cut a piece of barding fat to the desired size and place it on the top and bottom of the poultry and tie it down in two or three places.

Stuffing poultry

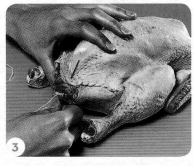

1 Place the poultry on its breast bone, pull the neck skin up and over the top then tie it closed using kitchen twine.

2 Turn the poultry over on its back and make a long incision across the tail end. Stuff the poultry with the filling, leaving some room inside the cavity to allow the stuffing to expand while cooking.

3 Close the cavity tightly using kitchen twine and a trussing needle, then truss the poultry as described on the preceding page.

Carving beef ribs

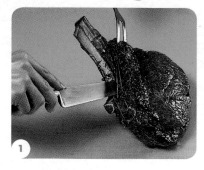

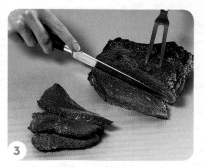

1 Use a large grilling fork to hold the beef ribs steady. Using a knife, cut away the meat from the backbone, if necessary.

2 Cut the meat completely from the rib bone using a knife.

3 Cut the meat evenly into thick or thin slices, as desired.

Carving a leg of lamb

1 After removing the meat from the end of the knuckle (considered a delicate morsel) using a long-bladed knife, rest the leg of lamb on the thick end and cut away thin slices, just behind the tip, with the knife moving away from you and parallel to the bone.

2 Make shallow incisions on each side of the bone and carefully detach the bone from the meat to allow for easy slicing.

3 Turn the leg of lamb over. Thinly slice the meat perpendicular to the bone. Sliced in this way, each serving will have a section that is cooked well-done and a section that is cooked rare.

Carving a cooked chicken

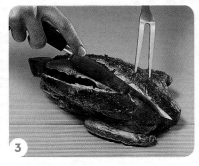

1 After removing the kitchen twine used to truss the chicken, secure the chicken by holding it steady with a grilling fork. Using a very sharp knife, cut through the skin and the flesh between the thigh and the breast meat then precisely slice through to cleanly separate the thigh from the carcass.

2 Separate the upper thigh from the drumstick.

3 Detach the breast meat from the breast bone then cleanly and precisely cut off each wing. Cut the breast meat into two parts.

Carving a cooked duck

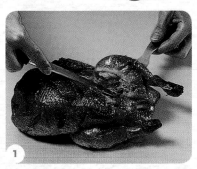

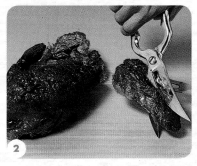

1 Place the duck on its back and hold it steady with a grilling fork. Using a very sharp knife, cut through the skin and the flesh between the thigh and the side of the duck, then precisely slice through to cleanly separate the thigh from the carcass.

2 Carefully cut away and detach the wings then cut each wing in half using poultry shears.

3 Cut away the breast meat from both sides of the carcass and slice it into thin portions.

Trimming and scaling a fish

Did you know?
The head, bones and the cuttings of a fish can be used to make an excellent stock or broth that can serve as the base of a sauce or a soup. You can freeze small portions of the stock in ice cube trays to use when you need it.

1 Using sharp scissors, remove all of the fins from the fish, cutting them flush to the body. Cut away the dorsal fins by lifting them and cutting them from the opposite direction. Clip off the tail fin.

2 Vigorously scrape the fish using a fish scaler (or a knife), scraping from tail to head. Rinse the fish several times under cold water.

Cleaning a fish

1 If the fish is small, it should be cleaned from the gills. Place your index finger inside of the opening (the operculum) around the gills and carefully remove the gills and the entrails.

2 Medium or large fish should be cleaned from the belly. Make an incision several inches along the belly then pry the belly open and pull out the entrails and the gills.

Tip
After cleaning the fish, rinse and carefully pat it dry using a paper towel. If you are not cooking it immediately, store it in the coldest part of the refrigerator.

Filleting a flat fish

1 Using a cleaned and scaled fish, make an incision from the head to the tail, following the spine.

2 Cut away the first fillet starting from the end under the head: make a cut between the spine and the flesh and remove the fillet while pressing down onto the spine with the blade of the knife to avoid tearing or cutting into the flesh.

3 Cut away the second fillet from the same side and on the other side of the spine. Turn the fish over and remove the two fillets from the other side in the same manner.

Filleting a rounded fish

1 Place the fish with the tail pointing toward you and make an incision along the spine from the head to the tail fin.

2 Make a wedge-shape cut behind the head then progressively cut underneath the fillet while sliding the knife down along the bones.

3 Once the first fillet is removed, place the fish bone-side down against the work surface. Hold the knife parallel to the spine and cut cleanly, moving from the tail toward the head to remove the second fillet.

Stuffing a fish

1 Hold the fish from the underside and make an incision along the back from the head to the tail fin.

2 Pry open the incision and detach the spine. Cut around the spine along the head and the tail and carefully pull the spine out.

3 Season the inside of the fish with salt and pepper. Stuff the cavity with filling and pack it in well. Use kitchen twine to tie the fish closed in several places.

Cleaning scallops

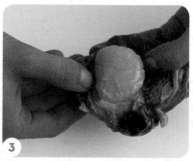

1 Place the scallop on a work surface with the rounded side down while holding the hinge away from you. Insert the blade of a knife between the shells. Locate the internal membrane attached to the top shell and detach it by sliding the knife all the way around the inside.

2 Pry open the shell and gently rinse the half containing the muscle under water to eliminate any sand that may be present. Detach the muscle using a spoon.

3 Applying slight pressure with your thumbs, remove the internal muscle as well as the surrounding membrane and the black entrails. Next carefully cut away the coral (roe). Soak the white portion of the meat for several minutes in cold water to clean it completely.

Shelling a crab

1 Insert the point of a knife between the top shell and the breast plate (apron) and run it all the way around to detach the shell.

2 Pull the shell and the breast plate apart and place the crab on its back and twist off the legs and claws.

3 Using a spoon, remove the meat from the cavity and from around the entrails. Remove the soft yellow material located between the meat and the shell. Crack open the legs and the claws using a nut or seafood cracker and pull out the meat from inside.

Fluting a lemon

1 Hold the lemon in one hand and a fluting (or cannelling) knife in the other and peel off strips of zest spaced evenly apart.

2 Slice the lemon into even rounds.

Did you know?
You can flute other fruits and vegetables in this way to give them a decorative appearance, such as zucchini, cucumbers, carrots and oranges.

Julienning a leek

Did you know?
The approach of cutting into a julienne typically applies to vege-tables, but you can also julienne other foods such as chicken breast, cornichons, ham, etc.

1 Cut the white portion of the leeks into sections measuring approximately 2½ to 4 inches long then cut them in half lengthwise.

2 Place the pieces flat-side down on a cutting surface and slice them into thin strips.

Removing an artichoke heart

1 After cutting off the stem, trim off the tough outer leaves from around the base of the artichoke and drizzle the entire artichoke with lemon juice.

2 Cut off the top two-thirds of the leaves, down to the top of the fuzzy choke.

3 Remove all of the choke using a knife until only the soft, white flesh of the artichoke heart remains.

Poaching eggs

FOR 4 PEOPLE

PREPARATION: 10 min

> ½ cup vinegar
> 4 very fresh and very cold eggs

1 Add 8 cups of unsalted water to a saucepan and add the vinegar. Bring to a boil then lower the heat to a gentle simmer.

2 Break 1 egg into a cup. Carefully ease the egg into the simmering water by holding the cup just above the surface of the water so that the yolk and whites stay together. If the saucepan is large enough, repeat with the other eggs; the whites will coagulate around the yolk.

3 Cook the eggs for 3 minutes without letting the water boil. When the whites are firm, remove the egg using a slotted spoon and place it in a bowl of cold water, then remove it to drain.

4 Using a knife or a pair of kitchen scissors, trim off the small strands that form around the edge of the poached egg to give it a uniform appearance.

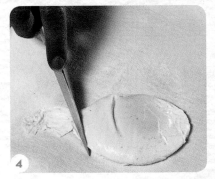

Successfully poaching an egg
The eggs must be very cold and very fresh so that the whites will not separate from the yolk. You should never salt the water because the salt will dissolve the egg white. To poach several eggs at once, use a large saucepan or a large sauté pan. Poached eggs should be served immediately. Serve with a sauce or on toast.

Cooking glossary

Al dente: a food such as pasta cooked until it offers slight resistance when bitten and is neither over- nor under-cooked. Italian for "to the tooth."

Bain-marie: also called a water bath. A process by which a container of water (such as a saucepan) is heated to hot or to simmering and a second container is set on top that contains ingredients for melting (such as gelatin or butter), keeping warm (such as already cooked foods) or for gentle cooking.

Bard: to wrap a thin strip of bacon or other pieces of fat (usually pork) around a piece of beef, game, fish or poultry to add flavor and to prevent it from drying out while cooking.

Barding fat: the piece of fat used to bard beef, game, fish or poultry (see Bard above). Commonly a piece of pork fat.

Baste: to spoon or brush foods with their cooking juices, other sauces or fats (such as butter) while cooking in order to add flavor and keep the food moist.

Blanch: the action of briefly immersing raw food into salted or unsalted boiling water or boiling water and vinegar then immediately stopping the cooking process by immersing in cold water and draining before cooking completely. Blanching helps to strengthen, purify, remove bitterness, assist with peeling fruits and vegetables and to remove excess salt as well as reduce the volume of the fruits and vegetables.

Blind bake: to partially bake a tart or pie crust. This method usually involves covering the unbaked crust with parchment paper or aluminum foil then placing weights such as metal pie weights or dried beans in the center and baking the crust until it is dried and light in color. The crust can then be baked further once the foil is removed and before adding the filling and baking to completion. A blind-baked crust will maintain better crispness when combined with a moist filling. Also referred to as prebaking.

Braise: to cook foods by first browning them in a fat (such as butter) then covering them tightly and cooking slowly over low heat. Braising tenderizes foods and helps develop flavor.

Brown: to cook foods over high heat to turn the surface to a brown color.

Bouquet garni: a choice of herbs, tied in a small bundle, used to add flavor to dishes. Generally a bouquet garni consists of 2 or 3 sprigs of parsley, a sprig of thyme and one or two dried bay leaves.

Caramelize: to convert sugar into caramel by heating it over low heat. Also refers to coating a pan with caramel or to covering fruits or pâte à choux in caramel. Caramelize can also mean to cook foods under a grill to give them color or to heat the top of a dessert that has been sprinkled with sugar to cook the sugar and give it color and crunch. Vegetables or nuts can be caramelized if cooked in a skillet with a little bit of sugar and butter.

Casserole dish: a baking dish with sides, usually oval or rectangular, that is usually made of clay or porcelain and designed to evenly bake and brown foods. Not all casserole dishes are broiler-safe.

Chervil: an herb with curly, dark green leaves and a delicate anise flavor. Chervil is a member of the parsley family and can be used in a similar way to parsley, either dried or fresh.

Clarify: to make a bouillon, syrup, or gelatin mixture clear by filtration or decanting. Clarifying butter consists of melting it over a bain-marie without stirring to eliminate the milk solids that give butter its solid appearance.

Coddle: to place a food (such as eggs) in an individual, covered dish and set the dish in water heated to just below the boiling point in order to cook the food gently. Eggs can be coddled in their shells or in separate containers called coddling cups. See also Poach.

Confit: to preserve meat such as duck, goose or pork by salting then slowly cooking it in its own fat. The cooked meat is stored in a container and covered in its fat in order to seal and preserve it.

Court-bouillon: a vegetable and herb broth used for poaching fish, seafood or vegetables. The vegetables and herbs (which usually include a bouquet garni) are simmered in water for 30 minutes before being strained and cooled.

Crème fraîche: a thickened, matured cream with a slight tangy flavor and very creamy texture. The tanginess of crème fraîche is more subtle than that of sour cream, but the two can be substituted for each other in certain recipes. Unlike sour cream, crème fraîche won't curdle if boiled and can be whipped like fresh cream. Commercial brands are available but you can make your own with 1 tablespoon buttermilk mixed with 1 cup heavy cream in a jar with a tight-fitting lid. Set the jar in a warm area such as near the stovetop, covered tightly, and leave undisturbed for 12 to 18 hours until thickened. Keep chilled after the cream has set.

Cutlet: a thin, tender cut of meat such as chicken or other fowl, veal or lamb. Cutlets are usually dipped in a coating of egg, flour and bread crumbs before sautéing or frying as their thickness makes them ideal for quick cooking.

Deglaze: to add a small portion of liquid such as wine or cream to a pan to dissolve and scrape up the browned bits of food that are left over from either sautéing, frying or baking. The liquid is then reduced and used as the base for a sauce to accompany the food cooked in the pan. See Cooking Class, p. 565.

Dice: to cut up vegetables, fruits or other ingredients into cubes of varying sizes for even cooking or easier eating.

Dutch oven: a heavy cooking pot usually made of cast iron or earthenware and having a tight-fitting lid. Dutch ovens distribute heat evenly and are usually adapted for both baking and stovetop cooking. Also referred to as a casserole dish.

Egg wash: a lightly beaten mixture of egg yolk or whole egg, either plain or with a small amount of water or milk, brushed onto the surface of pastry dough, bread dough or other baked goods to give them a glossy and browned appearance after baking.

Emulsify: to smoothly blend one liquid with another (usually liquids that do not easily combine, such as oil and vinegar) by slowly adding one to the other while mixing vigorously. Slow and vigorous mixing creates a suspension of one liquid in the other. When the liquids separate, the emulsion is said to be "broken."

En croûte: cooking food (usually partially cooked) that is wrapped in pastry and baked.

En papillote: (pa-pea-yote) a method of cooking that involves wrapping and sealing meat such as chicken or fish in a piece of oiled parchment paper, allowing the food to cook and steam while maintaining moisture. Vegetables are often added along with the meat to cook at the same time.

Feuilles de brick: tissue-thin sheets of pastry dough made from wheat, water and salt (similar to phyllo dough) used to wrap savory or dessert ingredients in many types of cuisine. When baked, feuilles de brick turns golden brown and crispy. Feuilles de brick does not contain butter.

Fillet: to cut sections of meat from the bones of beef or fish. A fillet (or filet) can also refer to the meat itself once removed. See Cooking Class, p. 571.

Flambé (Flamed or Flambéed): igniting warmed liquor (or a liqueur) that has been sprinkled or poured over a savory dish while cooking or a dessert dish while hot.

Flour: To cover a food with flour or to sprinkle or cover a work surface or a pan with a light coating of flour to prevent foods, such as doughs or cakes, from sticking.

Flute: to carve grooves or v-shapes into vegetables and fruits to make decorative markings using a fluting knife or other special tools. Fluting can also mean making a decorative border in pastry using a pastry wheel designed for this purpose. The surface of a mousse or a purée can also be "fluted" using a spatula or fork. See Cooking Class, p. 573.

Foie gras: (meaning "fatty liver" in French). The liver of a duck or goose that has specifically been fattened to achieve a creamy and buttery texture.

Fricassee: refers to a dish made from sautéed or stewed meats that are cooked slowly and served in a thickened sauce or gravy. It can refer to the name of a dish or the method used to cook a dish.

Fry: to cook a food or finish the cooking of a food by immersing it in a fat heated to high temperature. Fried foods are often first coated in flour or batters (such as beignets) and cooked in the fat until they obtain a browned and crispy outer layer.

Garnish: to add ingredients to a serving plate for decorative purposes or to add a little bit of flavor to a dish just before serving.

Homogenous: a mixture that is smooth and emulsified. A well-made vinaigrette is a homogenized mixture. See also Emulsify.

Immersion blender: a tall, narrow and portable hand-held blender used to chop, purée or blend foods in their containers (such as puréeing a soup in the saucepan).

Jerusalem artichoke: not related to the artichoke but actually a species of sunflower, sometimes referred to as a sunchoke. The flowers of the Jerusalem artichoke look like small, yellow sunflowers. The tubers of the plant resemble ginger root in appearance and have a potato-like texture.

Julienne: to cut sections of vegetables or other foods into very thin, uniform strips or matchstick-size pieces to be used for garnish, especially in soups. See Cooking Class, p. 574.

Knead: the method used to mix and work a substance such as butter or a dough either by hand or with a mixer or food processor in order to obtain a homogenous and pliable mass.

Macerate: to soak raw, dried or preserved foods in a liquid (such as a liquor, liqueur, syrup, wine or tea) in order to rehydrate it and infuse it with flavor. Similar to marinate.

Marinate: to soak foods (usually meats) in an aromatic liquid to tenderize them and add flavor.

Mince: to chop foods (such as onions, herbs, or citrus zest) into very small pieces using a knife or other chopping blade.

Parboil: to partially cook foods by immersing them briefly in boiling water. Parboiling is used to cook denser foods, such as potatoes or carrots, that take longer to cook in order to shorten their cooking time, especially when combined with other foods that cook more quickly.

Parma ham: considered the true prosciutto ham from the province of Parma in northern Italy. Parma is a non-smoked, seasoned, salt-cured and air-dried meat taken from pigs that are fed a special diet of chestnuts and whey, resulting in superior quality ham. Parma is usually very thinly sliced and eaten raw in appetizers or incorporated into pasta dishes.

Peel: to remove the skin of a fruit or vegetable (such as tomatoes, peaches, carrots) to clean them and prepare them for cooking. Peeling can be facilitated by blanching the food first. See also Blanch.

Poach: to cook a food gently in water heated to just below the boiling point. Poached eggs are cooked without their shells in simmering water. See also Coddle.

Puff pastry: a rich pastry comprised of chilled fat (butter) and pastry dough that have been folded together several times, producing hundreds of alternating layers of the butter and dough. When baked, the pastry puffs and becomes flaky. Puff pastry is used to make such pastries as croissants and also for baking dishes typically described as "en croûte."

Ramekin: an individual porcelain or earthenware baking dish usually 3 or 4 inches in diameter used for baking or cooking savory or dessert dishes.

Reduce: to decrease the volume of a liquid (such as a broth or a sauce) by evaporation from boiling or simmering therefore concentrating the juices and creating a smoother texture. A reduced liquid is called a reduction.

Roux: a cooked mixture of equal amounts of flour and fat that is used to thicken sauces. A roux's flavor can be deepened the longer it is cooked and by the type of fat used. Butter is the common fat used to make a light roux.

Sauté: to cook foods quickly in a small amount of oil or fat. See also Sauté Pan.

Sauté pan: usually a stovetop pan with straight sides and a lid but can also refer to a pan with sloped sides (sometimes referred to as a skillet or fry pan). Sauté pans with sloped sides are best for sautéing foods as they help with evaporation and therefore faster browning. See also Skillet.

Scale: to remove the scales from a fish by scraping. See Cooking Class, p. 570.

Sear: to start the cooking of a food (usually meats) by putting them in contact with a hot fat or a boiling liquid to cause the surface of the food to brown immediately.

Sift: to pass flour or other dry ingredients through a mesh-bottomed sifter or sieve in order to remove or break down lumps and to aerate the flour. Flour is often sifted prior to measuring its volume.

Simmer: to cook foods in a liquid over a low heat as to produce small bubbles. Generally used to slowly cook foods or to finish the cooking of sauces.

Skillet: a stovetop pan with sloping sides (sometimes called a fry pan or a sauté pan) and a long handle for easy gripping. Skillets with sloped sides are usually best for sautéing foods as they help with evaporation and therefore faster browning. See also Sauté Pan.

Skim off fat: to eliminate the excessive fat from a liquid (such as a sauce or broth) or other food using a spoon, ladle or absorbent cloth such as a paper towel. See Cooking Class, p. 565.

Speck ham: a salt-cured, smoked ham from Italy with a distinctive juniper flavor.

Squab: a young, domestic pigeon.

Strain: to pass foods or liquids such as broths, sauces, or syrups through a mesh-bottomed strainer or sieve to filter out unwanted particles and create a smooth mixture.

String: the action of peeling string beans (haricots verts) by breaking off the stem and pulling off the fibrous string that runs down the seam of the pod.

Sweat: to slowly cook vegetables (usually chopped) in fat so that they release all or part of their natural moisture to soften them and concentrate their juices.

Tagine: Moroccan stew made by gently simmering vegetables with meats such as chicken or lamb and often served with couscous. Tagine can also describe the vessel in which the dish is made.

Truss: to tie up the body of a chicken or other poultry or game bird using kitchen twine (and sometimes a trussing needle) in order to keep the wings and legs against the body while cooking. See Cooking Class, p. 566.

White stock: Broth or stock made from vegetables, veal and poultry meat and bones and used for cooking other foods or as a basis for soups and sauces to add richness and depth of flavor. Stocks are generally categorized as "white" or "brown" in reference to their color and how they are made.

Index of recipes from A to Z